EIGHTEENTH-CENTURY SPAIN 1700–1788

EIGHTEENTH-CENTURY SPAIN 1700–1788

A Political, Diplomatic and Institutional History

W. N. HARGREAVES-MAWDSLEY
M.A., D. PHIL., F.S.A., F.R. HIST. S.
Professor of History, Brandon University, Canada

ROWMAN AND LITTLEFIELD
TOTOWA, N. J.

© W. N. Hargreaves-Mawdsley 1979

First published 1979 by
THE MACMILLAN PRESS LTD
London and Basingstoke

First published in the United States 1979
By Rowman and Littlefield, Totowa, N.J.

Library of Congress Cataloging in Publication Data

Hargreaves-Mawdsley, W. N.
  Eighteenth-century Spain, 1700–1788

  Bibliography: p.
  Includes index.
    1. Spain—History—Philip V, 1700–1746.
  2. Spain—History—Ferdinand VI, 1746–1759.
  3. Spain—History—Charles III, 1759–1788. 4. Spain—
  Foreign relations—18th century. I. Title.
  DP192.H26   1978   946'.054   78–2831
  ISBN 0–8476–6048–6

Printed in Great Britain

A MARÍA TERESA DEÓ LAGÜÉNS,
mi cuñada, con afecto

Contents

Preface

This history of Spain is a straight presentation and interpretation of facts and was written for the English-speaking world to repair a yawning gap which at present follows Professor J. Lynch's *Spain under the Habsburgs*. My work ends at 1788 with the death of Carlos III, but I hope in another book to lead the reader through the reign of his successor Carlos IV and so up to 1808, the date of his abdication, when Professor Carr takes over with his *Spain, 1808–1939*.

The reader will here find a political and diplomatic history, prefaced by an account of governmental institutions, but he will not find cultural or economic history. The omission of the first I regret, but space did not allow it; and after all anyone who wishes to learn of it will find excellent accounts of the literature in E. Allison Peers and R. Herr, the music in G. Chase, and the art and architecture in S. Sitwell and M. Sori, to name a few. The author makes no apology for not having dealt with economic history, believing that it is an artificial and dangerous game to do as some writers have done in recent times and build up an armament of ideas based on economics which have led too often to the dehumanisation of history, in this author's belief an art and not a science, and which has led to a mere playing with data and to monstrous distortions. History is men and not metal.

The conclusions which have been reached and which I lay before the reader are founded on human endeavour. Human actions are my theme, and the theme is the more interesting because humanity is fallible.

I am not ashamed to find myself at one with Lytton Strachey when he wrote in his essay on Gibbon in *Portraits in Miniature* (1931): 'That the question has ever been not only asked but seriously debated, whether History was an art, is certainly one of the curiosities of human ineptitude. What else can it possibly be? It is obvious that History is not a science: it is obvious that History is not the accumulation of facts, but the relation of them'.

August 1977

W. N. HARGREAVES-MAWDSLEY

List of Maps

I. Spain in the Eighteenth Century

INTRODUCTION

Spanish Institutions During the Eighteenth Century

The absolutism of the Habsburgs who ceased to reign in Spain in 1700 was followed by the even more authoritarian and centralising stance of the Bourbons, for in this caesaristic attitude Felipe V followed the advice of his grandfather Louis XIV and transplanted French ideas of statecraft to Spain. Of institutions existing at the time of his accession the one that Felipe V made the most use of as an instrument of Bourbon autocracy was the Council of Castile, which was built up and strengthened throughout the eighteenth century as an antidote to regionalism. Practically all the notable statesmen of the period were associated with it, many becoming its president.[1]

Both Felipe V and his descendants pursued this method of ruling, although it was modified according to the characters of the various kings. Thus Felipe V, a weak character even though a sabre-rattler, was throughout his reign in the hands of a woman, first the Princess de Orsini and afterwards of his second consort Isabel Farnese; Fernando VI was jealous of his power, yet applied it carefully and intelligently; while Carlos III made use of his uncontested position to transform himself from a despot of the old school, though broadly speaking a benevolent one, into an enlightened one. During his reign (1759–88) Spain came nearest during the eighteenth century to approaching the contemporary thought of Europe. The point is that supreme power was vested in the monarch and was so great that, however it was administered, it was hard to dissipate it. Felipe, Ferdinand and Carlos, thanks either to their own or to others' wisdom, did not damage their power; and it took the disastrous Carlos IV twenty years to lose his throne.

In 1700 a French family took possession of the Spanish throne and, as is so often the case with foreigners coming to rule in a strange land, Felipe V wanted to graft himself and his family on to Spain and make it accepted as the one possible dynasty. In this he was eminently successful. Women were not excluded from the crown, for in 1713 the Salic law was introduced to Spain, by virtue of which women of the royal family could succeed to the throne, but only if there were a failure in the male line. Members of the

1

royal family born abroad could lose their rights of succession. The object of this was to preclude all danger of a foreign dynasty appearing in Spain,[2] as if Felipe's own were not a foreign one! He perhaps remembered that a Habsburg as popular as Carlos I eventually became had had to face rebellions in Spain in his early days.[3] Under the Habsburgs Spaniards had kept their jealously guarded identity free from the influence of other European states, and the reigning House was highly regarded because it had completely identified itself (at least in essentials, for Felipe IV could hardly be said to possess Spanish virtues!) with Spanish principles and values.

The Spaniard is proud and dislikes change. How then did the Bourbons so quickly impose themselves on the nation? In the first instance they did so because of the arrogant attitude of the Allies as personified in Charles, Archduke of Austria, during the War of the Spanish Succession. This arrogance appeared worse than that of France and, after all, had not the good but bewitched Carlos II, the last Habsburg, made the country over to the Bourbons in his will? Furthermore, Austria's allies England and the Dutch Netherlands were Protestant heretics; a Frenchman was better than that! In the long run the rise of the middle classes, following the pattern in the rest of Europe, in the enlightened reign of Carlos III, greatly benefited the Bourbons. *Los burgeses* provided a new strong arm for the crown and, in return, new privileges, even amounting to titles of nobility, were granted to the new professional class, which was increasingly called on to occupy positions of importance in the state and keep the old nobility in check.

A new and noteworthy feature of government under the Bourbons was the rise of a rank of professional statesman, unknown under the Habsburgs. Under the latter there had been *cancilleres*, or advisers, rather than executants of the sovereign, but there now appeared ministers who were auxiliaries of an absolute monarchy and who had wide functions and far more influence than the *cancilleres* ever had. Under the Habsburgs there had been favourites who had exercised a personal power over the king and who, being untrained in government, had usually wielded that influence with disastrous results. Now there were sober statesmen who after faithful and well-tried years as civil servants came to the front and enjoyed a far greater prestige in the eyes of the nation; such were Patiño, Campillo, Carvajal, Campomanes and Floridablanca. It is noteworthy that favourites of the old-fashioned type, the Princess de Orsini, Alberoni and Ripperdá, all bad influences owing their period of power to royal partiality, occur during the reign of Felipe V and not later. Felipe was indeed whimsical and wayward and a bad judge of men, while Isabel Farnese, whose insatiable egoism blinded her to the good of the country, was a bad influence on him. One could say that the King was not responsible for such choices of ministers as Alberoni and Ripperdá and that he merely accepted the Queen's nominees, were it not that he actively opposed good ministers such as Patiño even against Isabel's advice. It might be put like this: Felipe V himself rarely governed but rather ruled through women, whether through his first consort, María Luisa of Savoy, or his second, Isabel Farnese; and on the rare occasions when he did intervene such intervention was altogether bad. Fernando VI, until his health broke, and Carlos III were much better kings, the second an outstanding ruler. Although they were influenced by clever consorts they themselves did the ruling.[4]

The increase in ministerial power and the building up of an efficient civil service is a noteworthy feature of Bourbon rule during the eighteenth century down to 1792 when, under the feeble Carlos IV, the prototype of the unscrupulous favourite appeared in the person of Godoy.

As early as 1705 a start was made in building up ministerial and civil service power, when by royal decree the *Despacho universal* was split into two secretariats, one for War and Finance and the other for Public Administration. In 1714 this system became more intricate with three secretariats of State and Foreign Affairs, that is, for Ecclesiastical Affairs and Justice, for War, Navy and the Indies, and the Ministry of Finance with a *veedor* in charge, assisted by an intendant-general in case of disputed items, claims and threats of legal action. The next step of any significance taken in ministerial organisation was in 1755 when the secretariats of State and Foreign Affairs, Grace and Justice, Navy and the Indies, and War and Finance were set up.

In 1787 Carlos III made the Indies into a separate department, dividing it into Grace and Justice, and War, Finance, Commerce and Navigation, although in 1790 Carlos IV disbanded this special secretariat and placed Indies affairs with the Navy as before.

Until 1783 when Carlos III created the *Junta suprema* of State, a kind of council of ministers, each minister worked on his own, answerable only to the king; but with this significant reform the ministries were brought into contact with one another to their advantage. It might be imagined that this could diminish royal authority, since now it was possible for a united front of ministers to face the sovereign, whereas before the king might be expected to divide and rule as Prussian and Austrian despots did in the eighteenth century. This threat to royal authority never occurred in Spain during this period, but Carlos IV must have feared that it might when he suppressed it in 1792.

It is worth noticing that, although, of course, the absolutist Spanish Bourbons made and unmade ministers, there was a growing tendency during the century for court parties and groups of dissidents to help to bring about a ministry's or a minister's fall. An example of this belongs to Fernando VI's reign when we can see the manipulations of cabals influencing or even forcing the king to dismiss Ensenada; while in Carlos III's reign an almost party system appears with the Aragonese or Aristocratic party, as represented by Aranda, fighting for power with the *golillas*, the men of the ruffs, the professional lawyers like Floridablanca, who represented the rise of the new middle class.

Very different from the rich favourites of the seventeenth-century Habsburgs were the new hard-working, relatively poorly paid civil servants (even in the higher ranks) under the Bourbons. Some indeed died so poor that their families had to be aided from the privy purse.

Of the organs of government[5] the Councils were very important and characteristically Spanish, in fact vital to the administration. Under the later Habsburgs they had been increasing in power to such an extent as to be detrimental to royal authority. Under the eighteenth-century Bourbons, as one would expect with a caesaristic and centralising crown, all were brought under the king's private council, generally known as the Council of Castile before the death of Felipe V. The Councils were not only legislative assemblies but also administrative organisations and courts of appeal. When Campomanes, sworn to reform them, came to review their functions later in the century, he found that all their business was carried out in writing with abundance of red tape, that there was no personal access to any of them, and that whether a case was trivial or of the utmost importance and urgency it was subjected to the same maddening dilatoriness.[6]

In 1700 the following councils existed: the Council of State, the Royal Council, the Chamber of Castile (*Cámara de Castilla*), the Council of the Inquisition, the Council of the Indies, the Council of the Orders (*de las Órdenes*),[7] the Council of War, the Council of Finance and the Council of Aragón, this last suppressed by the vindictive Felipe V as being a danger to his authority in 1707. Below these were numerous committees, commissions and superintendencies.

The Council of State lost much of its power during Felipe V's reign, under Alberoni membership of it becoming purely honorific. There were fourteen members. In 1764 under Carlos III it was reformed and, consisting of the ministers of the crown, it met once a week; but in 1783 it was disbanded as being of little value. Then in 1787[8] the *Junta suprema de Estado ordinaria y perpetua*, a kind of cabinet, was set up, but was in its turn suppressed in 1792, when Floridablanca prevailed on Carlos IV to recreate the Council of State. The king was president of it and all the ministers of state were members. High hopes were entertained for it which were not fulfilled.

For all its outward dignity the Council of State was, however, cast into the shade by the Council of Castile which possessed the real power by reason of the importance of its jurisdiction and the variety of affairs over which it had control. So prestigious was it and so fine its tradition that it was able at times even to withstand Bourbon autocracy; and it is remarkable that although ministerial power increased and became a fundamental system of government the Council of Castile actually absorbed the ministers until all became members of it and worked through it and within it. It is interesting to see why the Council of Castile flourished while the Council of State decayed. It was because the former had always been concerned only with internal affairs, while the latter had had under its jurisdiction Spanish territory in Europe. When after the Treaty of Utrecht (1713) such territory was lost and when at the fall of Alberoni (1720) any aspirations to win back such territory were extinguished, the Council of State lost its *raison d'être*.

The Council of Castile had survived the change of dynasty in 1700. Seven years later, on the suppression of the Council of Aragón, the latter's jurisdiction was added to its own. In the reforms which it underwent in the following years it took on a character which was to make it an important vehicle for caesarism.[9] The members were chosen by the king, were well-trained functionaries, and consisted of four ranks: chief magistrates (*corregidores*), ordinary judges (*oidores*), intendants and advisory lawyers (*jurisconsultos*). Until 1717 the members of the Council had no fixed salary but enjoyed all kinds of perquisites, including a house; but in that year they were given a salary according to rank, which was significantly increased in 1763. Their dress of office consisted of a full-bottomed white wig, stiff and arranged round the head in horizontal curls, a white ruff (*golilla*) and a long black gown closed down the front with a loose black cape over it.[10] They carried a long staff with a round gold top.

The President of the Council was the most important person in the state after the king and he carried out the monarch's functions in his absence. Even if dismissed he always retained his title and rank.

The Council employed about one hundred and forty various inferior officials and clerks, and there was a constant relationship between it and various advocates, procurators and agents, generally in Madrid. All cases had to be presented to the Council by an advocate of the College of Advocates of Madrid. Poor clients—and this is in marked contrast to many countries then and since—had their own advocate chosen by the Council and paid for by the privy purse. The procurators brought together all documents concerning both sides in a case, thus forming a link between opposing parties.

The Council enjoyed legislative powers and was responsible for preparing ordinances, decrees, orders, rulings on matters and agreements carried out in the name of the crown. Its rulings and decrees had the force of law. As a high administrative tribunal the Council had a very wide area of jurisdiction. It was the President of the Council who received the will of a dead king and handed it, sealed, to his successor. It was he who convoked the *cortes*, checked the authority of the representatives and gave them permission to absent themselves from court. The Council turned itself into a High Court of Justice to judge cases of high treason and lèse-majesté. As to ecclesiastical affairs, the Council saw to it that the canons of the Council of Trent were observed and defended the rights of the king against the Papal Curia. Further, it received and allowed the publication in Spain of Papal bulls and briefs, protected bishops from seditious clergy, looked after monasteries and hospitals, supported the foundation of monasteries and administered the goods of vacant sees. In the educational field the Council held wide powers. It thus chose schoolmasters, approved the syllabuses of universities and was responsible for their inspection, and was in charge of the royal and provincial archives. It issued licences for the printing of books, pamphlets and newspapers, and ordered the seizure and destruction of such writings as were considered seditious or immoral. It even kept a watch on commerce and agriculture, mines, forests, roads and bridges, and municipal finances.

The Council was also the supreme court of justice and had the power to examine serious criminal and civil cases. It passed judgment on the quarrels between judges and courts and settled conflicts between differing tribunals. Claims to nobility, fishing rights, hunting rights and property also came under its jurisdiction.

Thus, as can be seen, the influence and power of the Council of Castile was almost universal and on occasion it was ready to stand up to the will of the king, as in 1726 when its president denounced the attempt to expropriate for the benefit of the state the funds of San Justo intended for widows and orphans, thereby refusing the application in which Felipe V was said to have had a part. The Council similarly opposed the concordat of 1737.

The[11] political privileges of Aragón and Valencia were abolished by decree on 27 June 1707 and Castilian law was forced on those recalcitrant regions by Felipe V, in consequence of the attitude that they had taken against him in a war in which he was fighting for his throne. Yet exactly a calendar month later, on representations being made to him that, whatever the attitude their governments had taken, it did not represent the Aragonese and Valencians at large, who were loyal *Felipistas*, the King softened the decree and restored the local privileges, but did not relax his hold on the form of government under which these areas should live. It was the French-born minister Amelot who, trained at the court of Louis XIV, impressed on the young King that, while he might indulge Aragón and Valencia in vague prerogatives, he must never let them off the reins of Madrid. When in 1713 the War of the Spanish Succession ended and, except in Cataluña and the Baleares, Felipe was victorious, the Spanish minister Macanaz, a disciple of Amelot, in drawing up a revised constitution followed this policy.

In 1707 High Courts (*audiencias*) were set up, one for Aragón in Zaragoza and one in Valencia for Valencia, their character and organisation being copied from the Chanceries (*chancillerías*) of Valladolid and Granada. How much regional autonomy was to be allowed could be seen in the following years, as when, for example in 1711 it was decided that, although criminal cases in Aragón could be judged by the High Court of Zaragoza, they were to be 'regulated in order to accord with the customs and laws of Castile'. Civil cases, on the other hand, could be judged according to municipal laws (that is, the laws of the city of Zaragoza) unless the crown intervened, in which case they were to be judged by Castilian law. The fact is that the real rule stemmed from Madrid but, as a gesture of appeasement to flatter local susceptibilities, privileges were extended where they could do no harm to centralism. The powers of the High Court of Valencia were similarly curtailed in 1716.

Cataluña and Mallorca did not feel the rigour of Bourbon centralism until 1714 and 1715 respectively. They had been hardened opponents of Felipe V and were made to smart for it. When on 16 September 1714 Barcelona capitulated, its three proud institutions, the Council of One Hundred, the *Diputación* and its Officer Corps (*Brazo militar* or *Brazo noble*) were dissolved. In their place a Royal Council of Justice and of Government was created; it was composed of six councillors and a secretary, all of them Catalans, with Patiño as President. Vengeance, however, lurked behind the apparent smile of Madrid, for when this Council was joined by another new institution, the Council of Administrators of the City of Barcelona consisting of eighteen members, both were seen as tools in the hands of the central government. Their very first acts showed that though all members except Patiño were Catalans they did not function *sua sponte*, but were puppets of Castile. For how could Catalans prohibit their own people from carrying arms, exact savage stamp duties, force citizens to make over part of their property to billet the occupying forces of Castile, order those who had gained titles and other privileges from the Archduke Charles of Austria to hand over their documentary evidence for these to be burnt and, perhaps most humiliating of all, insist that Catalans who wished to journey outside Cataluña should obtain a passport and that if they failed to do so execution would be their fate? All these laws were passed by mid-November 1714. The following year the University of Barcelona was disbanded, its members being banished to brand-new buildings, on which acroteria in the shape of crowns were abundant, in the country town of Cervera. Professors and students could do little harm in that remoteness except teach and study scholasticism. Only the Grammar School, a minor part of the old University which prepared students for matriculation, remained in the capital. At the same time the *cortes* of Cataluña was suppressed and its members were absorbed into the *cortes* of Castile at Madrid, which now became the only one, the *cortes* of the nation.

This curtailment of Catalan liberties was not enough for the triumphant Bourbons and in 1716 the so-called and euphemistically termed New Plan (*Nueva Planta*) was brought in.[12] All ancient Catalan usages and forms both political and economic, both procedural and legal, were to be abolished by it and new forms based on Castilian usage were to be imposed on Cataluña. Besides, it was forbidden to employ the Catalan language in administration and in the law courts. The law indeed was to be Castilian

law. The success of the New Plan, however, was never complete, and
Cataluña until the early nineteenth century continued to employ a great
deal of its own criminal law; and the office of Notary Public of Barcelona
survived. Civil and mercantile law remained exclusively Catalan and in
fact the New Plan expressly stated that the central government of Madrid
wished to respect those sections of Catalan law which dealt with the family,
property and the individual. The Catalan language continued to be taught
in a few private schools.

Closely associated with the government of Cataluña was the *Audiencia*
(High Court) sitting in Barcelona with the Captain-General of Cataluña
presiding,[13] but its decisions could be overruled by the central administration in Madrid. A modification to this was, however, brought in in
1740[14] when it was enacted that if Madrid contraverted Cataluña an
appeal could be lodged with the Council of Castile. Until 1768, when it
was suppressed as having really ceased to function and anyway being
contrary to the spirit of enlightened times, there existed in Cataluña a
feudal Tribunal of Peers.

Cataluña was divided into twelve magistracies chosen by the crown,
which also nominated the twenty-four aldermen (*regidores*) of the city
corporation of Barcelona. The chief officials of other Catalan towns were
nominated by the *Audiencia* of Barcelona.

Felipe V failed to keep the promises he had made at the time' of the
capitulation of Barcelona and many higher civil servants and officers were
imprisoned. General Moragas was one of four prominent nationalists who
between March and April, 1715, were shot for attempting to escape. So
zealous a *Felipista* as Bishop Taverner of Gerona at the Provincial Council
of 1717 drew attention to this failure of the victorious regime to honour its
word. Some citizens of Barcelona decided to emigrate to Sardinia rather
than see the new fortress (*ciudadela*) arise to overawe the city.

Mallorca was dealt with similarly late in 1715[15] when by decree the
Audiencia (High Court) of Palma was set up,[16] presided over by a *Felipista*
general. Mallorcan civil law, the *Consulat del Mar* and the *Gran i General
Consell*, however, survived until 1718. The city of Palma was controlled by
twenty aldermen (*regidores*), while Alcudia, the second largest town on the
island, had a council of twelve. All these were nominated by the crown. As
in Cataluña the *Audiencia* of Palma elected the officials of the other towns
and villages.

In the Basque provinces the settlement was somewhat different, for here
there was more eagerness on the part of the central government not to
upset local susceptibilities, since its hold over Basque territory was never
too secure. Even so, and in spite of much window-dressing and many
statements to the contrary, representatives of Bourbon authority were
intruded into local government throughout the century. The sovereign
was directly represented by the crown-nominated chief magistrate
(*corregidor*), who resided in Bilbao as Lord of Biscay. He had deputies in

Avellaneda and Durango. The proud nationalism of the Basques was always treated with caution, and no one before Godoy dared to place the Basque provinces under a military governor.

With this in mind the *Felipistas* in 1717 made a placatory gesture towards the Basques by moving their customs posts from the boundary with Castile to the French frontier and the coast, well out of the range of Castilian interference; but soon afterwards the government in Madrid was forced to abandon this policy owing to frequent instances of fraud and contraband on the part of the Basques; so back went the posts to their former positions under the eye of Castile.

The centralising policy of the Bourbons is to be clearly seen in administration. The War of the Spanish Succession was a wonderful opportunity, a pretext, to force it home. Under Felipe V this meant the autocratic despotism of Louis XIV and under Carlos III the enlightened despotism of the time. Both led to efficiency, to the destruction of regionalism and so of feudalism, and to the concentration of wealth and power in the crown. All the same, throughout the eighteenth century provincial administration in Spain remained as illogical as ever. Granted that in Madrid the administration was made much more efficient and more accountable than it had been under the Habsburgs, especially after 1766 when Carlos III underwent soul-searching as a result of the *motín de Esquilache*, yet this was not so in the provinces where a captain-general and a chief justice held all the power. Before these two officials assemblies and councils were powerless.[17]

The two most outstanding aims of the Bourbon administration are centralisation and uniformity, with the crown in reality being more absolutist than under the Habsburgs. The homogeneity of the Bourbon government was due to two Frenchmen, the great financiers Orry and Amelot who had learnt their craft under Louis XIV. Patiño, the Spanish disciple of Orry, was given his first chance of showing what the new civil service could do when he was sent to reorganise Cataluña after the War of the Spanish Succession. From that time onwards Castile pursued an ever-increasing policy of centralisation; but at the end of the century, and indeed for ever afterwards, this attitude was by no means accepted in the provinces.

Apart from the obvious difficulty of communication in a most mountainous country, there was another fact which militated against a tidy uniformity. In the eighteenth century Spain's territorial divisions still kept the feudal units of the Middle Ages, something so bound up with the jealously guarded traditions of Spanish culture as not to be lightly swept away. Confused and disorderly they may have been,[18] but they were Spain. Thus, to a would-be reformer of the Enlightenment it would appear not only ridiculous but a menace to improved government that the boundaries between the provinces should be so irregular, with portions of the territory of one intruded into the territory of another. For example, the county of Treviño was an enclave in the territory of Álava, the village of Llivia was and is Spanish although surrounded on all sides by French territory, while the district of Antequera, situated between the provinces of Granada, Cordoba and Sevilla, had nothing to do with any of them. Just as various as the shape and size of the territories were the constitutions of the local governments, so that some towns might be under the king's authority, others under the lord of a manor, others again under an abbacy and others under a military order.

Navarra had the distinction of being the only territory of Spain to have a viceroy, chosen by the crown. During the eighteenth century all who held this post were aristocrats of the first water or outstanding members of the military or civil service.[19] After all, Navarra had been a proud kingdom, it was in a strategic position between factious Aragón and the still more factious Basques, which made it worth a wooing by the central government, and moreover it had on the whole remained loyal to the crown in Castile whichever dynasty had ruled. It therefore retained this prestigious office. The viceregal palace was in Pamplona, where the viceroy governed with the assistance of a council and had the power when the occasion warranted it to convoke the *cortes* of Navarra, over which he presided seated on a low throne. Navarra enjoyed other privileges, such as having the right to coin its own money, exemption of its people from military service, control of its own finance, the maintenance of its own civil law, and the right to admit from outside Navarra only five officials and the viceroy who might or might not be a Navarrese.

In the rest of Spain it was the captains-general, the particular creation of the Bourbons, who had the supreme power under the crown, for not only had they all the military forces of their province under their control, but as *ex officio* presidents of the High Court of their province they overawed the whole administration. On the other hand during the eighteenth century they lost their control over finances to a civil servant new to Spain but old to France, in reality the creation of Richelieu, the intendant. In Spain there was much opposition to the intendants by the captains-general, as one might imagine, when that office was first introduced in 1718, and so strong at that time was the military interest that Felipe V suppressed intendancies shortly afterwards. When, however, in 1749 Fernando VI restored the office,[20] the power of the intendants of the provinces soon became great and ate into that of the captains-general as the latter had feared, often tipping the scales in favour of civilians opposed to military control of everyday life. They had judicial, administrative and even military authority, particularly with regard to stores and ammunition, and, of course, they had key control of finance. In their capacity as judges they held the title of chief magistrate (*corregidor*) and kept a vigilant eye on magistrates and mayors. In 1766, however, Carlos III deprived the intendants of their legal authority, although this still left them with enormously varied and far-reaching powers, beyond the task of an ordinary mortal, as Campomanes was wont to say.

Of the provincial bodies the most important was the *audiencia*, in certain areas termed *chancillería*. (High Court), which was both the political council of the province and the court of appeal. The term *audiencia* was modern, while *chancillería* was much older, and when from 1707, the year the tide of the War of the Spanish Succession turned in his favour, onwards Felipe V pursued a strict policy of centralisation, the second of these terms, much more common under the Habsburgs, was generally given up as signifying higher authority than the first. Only the *chancillerías* of Granada and Valladolid retained the prouder title under the Bourbons.

The *audiencias* were presided over by the captain-general of the province; if he should be absent his place was taken by his second-in-command. The exceptions were the *chancillerías* of Granada and Valladolid and the *audiencias* of Sevilla and Cáceres which had civilian presidents.[21] The presidents had the power of bringing magistrates, mayors and other judicial functionaries to trial, but could not imprison them without the authorisation of the crown.

The *corregidor* occupied the next position after the captain-general and the intendant; each district, into which every province was divided, had its *corregidor*.[22] Together they sat as an assembly of government. In 1783 Carlos III reformed certain aspects of this office, insisting that all candidates should be obliged to put in six years of theoretical and four years of practical study and to present a dissertation on a legal subject. Before that date *corregidores* could continue in office indefinitely, but now Carlos III allowed them to hold office in the first instance for six years only, although this could be renewed. He also enacted that they should not be natives of the province in which they were to serve and should not own any property in it, a wise rule which was very much in accordance with the spirit of the age.

In his district the *corregidor* was very powerful, seldom loved, but generally respected; and indeed well he might be, since he was in charge of police and the carrying out of the law, controlled hunting and fishing rights, could enact sumptuary laws respecting the very dress that might be worn, maintained the privileges of the Church, and was responsible for levies for the army and navy, forced labour and the galleys. As a financial agent taxation was in his hands and he was responsible for the stocking of public granaries and the avoidance of food shortages, horse-breeding, afforestation and irrigation. On official occasions the *corregidor* carried an elaborate staff of office (*vara*).

During the eighteenth century the national *cortes*[23] was a shadow of its former self. It retained its prestige by reason of its venerable age, but it was sick. It had been powerful and important in the seventeenth century, and it was to be so again in the nineteenth. For the present it was moribund. The Bourbons wanted it to be. Felipe V had no wish that it should have the importance it had held under the later Habsburgs and, soon after his accession, turned to his mentor Louis XIV for advice. Surely such an authoritarian monarch would have counselled dominating, if not suppressing, it; but no, the shrewed old king refused to give advice to his grandson on so delicate a matter, since he knew that the *cortes* was highly regarded by every Spaniard as a symbol of a proud independence. If the virtual suppression of the States General and the driving underground of the Paris Parlement had cost France the Frondes and Louis himself nearly the loss of his throne, then, in a Spain faced with a new dynasty with allied enemies clamouring outside, it would be dangerous to tamper with anything so revered.

Felipe V showed his ill-will towards all idea of tradition and even a measure of free representation when in May 1701 he convoked in Madrid the Three Estates of all Spain, for he pointedly omitted the customary formalities both before and after they were assembled. This was regarded as an affront by the members and also by the Spanish public at large. Alone of the provinces Cataluña took no part in this assembly, but held its own later in the year in Barcelona; the Aragonese, withdrawing from the Three Estates at Madrid, followed suit at Zaragoza in 1702. These two regional assemblies revealed all the characteristics of the general *cortes*, legally convoked, following traditional ceremonial to the letter, and widely representative. As if to show that while doing things better than the King could manage in Madrid and while proud of their liberty, they were yet loyal, but on their terms, both the assemblies voted the King a substantial sum in their own coinage, Catalan *libras* and Aragonese *reales*, to prosecute the war. Felipe, however, was not the man to accept such pride or insolence. He meanly bided his time and, soon afterwards, in the name of national unity in face of the enemy, suppressed both assemblies. Small-minded, vain, proud without reason and yet unsure of himself Felipe stored up the remembrance of Catalan and Aragonese defiance of him in his unbalanced mind and after he had won the war humiliated the two provinces.[24]

Felipe V had not done with the question, however, and perhaps influenced by his French ministers advising prudence he called together the general *cortes* of Castile and Aragón, in Madrid in April, 1709, Aragón having been forcibly brought in, Castile being the dominant partner. The rest of the provinces were not even mentioned. It was soon to be seen that the general or national *cortes* was to be nothing more than a body which gave its blessing to decisions already made, and so it remained during the eighteenth century. Thus at its session of 1709 it did no more than recognise the Infante Don Luis as *príncipe de las Asturias*,[25] while at that of 1712 with a great many flourishes Felipe V renounced his rights to the throne of France and was congratulated in rotund but hollow phrases.[26] It met again in 1714 and twice in 1724, on the first occasion doing no more than admit a new Aragonese deputy and discuss the Salic law question, on the second to swear allegiance to Luis I, and, a few months later on the young king's death, to swear allegiance anew to Felipe V who had reassumed the crown.[27]

The national *cortes* was not convoked again until 1760 when, on the entry of Carlos III into Madrid, it was required to swear allegiance to the príncipe de las Asturias (afterwards Carlos IV).[28] It was the latter who, having newly succeeded his father, convoked it in 1789 with Campomanes as President, but Floridablanca, scared by the French Revolution, urged that it should be dissolved, and dissolved it was. The *cortes* of Navarra, however, continued to meet as it had done for most of the century.

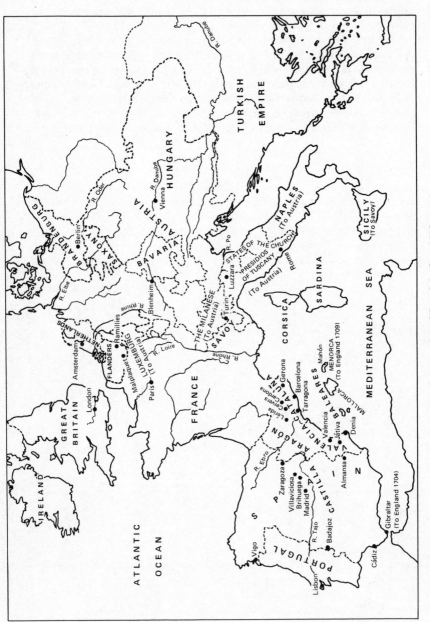

II. Europe at the time of the War of the Spanish Succession

PART ONE

The Reign of Felipe V
(1700–46)

In 1700 Louis XIV, 'Mars Christianissimus' as Leibniz had satirically called him, had been at work disrupting Europe for nearly thirty years. By 1688 France stood alone confronted by a coalition in which difference between Catholic and Protestant mattered not at all. The Emperor, the King of England, the Grand Pensionary of the United Provinces, the Great Elector of Brandenburg and others with various forms of statecraft and different churches were sworn to fight together to bring France down.

The Spanish Habsburgs, long tortured by France, were at an end in 1700. Poor, demented Carlos II, his death-bed surrounded by intriguing diplomats, had just breathed his last, by his will having left Spain and its huge and far-flung Empire to a French prince, young Philippe, duc d'Anjou, grandson of Louis XIV. After all, his grandmother had been María Teresa, daughter of Felipe IV of Spain, half-sister of Carlos II himself.

Thus Philippe could be said to have every right to this inheritance; but how could the rest of Europe acquiesce? A French prince, under the tutelage of Louis XIV, that hardened old warrior, ruling the Spanish Empire? What would that lead to but an aggressive France, one hundred times more dominant than before? It was something that the rest of Europe could not bear.

The Allies rallied round the House of Austria. Had it not claims to the Spanish inheritance too? The great drama of Habsburg and Bourbon was to be continued in the War of the Spanish Succession, out of which was to emerge a mercantile rivalry of great significance ending in the British Empire.

The House of Austria had firm claims. Emperor Leopold was the son of another of Felipe IV's daughters, Margareta Teresa, and, more than that, he could turn the pages of his family history much farther back to the fifteenth-century marriage of Philip of Austria and Juana la Loca of the Royal House of Spain. Since Leopold and his elder son Joseph the heir presumptive had abandoned their claims, it was the second son, the Archduke Charles, who was the figure round whom the Allies rallied. It was to be Charles and not Philippe for them. Pedro II of Portugal and Vittorio Amadeo of Savoy also had rights to that mighty inheritance, but they represented power too insignificant to matter. There was, however, no ignoring the final will of the dead king of Spain Carlos II,[1] which made over to Anjou not only Spain but the European possessions, the Spanish Netherlands, the Milanese, Sardinia and the two Sicilies, and the Spanish Empire of America and the Philippines. The fact that the will[2] stipulated that the Kingdoms of France and Spain were never to be joined did not comfort the rest of Europe, for even if the worst did not happen France and Spain would be close allies. Louis XIV was not slow to act, and Europe's nightmare of many years stood stark before them.[3]

The old French King presented his grandson Philippe in the palace of Versailles saying: 'Gentlemen, here is the King of Spain! His birth has called him to this crown; the Spanish nation has asked for him and has eagerly begged me for him; I concede to this with pleasure, actuated by the decrees of Providence,' and turning to Anjou he added: 'Be a good Spaniard; that from this moment is your first obligation; but remember that you were born French to preserve unity between both nations so as to make them both happy and to keep the peace of Europe'; while the Spanish ambassador, Castel de los Ríos, clinched this portentous announcement with words that, when reported, sent a shiver down the spines of the Allies: 'What happiness! Now there are no Pyrenees! They have sunk into the ground and we form only one nation!' He voiced what many had been thinking for many a year.

The will of Carlos II having been accepted by Louis XIV, the duc d'Anjou, grandson of the French king, took the high road to Spain, where he was to reign with the name of Felipe V. He[4] arrived in Spain on 28 January 1701 and the government of Louis XIV began there, a Spanish state to be governed from Versailles. The most important personalities who accompanied the new king were Cardinal Portocarrero, who was completely bound to the wishes of the French king and who would soon prove his lack of tact and his incapacity, the President of the Council of Castile, Manuel Arias, an intelligent person but one who envied the preeminent position of his colleague the cardinal, and the Secretary of State, Antonio de Ubilla. A respectable pension was given to Maria Anna of Neuberg, widow of Carlos II, who chose as her place of residence the city of Toledo. At the very beginning the representative of Louis XIV, the comte d'Harcourt held office. Taken ill a little time afterwards, his place was poorly filled by Blécourt, appointed by the impulsive confidant of the king, the marquis de Louisville.

The imprudent reforms of Portocarrero produced general discontent. Much reference is made to the economies which deprived the old courtiers of their emoluments, and many others were dissatisfied. Juan Tomás Enríquez de Cabrera, duque de Riosco and conde de Melgar, Admiral of Castile, was deprived of his post of majordomo; the banishment of Oropesa the Grand Inquisitor was confirmed, and he was relegated to his bishopric of Segovia. These methods were soon to be the cause of the unpopularity of Portocarrero and of Arias, and this was increased by the growing invasion of French adventurers and courtiers who came to Spain as to a conquered country. At fifty, Arias became a priest and obtained the bishopric of Sevilla, ambitious to obtain a cardinal's hat so as to gain a position equal to that of his rival. The *cortes* of Castile was called together on the advice of the marqués de Villena and met in the church of San Jerónimo in Madrid on 8 May 1701. There the King swore to abide by the laws and respect the privileges of the kingdom. The representative of the *cortes* swore loyalty to the sovereign. Later the marqués de Mancera and the duque de Montalto entered into office. Cardinal Portocarrero asked Louis XIV for an economist capable of putting in order the precarious Spanish finances. In answer Louis sent Jean Orry to Spain.

Orry was an obscure figure, known only to the great financiers, a man, in fact, who, as Saint-Simon put it, had started his career as a *rat de cave*: a businessman, a hard worker and with iron health. From now on he sought to build up the resources necessary for making war, for there was no doubt that France and Spain would now have to face a belligerent Europe. His enemies (and he had many) said that he was impatient and easily deceived and that he meddled with everything and finished nothing.[5] His rough manners and the way in which he flouted conventions and customs gained for him universal hatred, and the duque de Alba was his mortal enemy. Orry studied state revenues and expenditures; Louis was behind his back requiring that Aragón should share the weight of commitments that pressed exclusively on Castile and that the Church should contribute to State expenses, and finally that the abuses of the colonial administration should be remedied. F. Rousseau, the modern historian and writer on Orry, says that the financier's career was frequently interrupted by enemies who were always (and at times were on the point of succeeding) looking for an opportunity to overturn this disciple of Colbert.[6]

The circumstances in which the Spanish monarchy became involved were increasingly difficult, since neither the maritime powers nor the Emperor, the latter in reality being the more dangerous, were ready to allow the aggrandisement of France. Louis XIV lured to his political game Vittorio Amadeo II of Savoy, negotiating the marriage of his daughter María Luisa to the King of Spain. Felipe V placed government in the hands of Portocarrero and Arias, and left Madrid on 5 September to meet his new queen. Passing through Zaragoza he swore to abide by the privileges of Aragón and, having visited Lérida, he made for Barcelona where similarly he swore to the Catalan privileges. Afterwards he went to Figueras where he met his queen María Luisa and returned accompanied by her to Barcelona. With the queen came a personage, the Princess de Orsini, who well deserves some discussion.

Marie-Anne de la Trémoïlle,[7] of noble French family, had been married during the second Fronde, to Adrian Blaise de Talleyrand, Prince de Chalais, who, because of a duel, had to escape from French territory. The couple set out for Rome and on the journey Chalais died. Now a widow Marie-Anne, remaining in Rome came to know several Spanish diplomats and Cardinal d'Estrées, the French ambassador to the Holy See, and a little later married Flavio Orsini, duque de Bracciano, a Spanish grandee and the possessor of a considerable fortune. Marie-Anne de Orsini paid two visits to France and formed a deep friendship with the wife of maréchal de Noailles, making also the acquaintance of the marquis de Torcy, who had under his direction French diplomatic affairs. Torcy appreciated the talents of his compatriot, and Madame de Maintenon before long began to fear that her own influential position was being undermined. Back in Rome Marie-Anne made the friendship of Portocarrero, that scheming priest, and won him over to declare himself in favour of the candidature of a French prince for the Spanish throne. Louis XIV now rewarded Marie-Anne by naming her chief lady-in-waiting to the young queen of Spain. The mental agility, the spirit of intrigue and the great experience of the Princess were to be of great benefit to the Savoyard child who had come to be the consort of a young king entering upon his rule over a country whose throne was reeling under the fate of a worldwide war against the Bourbons.[8]

The Catalan *cortes* sat until 12 January 1702 and voted Felipe a million and a half *libras* and an extra sum of twelve millions payable in six years. The Catalans, jealous of their privileges, tried to make sure that King Felipe would respect them. During these discussions, events in Italy, where Prince Eugène of Savoy was gaining the Empire its first victories, forced Felipe to set out for that troubled area. Also he must have the advice of Louis XIV, since neither Marcin, the French ambassador to Spain, nor Louisville, faced with the opposition of Portocarrero, could reach agreement among themselves. The French courtiers, supported by Marie-Anne de Orsini, were keen for the Italian expedition. Louis XIV agreed with this as against all the Spanish courtiers led by Portocarrero. Leaving his young queen as regent, Felipe V embarked at Barcelona for Naples on 8 April 1702.

What had happened? It was not a question of Austrian schemes in the Viceroyalty of Naples, it was in reality the attitude of a Europe which, faced with the preponderance of the Bourbons, was working to counter the aggrandisement of Louis XIV resulting from his control of Spain through his grandson. France was indeed becoming an irresistible power.[9] The maritime states England and the Netherlands were anxious to destroy that power, and consequently united themselves with the interests of the House of Austria, which though not a sea power wanted to be, and above all desired to extend itself into Italy, an ever-present Imperial ambition. Louis XIV, far-sighted monarch that he was, desired to break up this coalition and, as was his custom, he had prepared the way for war, which he had irremediably brought close. He sought allies and found them: the Dukes of Brunswick-Wolfenbüttel and of Saxe-Gotha, the Bishop of Münster and the Electors of Cologne and Bavaria. In Italy, France had the friendship of the astute Vittorio Amadeo of Savoy who was father-in-law of the Duke Burgundy and Burgundy's brother, Anjou, now King of Spain. The Duke of Mantua also allied himself with France. Louis wanted to continue the traditional policy with regard to Portugal and at first pursued it, but before long the Iberian interests of Felipe V and the very firm and time-honoured friendship of the English, and indeed English threats to Portugal to abide by that friendship, brought hostility between Portugal and France. Spanish opinion in all parts of the country was unanimous on this point, that Spain should not be dismembered. On the other hand there was danger of civil war in Spain, for the rest resented a centralising policy emanating from Castile and were determined that Madrid should not deprive Cataluña, Aragón and Valencia of their privileges. If the rulers in Madrid wanted the provinces to forfeit their privileges for the sake of the preservation of a united country, then they would have to think again.

To the accompaniment of the protestations of the Emperor Leopold I French troops occupied fortresses in the Low Countries garrisoned by the Dutch. Louis XIV took it upon himself to protect the Spanish Netherlands, which were to be governed by the Elector of Bavaria, and this produced discontent in the court of Madrid. In view of what had happened, the Grand Alliance, brought about largely by William III of England, that implacable enemy of Louis XIV, was confirmed at The Hague on 7 September 1701. England, the United Provinces and the Holy Roman Empire bound themselves to fight against Louis XIV and his grandson Felipe V.[10]

While Felipe was on his way to Naples, a revolt against Spain, with Austrian help, had been with great difficulty brought about by the duque de Medinaceli, the Spanish Viceroy of Naples, more preoccupied with idle amorous pursuits and with continuing his scandalous life with his favourite mistress, la Giorgina, than with concerning himself with governing. The French ambassador, Marcin, Père Daubenton, Louisville, Medina Sidonia, the conde de San Esteban, and the Secretary of State, Ubilla, now made marqués de Rivas, had accompanied Felipe V on his journey to Naples. The marqués de Villena was at once made Viceroy in place of the treasonable Medinaceli, and Neapolitan affairs soon began to wear a better aspect; but war broke out in Lombardy, where Prince Eugène of Savoy attempted to seize from the Bourbons the Milanese which the Emperor claimed.

Prince Eugène forced the crossing of the River Adda at Carpi, the front commanded on the French side by General Catinat; Villeroy, the other French general in that neighbourhood, was surprised and taken prisoner at Cremona—a bad beginning to the campaign for the Bourbons. Maréchal Vendôme entered Italy with 50,000 men; but Prince Eugène raised the sieges of Mantua and Goito. Felipe, desirous of fighting, left Naples and after visiting the Spanish fortresses of Tuscany, disembarked at Finale; he was received by the Governor, Prince de Vaudemont, and soon afterwards entered Milan (18 June 1702). From there the King set out to join Vendôme. Vendôme surprised the enemy at Santa Vittoria, near the River Po, on 26 July and won the battle. The Bourbon success continued, and at the battle of Luzzara (14–15 August) the Austrians were defeated. In this battle maréchal Créqui was killed; and Vendôme, the Duke of Savoy and Villena distinguished themselves.

Louis XIV has continued to defy his opponents after the death of James II, dethroned King of England, in 1701, by recognising his son the Pretender, James III, instead of the actual ruling English King, William III. The English Parliament approved of the Treaty of The Hague, and the Earl of Marlborough left with an army of 10,000 for the continent. William III died childless on 8 March 1702, but his successor, Queen Anne, daughter of James II, continued William's policy, impelled by her strong Protestantism and her enmity towards France. The Grand Pensionary of the United Provinces, Heinsius, joined the coalition, and Marlborough began to win battle after battle against the army of the Duke of Burgundy, brother of Felipe V. The fortresses of Venloo, Roermunde and Liège fell to the Allies. The Emperor declared war on France and Spain at the Diet of Ratisbon held on 15 May 1702.

Meanwhile, in Spain the gentle and charming Queen María Luisa of Savoy stood out in the grey ambience of mediocrities. She had come to this new country with the decided intention of pleasing her husband and of governing and saving Spain; indeed at the age of thirteen she had the maturity of mind of a woman of thirty. Arriving in Zaragoza from Barcelona, she convoked on 18 June 1702, the *cortes* of Aragón, swore to Aragonese privileges and was voted a stingy salary of 100,000 *pesos*, which she sent to the King. Soon in Madrid she presided over a meeting of the cabinet, chief among the members being Cardinal Portocarrero, Arias, the archbishop-elect of Sevilla, Montalto, and strangely enough the fallen Viceroy of Naples, Medinaceli.

Serious problems arose. In August 1702 an Anglo-Dutch squadron entered the Bay of Cádiz, commanded by the Duke of Ormonde, Admiral George Rooke and the Dutch Admiral Allemond.[11] It was said that the plan had been prepared by the Prince of Hesse-Darmstadt and Riosco, Admiral of Castile, who was a partisan of the Austrians. Queen María Luisa showed her fortitude by presiding over the council of state for six hours with her sewing-needle in her hand. She took part in the deliberations, offered her jewels for the defence of the Andalusian coast, and gave proof of a perspicacity extraordinary for her age, no more than fourteen as it now was. Fortunately the enemy could hardly threaten the forts of Santa Catalina and Matagorda and did no more than sack the towns of Rota and Puerto de Santa María. But on the other hand, in

October 1702, Spain did suffer a disaster in the sinking in the Bay of Vigo on the north-west coast of the greater part of the Navy of the Indies by the Anglo-Dutch squadron, and the loss the treasure-ships, which would have already been unloaded but for bureaucratic interference. The duque de Riosco perfected his treason, after being nominated Spanish Ambassador to the court of Versailles, by altering his route and taking refuge in Portugal.

These events necessitated the return of King Felipe to Madrid, so he left Milan accompanied by the new French ambassador to Spain, Cardinal d'Estrées. On 16 November 1702 he set out from Genoa and made by land for Figueras, where he was met by the conde de Palma, Viceroy of Cataluña. Already there were signs of a revolt in Cataluña. Without delay the King went to Madrid by way of Barcelona and Zaragoza and, having on 13 January 1703 met the Queen at Guadalajara, the two of them entered Madrid on the seventeenth. What they now faced was the threat of civil war in Spain within the context of a general European war.

The year 1703[12] was one of trial, for Spain was both beleaguered abroad and without a stable government at home. The dissensions between the marquis de Louisville, the Princess de Orsini and Cardinal d'Estrées reached the point of seriously compromising the Bourbon cause in Spain, a cause magisterially directed from Paris by Louis XIV. Louis's viewpoint was represented by d'Estrées, whose haughty behaviour soon came up against the *camarera mayor*, as the Orsini was now dubbed, and the powerful stance of Cardinal Portocarrero, no less eminent a supporter of the Bourbons. Now, however, Louisville, no less a confidant of Louis than was d'Estrées, started to intrigue against Portocarrero, who began to resent Louis's influence and wanted Felipe to detach himself from French authority, working for a Bourbon Spain certainly, but one from which direct French control was excluded. Père Daubenton, a Jesuit and Felipe's confessor, joined with Louisville and d'Estrées in countering Portocarrero. In opposition to Louisville, d'Estrées and Daubenton, and on the side of Portocarrero were Princess de Orsini, carrying with her the young queen who was now falling further and further under her influence, and Orry.

Louisville, a foul-mouthed courtier, said of María Luisa that she dominated King Felipe with childish tricks, spending the day playing hide-and-seek, at a 'cuckoo' game and at a pastime called 'Do you like the company?'. These entertainments were termed by Louisville the sports of the seraglio. The Princess de Orsini fell from court favour, but in her fall dragged down with her Portocarrero and Louisville. Daubenton, alone of the group, survived, thanks to the intervention on his behalf of his brother Jesuit Père la Chaise, Louis XIV's confessor, and in high favour with him.

Spain's situation in international affairs was more precarious than ever. The Low Countries had been offered by Louis XIV to the Elector of Bavaria in return for his loyalty to the Bourbons. The defection of the Duke of Savoy, who looked to his own interests rather than to those of his daughter, now Queen of Spain, and the association of Portugal with the Allies, strengthened the Archduke Charles's cause, and he now decided to sail from the United Provinces to Lisbon. He disembarked in the Portuguese capital on 7 May 1704 and, welcomed by his new ally, Dom Pedro of Portugal, he launched a manifesto directed to the Spanish nation.

Elsewhere in Europe good fortune attended the Bourbons. The Elector of Bavaria and maréchal Villars fought against Ludwig of Baden, obliging him to retreat to Augsburg; the Duke of Burgundy fought with advantage on the Rhine, taking the fortress of Brissac; and Tallard, who succeeded him in command, took Landau after defeating the Princes of Hesse-Cassel and Nassau at the battle of Speier on 15 November 1703. The Spanish army of Italy entered Vercelli. Vendôme, after crushing the Piedmontese, took Asti, while Tessé took Chambéry by assault; and in the Low Countries the French led by Boufflers and the Spanish commanded by Bedmar had already beaten the English and the Dutch before Antwerp on 30 June 1703.

The year 1704 turned out to be very different with the loss of Gibraltar; yet the campaign in Portugal began with good auguries. On this front the Spanish troops were reinforced by 12,000 French commanded by the duc de Berwick. King Felipe of Spain placed himself at the head of his army on 4 March and the conde de Aguilar conquered Salvatierra, Penha-Garcia, and the castle of Monsanto. Meanwhile Prince de T'Serclaes, advanced as far as Arronches and Francisco Ronquillo to Almeida. The marqués de Villadarias penetrated into the south of Portugal, laying waste the country-side. The Dutch general Fagel fell back and Spanish troops invaded the Alemtejo on 30 May. Berwick took the fortress of Portalegre, and Castel-Davide, besieged by the marqués de Aytona, surrendered to the Bourbons. Montalvan and Marván were the two last Franco-Spanish gains of the campaign, and the only blows which the Bourbon allies suffered was the defeat of Ronquillo at Monsanto, which town they lost, as also Fuente-Guinaldo, won back by the Portuguese. Felipe V retired to summer quarters on 1 July and, owing to excessive heat, the campaign was discontinued.

For the allies the Prince of Hesse-Darmstadt appeared with a squadron in front of Barcelona, but in spite of the complicity of the inhabitants he was unable to take it. French reinforcements were sent to Velasco, Viceroy of Cataluña, but he refused to admit them. A little later, on 2 August, Gibraltar surrendered to Darmstadt's fleet. The Governor Diego Salinas who, with the sixty soldiers of the garrison and the civilians of the place, had at his command no more than a hundred men could only resist the English attacks for two days; then he capitulated realising that a continued show of defence was useless. Admiral Sir George Rooke occupied Gibraltar[13] in the name of England; but the English failed against Ceuta.

King Felipe now sent the marqués Villadarias with a part of the army of Extremadura to recover Gibraltar by land, while by sea a French squadron, under the command of the comte de Toulouse, blocked the coast. A naval battle off Málaga on 24 August between Toulouse's French navy and Rooke's and Shovel's English one was indecisive.[14] Villadarias failed and, early in 1705, Maréchal de Tessé besieged Gibraltar to no purpose, losing 9,000 men. On the Portuguese front Berwick remained on the defensive.

The new French ambassador, the duc de Gramont, arrived at a very difficult moment, since Queen María Luisa of Spain, disillusioned by the sudden removal of the Princess de Orsini, whom Louis XIV regarded as having become too powerful, was not inclined to maintain the old cordiality with the court of Versailles. In place of the Orsini, the dowager duquesa de Béjar was named first lady-in-waiting, but the Spanish King and Queen decided to oppose the instructions which Gramont had been ordered to carry out by Louis to reorganise the civil service. Defeats, however, soon led the Spanish couple to abandon their animosity to the old French King. Felipe bowed to the will of his grandfather, and a council of state for Spain was formed consisting of the conde de Montellano, the duque de Montalto, the conde de Monterrey, the marqués de Mancera, Manuel Arias Archbishop of Sevilla, and the duc de Gramont. The marqués de Rivas was named secretary, and the orders of Louis were carried out to the letter. Orry, such a good ally of the Orsini, set out for Paris. The true King of Spain was Louis XIV.[15]

Gramont combated the young queen's influence and tried to blot out the memories which she still preserved of the Orsini, but his plans came to grief. Maréchal de Tessé advised the return of the Princess, who had been received in Versailles with a great show of appreciation. Felipe V and María Luisa followed this up by inviting the former first lady-in-waiting back and they also obtained the recall of Orry. Gramont was dismissed, and a new ambassador, Amelot, marquis de Gournay, a cold and thoughtful legist and a Councillor of State, who had been French ambassador to the Venetian Republic, Portugal and Switzerland, accompanied the Princess de Orsini back to Spain, arriving there on 5 August 1705.

Louis XIV, his confidence in her renewed, now began to govern Spain through the Orsini, but he had to be wary since Spanish pride would not brook too clear a show of Versailles influence. All the same, Queen María Luisa every day had proof of the Princess's special talent and her decided fondness for political affairs. For their part the Spanish grandees, such as the duque de Beragua and the conde de Aguilar, both intelligent men and devoted to the house of Bourbon, suffered from the intervention of Louis XIV. The Papal nuncio, Acquivia, enjoyed a certain influence on the Queen. Of the rest, the proud Medinaceli can hardly be counted among the faithful adherents of Felipe or the French connexion. The conde de Palma and the marqués del Carpio detested France. On the other hand Medina Sidonia, Villafranca, Benevente and de Sessa were devoted to the young Spanish king. Although San Esteban made a great show of ardour towards the Bourbons, what he really sought was self-interest. Castel-Rodrigo, adulator and good courtier, was not someone to trust very much. The conde de Montellano, President of the Council of Castile, gifted with unusual intelligence and of the utmost loyalty, shared the direction of affairs of state with the weak but able duque de Montalto, the variable Monterrey, and the experienced (and surely as a nonagenarian he should have been!) marqués de Mancera. The marqués de Rivas had the advantage over all the rest so far as intellectual qualities and activity went, but he was astute and egotistical and, with reason, the French agents had no confidence in his loyalty to the Bourbon dynasty.[16]

The arrival of Amelot and Orry at once changed the composition of the royal cabinet (*Despacho*); the marqués de Rivas not surprisingly was replaced by the marqués de Mejorada, and there now came upon the scene the hitherto obscure José Grimaldo, upright and hard working. At this point Montalto and Monterrey retired, while Montellano and Mancera remained in office. The two great supporters of the Bourbons in Felipe's first difficult days in Spain, Portocarrero and Arias lived respectively in their episcopal seats of Toledo and Sevilla. Meanwhile Orry and Amelot tried to bring about a constitutional revolution by suppressing the privileges of the three ancient realms of Aragón, Valencia and Cataluña, since they felt it to be unjust that they did not bear the financial burdens of the country equally with Castile. Other points in their programme were the weakening of the power of the nobility and the keeping of the religious orders in subordination. Orry wanted to introduce the French system of bourgeois bureaucratic government directed against the traditions of Spain, as in France it had been directed against the feudal nobles and regionalism. The reformers sought an early confrontation with the grandees and the Church.

The war continued intermittently. The Portuguese recovered Marván and Salvatierra and, in May 1705, took Valencia de Alcántara and Albuquerque. By autumn the Portuguese were over the frontier besieging Badajoz, but were driven off by Tessé.

Now there arrived in the Austrian headquarters at Lisbon that extraordinary Englishman, Charles Mordaunt, Earl of Peterborough, extravagant and a genius. He was brave and impetuous like a Frenchman, but had plenty of British tenacity. His abilities were profound as they were varied, but he could stick at nothing for long, and he suffered from a wanderlust which prompted him constantly to change his occupation and his place of residence. He liked to rush over Europe like a courier, one Sunday in Vienna and the following one in The Hague; now he wanted to see Madrid, the next moment Copenhagen. Macaulay calls him the last of the wandering knights, brave to temerity, liberal to profusion, courteous in his relations with his enemies, protector of the weak, passionate in love. Before this extrovert there had arrived at Lisbon the Archduke Charles, a man his very opposite, reserved, pompous and pious. The Archduke and the Earl set sail for Gibraltar where they took on board the Prince of Hesse-Darmstadt whose advice was to make for Cataluña.

The north-eastern part of Spain felt warm sympathy for the Archduke. The English were driven from the Isla de León but, on the other hand, in Altea and Denia they were received with delight on 8 August 1705. The conde de Cifuentes prepared the uprising in the Allies' favour of the whole of the province of Valencia, which was overrun by the troops of Juan Bautista Basset y Ramos and Juan Gil. The efforts of the marqués de Villagarcía, Viceroy of Valencia, Luis de Zúñiga and the duque de Gandia to stop them were vain. The Catalan José Nebot and the Valencian Juan Basset took Zúñiga prisoner at Oliva on 12 December. Soon they had entered Gandia and, before long, Valencia, where the conde de Cardona was nominated Viceroy by the Archduke. Alicante, La Hoya, Cartalla, Peñiscola and Montesa held out for Felipe V, but Juan Tárrega captured Játiva and the marqués de Rafal took Orihuela, both of which declared for Charles of Austria.

Great misfortunes overtook the Bourbon cause in Cataluña. The Anglo-Dutch fleet appeared before Barcelona on 22 August and, with the aid of the peasantry, who had rebelled in his favour, the Archduke was able to disembark near the capital and soon afterwards set up his court at Sans.[17] The Bourbon Viceroy Francisco Velasco could rely on little support in Barcelona; but the Earl of Peterborough remained inactive before the city, deaf to the reproaches of Hesse-Darmstadt. Then suddenly one day, true to his impulsive nature, he invited the Prince to lead a reckless assault on the castle of Montjuich with cavalry. Hesse-Darmstadt accepted the challenge and carried out the seemingly incredible, paying however with his life, and on the 14 September 1705 it was the dashing Peterborough who found himself master of the outworks and the trenches. Three days later the English had captured Montjuich itself. Garacho, the commander of the fortress, had been killed and, on the 9 October, Barcelona capitulated. In the whole of eastern Cataluña only Rosas recognised Felipe V.

The example of Barcelona led to uprisings in central Cataluña,[18] and Lérida fell to the Austrians in spite of the brilliant defence of the Portuguese general in Bourbon service, Álvaro Faria de Melo; Aragón followed suit and the towns of Alcañiz, Caspe, Monroy and Calaceite fell. The conde de San Esteban de Gormaz, named Captain-General of Aragón, managed to check the general desertion from the Bourbons to the Austrians; but the whole region of Ribagorza revolted and Monzón fell to the Austrians in October 1705. Two months later, in December, there were disturbances in Zaragoza directed against Tessé and his troops. It appears that these riots were due to the intrigues of the conde de Sástago and the marqués de Coscojuela who were in touch with the conde de Cifuentes, all of them secretly working for the Austrians. By early 1706 a civil war between the supporters of Bourbons on the one hand and Austrians on the other had developed with all the cruelty on both sides that is usually so marked a feature of internecine war. By February 1706, when Felipe V took command of his troops in this theatre of war, it reached the borders of Cataluña and Aragón in the north-west, and in the south it had almost entered Murcia. On 23 February he made a bid to recover Barcelona, but the assault failed for all his personal bravery. By this time the duc de Noailles had arrived from France with reinforcements, while the comte de Toulouse, bastard son of Louis XIV, came with his fleet, bringing with it a hope soon to be extinguished when it turned tail at the sight of the Anglo-Dutch fleet which was patrolling the coast of Cataluña. For the moment Felipe felt that all was lost; in May 1706 he called off the siege of Barcelona,[19] and drawing out his northern army from Cataluña retreated to Roussillon. Thence, taking a roundabout route by which he avoided Cataluña and Aragón, he advanced rapidly on Madrid, where his queen María Luisa as Regent had given new proof of her talent and serenity of mind.

The war had already flared up in the province of Valencia, where the Portuguese army, commanded by Lord Galway and the Portuguese marquês de las Minas, had captured the fortified town of Alcántara on 14 April 1706. In the following months matters were still more serious for the young Spanish sovereign. The duc de Berwick's army was forced to retreat and there was talk of his treason. Ciudad Rodrigo fell into Galway's hands and, on 20 June, Felipe and María Luisa hurriedly left Madrid, which the Allies entered shortly afterwards. On the twenty-fifth the Archduke Charles in his absence was proclaimed Charles III in the capital.

In Valencia the leaders Basset and Nebot were masters of the situation, and Peterborough proceeded there to organise the region. The city of Orihuela, at the instigation of the marqués de Rafal, had declared for the Archduke, as had the conde de Santa Cruz, commander of the Spanish galleys. On 29 June, Zaragoza joined the Austrian cause, and the whole of Aragón followed suit except Tarazona, Borja, Jaca, Ainsa and Canfranc, thanks to the French troops which the governor of Béarn sent across the frontier to the help of the Bourbons. Feted everywhere on the way, the Archduke arrived at Zaragoza, whence he decided to go to Madrid, certain that Spain was now in his hands. He could rely on three armies, the Portuguese army, that of Zaragoza, which was directly under his command, and that of Valencia commanded by Peterborough. By July, Charles of Austria had entered the capital.[20]

Galway, after taking Toledo, turned eastwards and advanced by way of Alcalá to Guadalajara and Jadraque. Felipe V awaited him at Atrinza with troops sent by Louis, and it was soon seen—something which the slow-witted Archduke Charles had failed to see—that Castile, unlike Aragón, Cataluña and Valencia, was loyal to him. Castile was Spain, the rest were in the pay of the despised and unwanted foreigners. The Castilians were too proud to allow a French army to do their fighting for them: men and money flowed into Atrinza, and Galway's army which in the morning had been the pursuer was by the evening itself pursued. So dramatically had the fortune of the war changed that on 4 August 1706 the Bourbons recovered Madrid. Many nobles such as Oropesa and Sástago had committed themselves to acknowledging the Archduke Charles as their king, others such as Medinaceli, if they could not reach Felipe at least kept in touch with Queen María Luisa who held court Burgos. The majority of the grandees, however, having retired to their estates, without committing themselves, quietly awaited the result of this struggle between Habsburg and Bourbon, ready, of course, when this was decided to go over to the victor. The Archduke had finally come to see that Castile was hostile to him and ordered on 7 September a general retiral on Valencia against the advice of the marquês de las Minas, who advocated a retreat to Portugal.

The Austrians, therefore, crossed the Tajo and the Júcar, their rearguard harrassed by Berwick's army, for the rumours about Berwick's treachery to the Bourbons had been totally false. Both armies took up winter quarters in the neighbourhood of Alicante (still held by the Allies) and along the Valencian frontier. By the end of the year Felipé V had re-established his court in Madrid and looked forward to 1707 as the year of decision. Yet the situation outside Spain was by no means propitious for the Bourbons. The Duke of Marlborough had routed maréchal Villeroy at Ramillies in May 1706. A combined army of the United Provinces and Prussia occupied practically the whole of Spanish Brabant, and Luis de Borja, marqués de Caracena surrendered Antwerp, with the result that the Elector of Bavaria with his Walloon and Spanish troops fell back on Mons. Shortly afterwards Marlborough took Menin and Dundermonde. On the other hand maréchal Villars held German territory from the Rhine to Philipsburg.

In Italy also affairs went very badly for Felipe V. The advantages obtained by Berwick and Vendôme after the capture of Nice were lost by the calling away of both commanders, the first to the army of Extremadura and the other to Versailles. Vendôme before long returned to Italy, but just as he was laying siege to Turin he was again summoned away, this time to replace Villeroy in Flanders. Prince Eugène in September 1706 forced the siege of Turin, and in that battle General Marsin was mortally wounded, the consequence being that the French army retreated across the Alps, abandoning Piedmont and the Milanese, which territories Prince Eugène and the Duke of Savoy occupied in the name of the Archduke Charles of Austria. In March 1707, Louis XIV officially gave up the Milanese by a treaty of neutrality, and the Spanish evacuated the last of the fortresses which they still held there. Besides, Spanish control of Naples was lost in spite of the heroic efforts of the marqués de Villena and in spite of the defence of Gaeta by Walloon and Spanish forces. Only Sicily remained in the hands of Felipe V thanks to its Viceroy, the marqués de los Balbases.

At this lowest ebb of its fortunes the Bourbon cause was suddenly given new life by the unlooked for and extraordinary victory of Almansa,[21] gained by the duc de Berwick on 25 April 1707. A cynic will note that at this battle the British army was commanded by an emigrant French Protestant, Ruvigny (for such was the original name, country and church of the man we know as Lord Galway), and the French army by an emigrant English Catholic, Berwick, peer and marshal of France. The strange inaction of Peterborough who remained in Valencia reading *Don Quixote* and dallying with the Valencian girls, and the inactivity of Castile, had already the year before seriously impaired the cause of the Archduke Charles, whose armies had retreated from Madrid to Valencia. From the Allies' point of view it was imperative to open the road between Valencia and Madrid which had been closed by Berwick's army. They knew that the duc d'Orléans, the new commander-in-chief sent from France to join forces with Berwick, was on his way. Berwick alone might well be defeated, but with d'Orléans at his side victory for the supporters of the House of Austria was slender. Therefore Minas and Galway decided to give battle before he arrived. They did so, and in fact even by forced marches d'Orléans himself did not reach Berwick until twenty-four hours after the battle; but that made no difference, for his main forces arrived in time. Berwick alone turned out to be more than a match for them. He did not need d'Orléans's generalship.

The affray at Almansa began with the usual cannonade. Before long Lord Galway's cavalry was routed by the second Franco-Spanish line. Then the *Felipista* front was broken in two by the enemy's thrust, but the infantry wheeled round while the defeated cavalry was overpowered. Finally the Imperialists were pursued along the Alicante road and thirteen battalions were captured. Berwick had distinguished himself beyond all doubt in a battle which turned the tide in the Bourbons' favour. Almansa is the one decisive battle of the War of the Spanish Succession in Spain and, as a result of it, the Allies lost the whole of the province of Valencia and had to rely on their Catalan supporters alone for the rest of the campaign. The Spanish infantry, with José Amézaga at its head, had turned what had begun as a disaster into a triumph. True enough, the Franco-Spanish army of about 25,000 men was far larger than the Allied army, which can be computed at about 15,000, according to Berwick, for the main French army of d'Orléans had arrived in time for the battle, although d'Orléans himself had hung behind in Madrid; but, all the same, the Bourbon victory had been won without him. The losses, however, for the Bourbons had been much greater than for the Allies, in fact about twice as great. Berwick was rewarded by being created a grandee with the title of duque de Liria.

The immediate consequence of Almansa was the capitulation of General Requena and the entry of the duc d'Orléans into Valencia on 8 May 1707, the Archduke's Viceroy, the conde de la Corzana, having fled. The conde de Mahoni recovered Alcira, while Darfeld, who had already distinguished himself at Almansa as one of the cavalry commanders, took the heroic town of Játiva, which had put up a firm resistance. On 26 May, d'Orléans, having in the meantime reduced Calatayud, entered Zaragoza. Berwick[22] and d'Orléans, now united, decided to besiege Lérida. At first Berwick had to absent himself from this action in order to bring help to Toulon, menaced by the Allies; but he was still able to return in time to be present at the capitulation of Lérida on 14 November.[23] After this the plain of Urgel and the towns of Cervera, Tárrega and Morella fell into the hands of the Bourbons, as did Ciudad Rodrigo on the far away eastern front in Extremadura near the Portuguese frontier.

At court the Orsini continued in favour, having as excellent auxiliaries Orry and Amelot. Amelot, diplomat and statesman, was more flexible and balanced than Orry, and his conduct proved him to be a man of honour, sensible, kindly yet firm, prudent and modest, an instance of the best type of a man of law. He had no ambition for honours, and, besides, he had no family to consider. Amelot's influence was deep and lasting. He sought to modify the Spanish political system, replacing its feudal character by French absolutist doctrines, which meant a reliance not on great nobles and churchmen with their selfish, vested interests, but on an enlightened civil service of broad views, recruited from among men of merit of the professional classes. From the first he naturally met with the opposition of the grandees, the ecclesiastical hierarchy and members of the religious orders, and of the provinces. After the battle of Almansa, which had brought to account the age-old menace of regionalism as against unity in Spain, the latter exemplified by the patriotism of Castile, he felt emboldened to declare himself to be opposed to the selfish interests of Aragón, Valencia and Cataluña. He was the author of the suppression of provincial privileges, and has been vilified understandably by Catalans, the most emotional and vociferous on the subject, but he laid the foundations for a better-administered Spain. The famous Pragmatic doctrine of 1707 is due to him. Amelot was the creator of concentration camps to save the civilian population from the ravages of war, he created inspectorships and intendantships of the army, and ordered a revision of conflicting laws to bring about uniformity, by that means creating a national law for Spain. As an upholder of French ideas he had many difficulties with the grandees to overcome; but to him Spain owed the general improvement in incomes and taxation policy, and in the organisation of the army. One can certainly affirm that by his reforms he prepared the way for the victory of the Bourbon cause in Spain.

Amelot's great helper was the Spanish lawyer Melchor Rafael de Macanaz, who went to Valencia[24] to reorganise that province, in particular to deal out destruction to the city of Játiva for having remained perhaps recklessly faithful to the Archduke Charles. Many historians, especially and naturally Catalan ones, have indignantly described how on the ruins of this city was built the town of 'San Felipe', but it is certain that only some quarters were razed and medieval monuments remain. The duc d'Orléans, in command of the army of occupation, was charged with modifying and softening the reforms imposed from Madrid and not carrying out the orders of confiscation emanating from the court, which very much disgusted King Felipe, who suspected that his uncle, the duke, was aiming at creating his own following in this area. On 25 August 1707 the elder son of Felipe and María Luisa was born and was called Luis, automatically assuming the title of príncipe de las Asturias. Peace between Felipe and d'Orléans seems to have been re-established and d'Orléans became the child's godfather.

The bravery of the Catalans and Valencians upheld the Archduke's interest, and they did not lose heart as a result of Almansa. On 9 January 1708 the conde de Mahoni retook Alcoy, and shortly afterwards the Moors captured Oran held for the Archduke. At this period Orléans's actions appear to be somewhat equivocal as if he were eager to assure for himself the succession to the Spanish crown if the Allies were ready to treat with him. The historian Baudrillart defends the Duke against these charges, but even though in other respects his conduct can be justified as regards the question of the succession, his ambitions are clear enough.[25] Apart from this, his licentious life in Madrid had scandalised the court.[26]

At this point Queen Anne of Great Britain sent General Stanhope to Cataluña with money and an army, and soon afterwards on 20 June Princess Isabel Christine of Brunswick, recently married to the Archduke, disembarked in Barcelona where she was received with all the honours of a queen, her husband being openly called Charles III of Spain.[27] Stahremberg with an allied army could not, however, prevent Tortosa falling into d'Orléans's hands on 19 July 1708, and the following autumn a campaign began which ended, on 2 December, in the reduction of Alicante, except for the fort; on 17 April 1709 that also fell to the Bourbons. Stahremberg's attempt to recover Tortosa met with no success but, on the other hand, Admiral Leake gained possession of Sardinia and Stanhope took Menorca in 1708.

Now Felipe found himself at loggerheads with Pope Clement XI,[28] since the Pope was alarmed at the Gallican tendencies of Orry and Amelot as regards ecclesiastical matters. The rupture between the Bourbons and the Vatican ended in the latter's recognition of the Archduke in 1708;[29] but soon the proceedings of the Austrians in Italy, where they had taken the Milanese and Naples and now invaded the Papal States, made the Pope repent of his recognition of the Habsburgs. Nonetheless, it was difficult for Clement XI to change his policy, since France was worn out, and Felipe V with only moderate resources could not stand up to the power of the Imperialists and the maritime nations united against the Bourbons. The most recent events confirmed the situation. The Duke of Burgundy and maréchal Vendôme had gained some successes in Brabant by taking Ghent and Bruges, but shortly afterwards the French were defeated by Marlborough and Prince Eugène at the battle of Audenarde on 11 July 1708, and on 22 October maréchal de Boufflers capitulated at Lille. When on 29

December Ghent fell, Artois and Picardy were left defenceless against the victorious Allies.

In such an overwhelmingly disastrous situation, Louis XIV decided to negotiate with his enemies. At first the maritime powers, Great Britain and the United Provinces, demanded that Felipe V should renounce the Spanish throne; but when Louis consulted his grandson, he found that the young king was energetically opposed to any such thing, and the negotiations took another direction. What was now considered was the dismemberment of the Spanish Empire, and on this basis Great Britain and the United Provinces agreed to parley. Felipe V, however, leaning on his Spanish advisers, resolved to free himself from French tutelage. A Franco-Spanish conference at The Hague was therefore arranged.

The majority of Spanish statesmen hated France's intervention in the government of Spain, and such were the President of the Council of Castile, Francisco Ronquillo, the duque de Medina Sidonia, the duque de San Juan, the duque de Veragua, the conde de Aguilar, the conde de Monterrey and the duque de Montalto. The two last wanted above all at whatever cost to destroy the French diplomat Amelot. The time was propitious and, realising this, the clever Princess de Orsini, who dominated both Felipe and María Luisa, placed herself at the head of the cabal, with the result that soon Amelot was left out of the Royal Council, being replaced by Blécourt.

Thereafter a government comprised solely of Spaniards was formed. The duque de Medinaceli, in reality the head of government, took over affairs of state, while the marqués de Bedmar was placed in control of the War Department and the other ministers were confirmed in their positions. Nonetheless, the Princess de Orsini, though remaining in the background, enjoyed an all-embracing influence. It is true that now Louis XIV no longer governed Spain and that he was to go so far as to abandon it to the claims of the Allies, but their demands would be intolerable if followed to the end. The old King regarded it as especially hateful that he should be forced to hand over the Spanish fortresses held by France. Finally Louis refused to give in, and the contestants prepared for a new campaign.

In the renewed hostilities Spain now fought on her own account. The feeling against the French was great, and moreover Louis XIV wanted to base future negotiations on a French policy which had nothing to do with the particular interests of his grandson. For that reason he was ready for compromises, which after all might be advantageous to him since he did have troops in Spain. He now had no concern for Spain's future. Besides, he was willing to go so far as to dissimulate the supposed intrigues of his nephew the duc d'Orléans to become King of Spain, since these pretensions, kept up his sleeve, might be a motive for early negotiations, he felt, with the Allies. The culpability of d'Orléans rested on the declarations of his secret agents Regnault and Flotte, retained at the instigation of the astute Princess de Orsini; but the historian Baudrillart shows that d'Orléans was in no way criminally involved and that the case against him was forged by a monk Le Marchand.

The conditions of peace were unacceptable. France was about to make a supreme effort against formidable enemies and, exhausted and weary as she was, she now fought on all fronts to free her very soil from invasion. Marlborough took the fortress of Tournai and near Mons on 11 September 1709 he defeated maréchal Villars[30] in the bloody battle of Malplaquet. Mons was won for the Allies, yet Berwick in the Dauphiné and on the slopes of the Alps held the Duke of Savoy, while in Germany the duc d'Harcourt dug himself in along the lines of the Lauter in Westphalia.

In Spain the Bourbon army commanded by the marqués de Bay, won the battle of Gudiña in the province of Orense, and as a result the Austrian danger from the Portuguese frontier was staved off for the moment. On the other hand the conde de Aguilar, in command of the Spanish Bourbon army in Cataluña, found himself in the position of being unable to do anything to prevent Balaguer from falling into the hands of Stahremberg. The reason for the inaction of the Bourbons in this region was the attitude of the maréchal de Bezons, now commander of the French army there, who had received orders from Louis to remain on the defensive, perhaps to second the projects of Orléans who, it was murmured, maintained a correspondence with Stanhope, the English general. King Felipe, on 2 September 1709, put himself at the head of his army of the north, but the Allies were very well entrenched and it was impossible to break their lines. Meanwhile, the duc de Noailles entered Spanish territory from Roussillon and recovered the important fortress of Figueras. In spite of the unexpected vigour shown by France in this last event, the attitude of the French court reflected the longing of the whole nation for peace. Madame de Maintenon used all her influence with Louis to bring it about, and the Royal Council decided to parley with the enemy. Negotiations were opened at The Hague, but the Allies insultingly demanded that Louis should declare war on his grandson, and the old man's reply was to break off all negotiations, although soon afterwards he began to waver.

The year 1710 was to be decisive for the cause of Felipe V. The loyalty of Castile and the gold of America led to the raising of a new army, organised by the conde de Aguilar, who was, however, soon afterwards deprived of his command as a result of his outrageous pretensions. A far worse fate awaited the duque de Medinaceli who, accused of having relations with the Allies, was first confined in the Alcázar of Segovia and afterwards sent to the castle of Pamplona, where he died. Medinaceli's fall brought down other grandees who were similarly inculpated in plots against the Bourbons. Felipe, having by a great error of judgement given the marqués de Villadarias, the general who had performed so badly at the siege of Gibraltar, command in Aragón, departed from Madrid with him on 3 May 1710 to join his troops in Cataluña, leaving María Luisa as Regent once more.

Villadarias soon showed his imprudence by attacking the Allies, who had all the advantage of holding strong positions, and the result was a struggle on the heights of Almenara, a little to the north of Lérida, in which the Bourbon armies were defeated by Stanhope and Stahremberg on 27 July 1710. The British, German, Catalan and Dutch followed up their victory by pursuing the conquered Bourbons along the road to Zaragoza. In front of the city another battle took place, the marqués de Bay commanding the Bourbons, on 20 August. Although the right wing of Felipe's cavalry broke the Allied left, everywhere else the *Felipistas'* lines were broken by the Allies who gained the final victory. The rout and flight of the Bourbon armies was so inexplicable that it was openly said that it was the result of the treason of some of the grandees. The situation for Felipe was now as disastrous as it had been right at the beginning of the war. Indeed the battle of Zaragoza could have been decisive and could have cost Felipe his throne.

After delaying his march on Madrid for no apparent reason, the Archduke Charles, now at the head of the Allied armies, lingered for some time in Zaragoza, and it was not until 21 September that he entered the capital in triumph, Felipe's court having in the meantime had ample opportunity to make for Valladolid, something which it would have been unable to do if the Archduke had pressed on to Madrid immediately after the victory. Master of the capital, he now gave ample proof of his cold, unsympathetic and tactless character by adopting policies which ended by alienating his Aragonese and new Castilian supporters. When he should have been most careful not to offend the religious susceptibilities of the Spanish he gave free rein to Imperialist armies, the majority of them Protestants, to plunder churches and convents and commit other outrages, which led to a rising tide of guerrilla warfare, of surprise attacks, and ambushes carried out against the Imperialists by small detachments of roving soldiers aided and abetted by the peasantry.

Nonetheless, the reports which reached Versailles about the position of Felipe V were each time more alarming. Louis XIV before the insistence of his grandson and in view of his downright refusal to abdicate, sent to Spain the duc de Vendôme to take command of the Bourbon army. Noailles was also sent, his original mission being to report to Louis on the true state of Felipe's situation and to let the French court know what his resources were. The information that Noailles provided was encouraging, since as if by magic new battalions had been raised and the defeated army had been reorganised thanks to the fidelity and talent of the conde de Aguilar and to Castilian tenacity. The queen retired to Vitoria, and Noailles decided on a plan of strategy, which was to attack Cataluña while Vendôme dislodged the Imperialists from Castile.

Stahremberg's plan as commander-in-chief of the Imperialists was to join the Portuguese, hoping in this way to dominate the centre of the peninsula. Felipe, having gained information as to his intention, took up his position on the right bank of the Tajo at the bridge of Almaraz.[31] The hostility of the Castilians to the Imperialists now forced Stahremberg, who could not face a battle with the Bourbons since Felipe, now in Valladolid, had the army of Extremadura intact, to abandon Madrid and retreat towards Aragón. Felipe, who could now count on a general of such experience as Vendôme, pursued the Allies, and having roundly defeated them at the battles of Brihuega and Villaviciosa, (9 and 11 December 1710),[32] definitely gained control of Spain for good and all. The details of the events leading to this extraordinary change of fortune are as follows.

The Archduke Charles, with a cavalry corps, had set out, after Stahremberg's abandonment of Madrid, from Zaragoza to Barcelona. Felipe at once occupied Madrid and, without a moment's delay, attacked the British army under Stanhope who, after three days of stubborn battle, capitulated at Brihuega, having fought to the last cartridge. The fort was taken by assault and, at the surrender, Generals Stanhope, Hyl and Carpenter and all their troops were captured.

When Stahremberg came to the aid of Stanhope, great was his surprise to find the enemy in line of combat, commanded by Vendôme, along the plain of Villaviciosa. The battle was joined on 11 December 1710, and the marqués de Valdecañas with his cavalry charge drove back the Imperialists, only to endanger the Bourbon position by pursuing the wing he had defeated too far from the battlefield, thereby taking out of action some valuable forces which the Bourbons vitally needed. Meanwhile, the Spaniard Antonio de Villarroel, who commanded the Imperialist centre, delivered some hammer-blows to Felipe's forces, obliging them to retreat in disorder and capturing their artillery. This Bourbon centre now reformed itself and attacked Villarroel, who resisted stoutly. At that moment the flank attack of a section of the Spanish cavalry, which had become detached from the rest the day before but now opportunely flung itself into the fray, and the return of the imprudent Valdecañas decided the victory in favour of Felipe. The Imperialist right, however, commanded by Stahremberg, formed itself into squares which resisted the attacks of the victorious Bourbon cavalry, and, night intervening, the Imperialist army, under cover of nearby woods, was able to retreat without further harm.

Some Spanish historians are critical of Vendôme,[33] saying that his own front line was broken and that the Bourbon left retreated; but these are surely minor blemishes in an otherwise undoubted Bourbon victory which was due to his master mind. What one notices about Villaviciosa is the superiority, both in quality and number, of the Bourbon to the Imperialist cavalry.[34]

Noailles was meanwhile invading Cataluña, and after the capture of Gerona on 25 January 1711, Felipe V's power reached Ampurdán. The Imperialists continued to retreat, while the Bourbons under Valdecañas took Estadilla, Benabarre, Graus and the whole county of Ribagorza, continuing their mopping-up operations with the capture of Balaguer.

Soon in the whole of Cataluña the Archduke held little more than Barcelona, Tarragona and their environs.

In one year the fortunes of the Spanish Bourbons had soared while, ironically enough, those of the French Bourbons had sunk, for the war in the North, in Flanders, had meant the loss of Douai, Béthune, Saint-Venant and Aire-sur-la Lys, all captured by the Allies. Then the war languished. In Spain the Bourbon cause suffered from the growing rivalry between Vendôme and Noailles, and throughout 1711, its successes amounted to little more than the capture of such unimportant towns in Cataluña as Benasque, Castel León and Prats del Rey, while an attack on Tortosa broke down.

The Archduke Charles, whose heart had already become faint enough, now had greater matters than a Spanish throne, practically lost anyway, to consider. His brother Joseph I had died on 17 April 1711, and now the Imperial crown was in his hands. He could no longer afford to wait in Cataluña and, 27 September, he set out for Vienna, leaving Stahremberg in command of the Imperial army, encamped on the outskirts of Barcelona.

As for the Spanish army of Portugal, commanded by Alejandro, marqués de Bay, it did nothing of importance beyond capturing some small towns from the Allies. Yet, such as they were, these small victories were all grist to the mill of Bourbon success.

After the victory of Villaviciosa Felipe decided to reorganise the Kingdom of Aragón, respecting private law and civil privileges, but insisting on the suppression of the particular laws of Aragón both of a political or constitutional character and everything that concerned primitive law. In these areas Castilian legislation was imposed. While he was looking into these matters, he and his court stayed in Zaragoza, which now became a hotbed of intrigue, dominated by the Princess de Orsini, who still influenced the King and Queen beyond anyone else. In the summer of 1711, Queen María Luisa's health, undermined by constant application to affairs of state for many years past, broke down, a presage of the coming of her serious illness. But, after staying in the cool of Corella de Navarra, she was able to return by autumn to Madrid, to which the court had in the interval gone.

Uppermost in everyone's mind now was peace.[35] In a war which had lasted so long and which had ruined continental Europe, Great Britain emerged as the sole winner. Having already adopted a policy of only partial involvement, subsidising her Allies but only partly committing her forces to the fray—a policy which she had assumed during William III's reign and which she would continue until the Peninsular War—she had been quietly building up the commerical foundations, backed by an increasingly strong navy, on which she was to erect her empire in the course of the eighteenth century. She had become a major power and, for the first time in history, her home politics were of vital importance to Europe.

As to peace, already in 1705 France, seeking to divide the Allies, had tried to treat with the United Provinces in the person of the Grand Pensionary, Heinsius. It had seemed that these two old adversaries, so diametrically opposed in their ideologies, might come to an understanding; but the other members of the alliance had refused to allow it. Marlborough and Eugène, tired of the interference of Dutch civilians in their war affairs in the Low Countries, insisted that any negotiations with the enemy must be carried out by all members of the Grand Alliance. Twice a peace treaty seemed close; but at the negotiations at The Hague the Allies had posed the demand—an impossible one surely—that Louis should fight against his grandson. It was stoutly refused by the old king; but not long afterwards, at Gertruydenberg, that same aged monarch, war-weary at last, had shown himself ready to abandon Felipe. This time, however, filled with the new courage of his growing success, that same Felipe had dared to threaten to destroy those negotiations.

The death in the spring of 1711 of Emperor Joseph I had, however, changed the position. The Archduke Charles was now Emperor, his new office lessening his interest in a Spanish crown which after eleven years still eluded him. With that stiff, cold presence removed, and a Tory government, sworn to isolationism, lately come to power in Westminster, the way seemed clear for some understanding between Great Britain and France, and preliminaries opened in London. The Whigs had fallen and with them the war party and Marlborough.[36] After a long eclipse the landed interest was asserting itself against the commercial one, which had found in the war golden opportunities to expand trade in the wake of victorious navies, while in clothing and feeding armies many a London merchant had made his fortune to buy land and vie with the old gentry. On the other hand, to the landowner the war, growing more bloody and indecisive in each campaign, meant not glory but more taxes. Malplaquet had been a gory and apparently useless business. Swift's pamphlet *The Conduct of the Allies*, in which he condemned Marlborough for seeking personal prestige at the expense of the nation, had found an echo in many war-weary hearts. Queen Anne herself, tired of the insolence of the Marlboroughs and concerned to preserve the essence of national integrity and above all the Church of England, which had been threatened by Whiggish nonconformists, had dismissed the Whigs, virtually in power since 1689. Indeed if there had been any doubt after Malplaquet in 1709 that the war had reached a stalemate, after the Bourbon victories of Brihuega and Villaviciosa the public came to realise that the Allies were now losing battles.

Furthermore, while Charles remained Archduke his candidacy as King of Spain did not seem dangerous. He would surely not succeed as Emperor as well; but the sudden and unexpected death of his brother Joseph I was another matter; as Emperor and King of Spain he would be a new Charles V, and the balance of power in Europe would be overturned. This last consideration impelled Great Britain to leave the coalition.

It was difficult to induce Felipe V, and indeed stubborn little María Luisa, to agree to the dismemberment of his possessions. The ability of the French agent Bonnac overcame his first resistance and the King nominated the conde de Bergerick as his plenipotentiary; but the Spanish negotiators were not allowed to treat. Louis XIV pressed his grandson to act, to the great disgust of the latter, who, however, finally consented[37] to cede the Low Countries to the Elector of Bavaria and in this way an obvious dismemberment began. The Princess de Orsini sought a profitable recompense consisting of a Flemish principate. The year 1711 ended with these preliminaries, and on 22 December the Emperor Charles VI was crowned at Frankfurt-am-Main. The congress was set to begin in January, 1712 in Utrecht, the city chosen for it by Queen Anne. The peace treaty there negotiated was to transform the world, and as a result of it the Spanish power in Europe was to disappear and Spain's American Empire was gradually to decay. New powers were to arise, with the preponderance of Great Britain the most striking feature of the change.

After the sessions had opened on the 22 January 1712 it was soon seen how exorbitant were the pretensions of the Emperor, while the British and Dutch seemed disposed to drive a hard bargain. The recent death of the French Dauphin had made the British suspicious of the possible union of the French and Spanish crowns, which increased to a desperate fear when two more deaths in Louis's family occurred soon afterwards, that of the heir presumptive the Duke of Burgundy on 18 February and that of the Duke of Brittany, the new Dauphin, on 8 March 1712. The possibility that the French throne would fall to Felipe V of Spain seemed imminent, and British delegates were determined to force him to renounce all claim to it. Felipe, under pressure again from Louis XIV, who advised him that it was impossible to wear both crowns, unwillingly agreed; but when his grandfather suggested that he might succeed him in France, Felipe had no hesitation in choosing to keep the Spanish throne.[38]

Faced with this renunciation, Felipe sought from the British in compensation both Gibraltar and some Italian territory, but Great Britain refused to accede to such claims. On 5 November 1712 the Council of Castile and the *cortes* met in Madrid, at which gatherings Felipe formally renounced all claim to the French throne in the presence of the French and British ambassadors.[39] The duc d'Orléans and the duc de Berry, for their part, renounced their rights to the Spanish throne on 19 November, and it was decided that if Felipe's line failed, then the Spanish crown would pass to the House of Savoy. Felipe then promulgated a law of succession, called by Baudrillart[40] 'semisalic', in virtue of which, contrary to traditional Spanish custom, preference in the succession would be given to the male descendents of Felipe V whether of the direct or collateral lines, thus giving them right before all infantas. By December 1712 the Council of Castile had sworn its oath to this, and on 10 May 1713 this law of succession was given final approval.

Although peace negotiations were in progress, the war had not completely ended, for while Great Britain had observed a truce, Prince Eugène, commanding the Imperialists and Dutch, was still pursuing hostilities in the north. He took Quesnoy, but while he was laying siege to Landrécy, maréchal Villars, in command of a French army, forced the Imperialist lines at Denain and won a resounding triumph on 24 July 1712. The consequence of this victory was that the French gained Saint-Amand, Marchiennes, Douai, Quesnoy and Bouchain. Eugène's almost psychopathic hatred of Louis XIV and all things French was something for which the Allies had to pay dear. The wavering Dutch now eagerly sought peace, Portugal made a truce with Spain, while the Imperialists, with bad grace, unwillingly agreed to evacuate Cataluña on 14 May 1713.

Already, on 11 April 1713, the Imperialists being conspicuously absent from the negotiations, the Peace of Utrecht had been confirmed.[41] By this the Spanish monarchy, shorn of its wider pretensions to further territory in Europe, notably Italy and the Low Countries, was allowed to stand with Felipe V as master of Spain itself. France treated separately with Great Britain, the United Provinces, Prussia, Portugal and Savoy. Soon after this Louis XIV, weary at last, used all his power and influence to force Felipe to make peace with this array of the Allies, and Felipe, through his plenipotentiaries the duque de Osuna and the marqués de Monteleón, concluded peace with England (10 July 1713), Savoy (13 August 1713) and the United Provinces (20 July 1714). The Emperor Charles VI, however, disgusted with the whole proceedings and refusing to renounce his pretensions to Spain, the Spanish American Empire and Sicily, continued the war on the Rhine; but it was a foolhardy and disastrous campaign for the Imperialists. Maréchal Villars at once gained the upper hand, taking Speier in June 1713, Landau on 29 August and Freiburg the November following. As a result Prince Eugène came to terms with Villars in the palace of Rastatt-im-Baden and, after the preliminaries were confirmed on 1 March 1714, negotiations of peace between France and the Empire were completed on 7 September of the same year.[42]

Thus Rastatt had nothing to do with Spain's peace settlement. It was Utrecht which concerned her; and the clauses in the latter treaty which affected her were as follows: Felipe V, King of Spain and the American Empire, was recognised as the heir of Carlos II. So far, so good; but in Europe Felipe was deprived of all his possessions outside Spain, for he was obliged to cede the Spanish Netherlands, Naples, Sardinia, the Presidios of Tuscany and the Milanese to the Emperor, Spanish Guelderland to Brandenburg-Prussia and Sicily to the House of Savoy, while even her truly Spanish territory was not inviolate for Great Britain kept Gibraltar and Menorca. Britain as the rising commercial power was still further triumphant, gaining a privilege which no other member of the Grand Alliance could boast of, for by the *Asiento*, which gave her the unique opportunity to trade in slaves in the Spanish American Empire and to send one ship a year for that purpose to the West Indies, she had broken through a hitherto jealously guarded embargo on Spain's rich New World. Other questions dealt with at Utrecht were those of Catalan rights which, with a scandalous lack of good faith on the part of the Allies towards faithful friends, were not honoured. Cataluña was abandoned to its fate, which meant a vindictive policy towards it, on the part of Felipe and his advisers, lasting for years. As to Gibraltar, it was agreed that Great Britain would not interfere with the Catholicism of its inhabitants.

At Rastatt the Emperor Charles VI accepted the Treaty of Utrecht, but even yet he refused to recognise Felipe V as King of Spain, no doubt out of vanity and pique, and was not to do so without reservations until 1725.[43] Portugal made a separate peace with Spain in 1715, renouncing such conquests as she had made in Spain during the course of the war, and withdrew to her frontiers.

The Catalans, realising already in 1712 that they were going to be abandoned, decided to continue the war against Felipe.[44] Great Britain interceded with the triumphant Spanish King to show them clemency, while the Emperor Charles VI remembered[45] with a twinge of conscience that he had lived for five years in Cataluña and had restored to the Catalans those privileges which had been snatched away from them by Felipe and his ministers. Was it not cruel to make use of their support to dangle before them the prospect of freedom, only to throw them at the feet of this Bourbon enemy of his at the end? A Catalan deputation, headed by the marqués de Rialp now besought the Emperor to act on their behalf, but all that he could now do (and the other Allies, their consciences also smitten as, for example, one can see from the pro-Catalan books and pamphlets which now issued from the London presses, supported him as best they could) was to try to win over Felipe to promise to preserve Catalan privileges and to show mercy to the kingdom. Felipe, while agreeing to an amnesty which should apply to all except the foremost Catalan leaders, would go no further, and his little Queen María Luisa was just as severe.

Thus Cataluña fought on alone save for diminishing Imperial support.[46] When on 11 June, 1712 Vendôme died at Vinaroz, a port on the central east coast of Spain, Prince de T'Serclaes took command, and soon, since the British troops had melted away, the situation of the Imperialists was precarious. All the same, Stahremberg made one more effort and with Baron von Vetzel besieged Gerona, which by 15 December 1712 was on the point of surrendering when the advance of Berwick's troops saved the fortress and Stahremberg retreated. In virtue of the peace terms now being discussed at Utrecht, the Imperialists, who were not directly involved in this treaty as has been seen, nonetheless evacuated Cataluña. The Empress

Isabel Christine on 19 March 1713 embarked in a British ship from Barcelona, assuring the people who came to bid her farewell that she would never forget the days she had spent on Catalan soil.[47] Felipe V nominated the duca de Popoli Viceroy of Cataluña. The Catalans, however, did not lose heart and elected Antonio de Villarroel commander-in-chief, supported by the three generals, the conde de la Puebla, José Nebot and Juan Basset. On 29 July 1713 Cataluña officially declared war on Felipe V.[48]

Popoli advanced against the Catalans and, having taken the plain of Vich and the city of Manresa, soon began the blockade of Barcelona, which alone had resisted every attack of Felipe and the powerful reinforcements of the French. Nebot with his terrible guerrillas wrought destruction on the enemy, and it was with great difficulty that the Castilian general Feliciano de Bracamonte, a specialist in guerrilla fighting, was able to hold back the Catalans. Barcelona received help from Mallorca and Sardinia during October and November 1713 and Felipe's armies found themselves fighting greatly augmented Catalan volunteers in Solsona and Cardona, the latter bravely defended by Manuel Desvalls. Felipe decided to tighten his grip round Barcelona with Flanders and Sicilian troops, and the scene of hostilities spread to embrace the regions of La Plana, the mountains of Vich, Manresa, Cervera, Puigcerdá, Solsona and the banks of the River Segre. The plan was to blockade Barcelona by sea with a fleet of fifty ships.

In the Treaty of Utrecht there was a clause[49] in which Felipe, thanks to the intercession of Anne of Great Britain, promised 'to grant not only that these rights and estates be fully restored unto them but that they [the Catalans] shall henceforth enjoy all those privileges that do attach to the inhabitants of the two Castiles', which sounded magnanimous until one realised that *Catalan* privileges were not conceded at all. On 4 March 1714 the people of Barcelona sent a message to the duca de Popoli offering three million pounds (*libras*) to cover the expenses of the siege and for the recognition of their privileges. This proposal was rejected, and shortly afterwards the bombardment of Barcelona began, only to be interrupted soon afterwards by the treaty of Rastatt. The deluded inhabitants of the besieged city believed that the Emperor had been recognised as Count of Barcelona and with great jubilation celebrated the false news. The rich Barcelona merchant Sebastián Dalmare, who had recruited the regiment *de la Fe* at his own expense, went out to parley with the enemy in the name of the *Diputación*. When the disillusioned Catalans learned the sad truth, however, they refused to accept the general pardon offered them by Felipe V.

On 9 May 1714 a new bombardment of Barcelona began and the Capuchin monastery was taken by assault. The Catalans vainly hoped that the allied powers would take pity on them, and it was a cruel deception for them to learn that an army of 20,000 French under Berwick's command was making for the city. On 7 July Berwick arrived before the city, accompanied by Orry, the Spanish Minister of Finance, determined to take the place, and on the twelfth began the attack on it from the eastern or coastal side. Berwick was now in savage mood; prisoners were given no quarter, and on the twenty-fourth a breach was opened in the walls by the discharge of thirty cannon. The besieged made valiant sallies against the enemy, but it cost them dear. When on 4 September 1714 Berwick called for a surrender, the reply came back to him soon enough: that the besieged would rather die in arms. At this he ordered a general assault.

It was not until 11 September that French and *Felipistas* advanced to the final assault with fifty companies of grenadiers, forty battalions and 600 mounted dragoons. The defence was admirable. Already the standard of King Felipe fluttered on the bastion of Santa Clara and the Puerta Nueva, and the besiegers believed themselves to be masters of the city; but it was then that there began the bitterest part of the fighting, street by street, house by house, for everywhere the people of Barcelona showed a tenacious resistance. The Catalans indeed resisted their attackers from one end of the city to the other, but the enormous numerical superiority of the besiegers, who now held the bastion of San Pedro, was against them. The *Conseller en Cap* Rafael de Casanova and the Catalan commander-in-chief Antonio de Villarroel grouped their troops and attacked the French. The fight lasted for twelve hours, and even when at the end of that time the white flag was raised on the City Hall, armed civilians continued to fight everywhere. That night Berwick ordered that the city should be set on fire. The following day, to save the city from complete destruction, the deputies surrendered to the King. The conqueror promised to respect the lives of the population if Montjuich and Cardona were surrendered, and this was done. The leaders of the rebellion, Villarroel, Armengol, the marqués de Peral and a brother of Colonel Nebot were sent as prisoners to various fortresses, to Alicante, Segovia and Pamplona. The besieged had gone on fighting heroically. Neither the demands of Berwick nor his assaults on the city had daunted the people of Barcelona. They were defeated only because they were so heavily outnumbered.[50]

It has been wrongly stated[51] that in 1714 Felipe V was already completely Spanish, either for interest's sake or as a matter of convenience; for his advisers were of many nationalities, and only two Spaniards, the duque de Veragua and Alonso Manrique, enjoyed influence over him. A French woman, that Princess de Orsini who had already been such a great force in the state, continued to hold a high place in his regard, if anything increasing it. In fact it is remarkable how many foreigners were winning positions for themselves at court, notably the Italians, the duca de Popoli and principe de Cellamare. Three Flemings also came to the fore at this time, Baron de Capres, the Chevallier de Croy and the duc de Havré. Then there was the Irishman, Bourke, and, as for the French, the two with the most considerable influence were Père Robinet, the King's confessor, and the marquis de Caylus.

At the head of the royal cabinet was the very odd and inept duque de Medina Sidonia, the other members being the conde de Frigiliana, the marqués de Bedmar, the conde de Bergerick, the marqués de Mejorada (secretary) and José Grimaldo. The President of the Council of Castile was the harsh Francisco Ronquillo, while the members of the Council of State were, besides the cabinet ministers Bedmar, Medina Sidonia and Frigiliana, the intelligent duque de Montalto, the old and discredited conde de Monterrey, whose ambition it was to obtain the Archbishopric of Toledo, and another old man Mancera, who by now had ceased to attend the meetings. A person of importance was Cardinal Giudice, the Grand Inquisitor, who hungered after the post of first minister. There were two talented secretaries of state, who fortunately had control of their offices, and these were Manuel Vadillo, Secretary of the Council of State, and Bernardo Tinajero, Secretary of the Council of the Indies; but it was above all Orry who had the control of policy making.

This 'universal minister', who had been called away to France in 1704 and again in 1712, returned to Spain in 1713 at the urgent request of Felipe V. His earlier associates did not re-enter Spain, and now Orry, fully supported by the Princess de Orsini, held undisputed power over the King; but no one else liked him, for he was no courtier and, good and intelligent administrator though he was, his brusque manners and the contempt which he evinced for Spanish customs, led to a general opposition to him which dogged him for the rest of his career.[52]

Meanwhile Queen María Luisa of Spain, ill since 1710, was failing and on 14 February 1714 she died.[53] Felipe's grief for her loss was deep and sincere and he turned more than ever to the Princess de Orsini who made the most of her opportunity to strengthen her power, which grew and grew. Felipe, already prone to that melancholy which increased towards madness with the years, left the palace of the Alcázar for that of Medinaceli, which had been confiscated from the family of that fallen statesman, and there he began a life of great intimacy with the Orsini. This astute woman used all her arts and inventions to distract him, especially organising what were known to the Court as *recreadores*; she had a wooden gallery made which formed a link between her apartments and the King's, a place in fact where they could gossip together. The Princess became the arbitrator of everything and the protectress of Orry; indeed, this has been called the era of 'Orry's despotism', during which he carried out all kinds of projects. One of his victims was Francisco Ronquillo, President of the Council of Castile, who was driven from court.

On the death of the duc de Berry on 4 May 1714, the ambitions of Felipe V for the French crown rose again and, in order to circumvent the thorny question of his former renunciation, he made use of an ambassador of great ability, Cardinal Giudice, who as a result gained great prestige in both courts.[54] Louis XIV opposed Felipe's French claims; but the Orsini, with her pretensions to a Netherlands duchy, worked to destroy France's negotiations with Holland. Louis, however, exerted his authority, and Felipe V made peace with the States General on 26 June 1714.[55]

Giudice returned from Paris, having been told to break off his journey, and return to explain the sentence of condemnation, pronounced by the Inquisition, against a memorandum of royalist character published by Melchor de Macanaz, friend and protégé of Orry and the Princess de Orsini. The Princess had discovered a dangerous enemy, none other than the Abbate Alberoni.

Julio Alberoni,[56] son of a gardener of Fiorenzuola in the Duchy of Parma, was born there on 30 March 1664. His first official position was that of acolyte in Piacenza, Lombardy, and the sharp intelligence of the boy roused the attention of conte de Barni, Archbishop of Piacenza, who ordained him priest, gave him a canonry and named him his steward. Alberoni went to Rome with Barni and studied French there. When Vendôme went to Italy, Alberoni, supported by Roncovieri, agent of Parma, presented himself to him, and it is related that Vendôme, a great gastronome, took a liking to the Italian priest, not only because of his excellent French, but because he proved himself to be an outstanding chef, preparing for Vendôme the best macaroni that, he declared, he had ever tasted in his life.

Protected by Vendôme, Alberoni travelled to Flanders with him, visited Paris, and later accompanied him when he went to Spain. He served as intermediary between his benefactor and the Princess de Orsini; but when Vendôme died in 1712 he returned to France. Louis XIV was impressed by him enough to send him back to Spain as adviser to Felipe V, but his official standing was that of agent of the Duke of Parma. Following the death of Queen María Luisa, Alberoni, now on good terms with the Princess de Orsini, discussed with her the marriage of Felipe V and Isabel Farnese, daughter of the Duke of Parma.

The sagacious Princess was not, however, wise enough for the part she was playing with the astute Alberoni. She believed that the heiress of a small dukedom, brought up under the abbate's influence, would be manageable, and the accounts of Isabel which Alberoni gave her deepened this feeling. He said that she was young, simple in her tastes, and without ambition. Alberoni praised his countrywoman and promised incalculable advantages from such a union. The Princess de Orsini was in fact outplayed by Alberoni, being at first completely taken in. The comte de Chalais, her nephew, was sent to France to gain Louis XIV's assent; but too late she realised that she was digging her own diplomatic grave and that this unknown Italian princess might well supplant her. What was more, contradictory accounts of Princess Isabel were reaching her; she tried to break the match, but that opportunity was past. Isabel Farnese had set out on her journey, at the end of which she would become Queen of Spain. Alberoni hurried to meet her, being in time to greet her at Saint-Jean-Pied-à-Port, where he was made a count.

The Princess Isabel of Parma knew all about the Princess de Orsini, having received a letter outlining her attitude towards her from Felipe V himself. Consequently their meeting at Jadraque could hardly be pleasant. After formalities, the two princesses talked together; but as this led to the Orsini's making some criticisms of the Princess of Parma's coiffure, the latter raised her voice, cut her off and ordered her to leave her presence (10 February 1715). Isabel, according to Saint-Simon, ever afterwards referred to her as 'the old madwoman'. Smarting under her treatment the Princess de Orsini set out on a painful journey to France in full winter, hoping every instant that Felipe V would recall her to court; but he, ungrateful to her and forgetful of all the services which she had given to the Bourbons in Spain, abandoned her, overawed now, as he always was to be, by his future second consort.[57]

As she now vanishes from the scene this remarkable woman deserves a parting word. The Princess of Orsini, according to Saint-Simon, had an attractive face, was dark-haired, yet had large blue eyes with which she could convince anyone she wanted. She was on the tall side and her figure was perfect; indeed without being a beauty, she was most attractive. Of noble carriage, with something majestic in her elegance, she had a natural grace in everything she did down to the least important. Insinuating, courteous, affectionate, seeking to please if she was agreeably treated, when she was bent on winning anyone over it was impossible to resist her. She had about her an air of grandeur which, instead of repelling, attracted. Her conversation was delightful, inexhaustible and entertaining, since she had travelled in many countries and had known a variety of people. Her voice was sweet, she had read much, and was reflective. Saint-Simon adds that she was highly suited to intrigue, had great ambitions, and that the scope of these ambitions lay far beyond the grasp of most women. Like some men (and not so many of them) she wanted to command in the world. She[58] possessed much subtlety without allowing it to appear, and was nimble enough for intrigue, possessing a singular talent for knowing which people she should make use of for her own benefit. Her predominant weaknesses even into old age were an inclination to love affairs, and obstinacy. Basically she was proud and haughty, and liked to preserve an appearance of morality. A warm and excellent friend, but a cruel and implacable enemy, she was an intelligent, energetic and prudent woman. Professing a great affection for the royal family, she twice saved the crown of the Spanish Bourbons, laid the foundations of the Family Compact, and realised, in Amelot and Orry, men useful to the government. Her seductive nature contrasted with her ambition and pride, for she believed herself to be more powerful than the Inquisition and hungered for a sovereign principate. The shock of her fall from power destroyed her dreams of glory, and she died disillusioned and in complete retirement in Rome in December 1722.

From 1715 onwards until the end of the reign of Felipe V the true ruler of Spain was Queen Isabel,[59] mistress of the King's will from the very moment of their marriage. A letter of the Prince of Monaco describes her as of medium height, well-built, and her face oval in shape but pock-marked. She held her head well, and her blue eyes, although small, were expressive; her mouth was large, her teeth excellent and her smile was very pleasant. The Prince of Monaco goes on to say that she liked music, painting, horse-riding and hunting, and spoke several languages, adding that, her heart being Lombardic and her spirit Florentine, when she wanted something she wanted it strongly.[60] Other contemporaries complete the picture by telling us that she was brusque and violent in her manners, which quickly brought her unpopularity.

Spanish politics changed violently with her arrival: Orry, Macanaz and Père Robinet left Spain, while Père Daubenton, who had been removed by the Princess de Orsini, returned to the Spanish court, to be confessor to the King. The fallen of yesterday were now triumphant. Cardinal Giudice took over the post of tutor to the príncipe de las Asturias, and Grimaldo regained his old position. On 2 March 1715 peace with Portugal was signed, by which the Portuguese restored to Spain the American colony of Sacramento and the fortresses of Albuquerque and La Puebla and Spain paid what she owed to the Portuguese Company for the *Asiento* of negroes. With the help of France Felipe regained Mallorca and Ibiza where the duque de Rubí held out against the Bourbons (15 June 1715).[61] Over two months later, on 1 September, Louis XIV died.

Lately Felipe V had looked forward to taking over the regency which was bound to be necessary on the death of the old king; indeed the French ambassador to Spain, Saint-Aignan as well as the principe de Cellamare were in on the secret; but Louis XIV had assured the regency to his nephew, Philippe, duc d'Orléans. This did not prevent Felipe V from insinuating his pretensions to the French throne, the while declaring his hatred of Orléans.

Meanwhile someone was assiduously bowing his way into the court circle, none other than Alberoni, quietly supplanting his rival Cardinal Giudice. The abbate, who hated Giudice, maintained on the other hand a great friendship with Cellamare, the Cardinal's nephew. Alberoni fomented the opposition of Felipe to Orléans, and Spanish politics again changed course in the direction of withdrawing the country from French influences, in spite of the efforts of Orléans, well seconded in his purpose by his ambassador the marquis de Saint-Aignan.

Alberoni's plan was to bring Spain and the Protestant powers, Holland and Great Britain together; and while the Regent Orléans refused to treat with the British separately, Alberoni started negotiations with the Dutch States General, the Republic of Genoa and Great Britain in September

1715. He therefore entered into relationship with the Dutch minister, Baron de Ripperdá, and with the British envoy, Bubb-Dodington, later Lord Melcombe Regis. Alberoni, for once completely outwitted, conceded on 14 September 1715 to the *explicative articles* of Utrecht which were favourable to Great Britain in the highest degree since they contained the implicit recognition of George I, as against Stuart pretensions which until then Spain had supported.[62]

Alberoni greatly influenced the Queen from the start and, after the birth of Prince Carlos on 20 January 1716, did so even more. He now began his projects concerning Italy. It was necessary for him to ingratiate himself with the Papacy, and so he sent the Spanish galleys, commanded by Baltasar de Guevara, and six warships, commanded by the marqués Esteban de Mari, to join the Venetians in freeing Corfu from the Turks in August 1716. In a few months he had healed the bad relations which had existed between Spain and the Papacy and, as a reward, was made a cardinal.

On other fronts Alberoni's perspicacity often failed him. The British profited from the facilities granted to their commerce and treated directly with the Emperor, abandoning and making a mockery of the abbate's intrigues to isolate them. It was France which was isolated and now wished at all cost to recover her prestige in Spain. For this reason the Regent sent the marquis de Louisville to Madrid with express orders to destroy the Italian cabal. A fortnight before Louisville's arrival, in July 1716, Giudice had fallen from power, the duca de Popoli taking his place as the royal tutor, and had resigned from his post of Inquisitor-General and left Spain. Alberoni, now commanding absolute power, was the author of this plot. Louisville was not received by the King and soon returned to France; this led to the schemes for Alberoni's fall which the Regent Orléans now began to lay, aided thereto by his ambassador in Spain, Saint-Aignan. In Spain itself there were many at court, among them the conde de Aguilar, the duque de Veragua and the conde de las Torres, who were only too ready to ruin Alberoni, proof of with what general disgust the grandees regarded the power of the Parmesan gardener's son. In truth, however, the only persons at court who had true influence were Père Daubenton, the King's confessor, and Laura Piscatori, long since the Queen's wet-nurse, and both were entirely under the influence of Alberoni.

During 1716 and 1717 Felipe V, in broken health and prey to black melancholy, was not expected to survive for long owing to the excesses of his marital life. In October 1717 his illness caused great anxiety, and it was believed at court that he had dropsy. Meanwhile Isabel governed and the French ambassador conspired.[63]

France came out of her isolation through the ability of Cardinal Dubois, the unscrupulous confidant of the Regent Orléans, who was able to form an alliance with England; on 14 January 1717 this was converted into a triple alliance at The Hague when the United Provinces joined. A few months afterwards, in May 1717, the Inquisitor-General José Molines was detained in Lombardy by the Austrian governor of the Milanese. Alberoni retaliated by ordering José Patiño to make ready a fleet of warships in Barcelona, and was astute enough to trick everyone into believing that he was actuated by peaceful motives and that he was preparing an expedition against the Turks.

On 22 August 1717 a squadron with 9,000 men, commanded by the marqués de Lede, left Barcelona.[64] Disembarking at Sardinia they set about conquering the island. Cagliari, Castel-Aragonese and Alghero capitulated, and by November the whole island was in Spanish hands. What amounted to an attack on the Emperor Charles VI, for after all the island was now his, shook all the courts of Europe; but neither Great Britain nor France wanted decidedly to support the Emperor who had finally triumphed over the Turks in the Balkans and whose increase in strength alarmed the maritime powers. The consequence of these diplomatic vicissitudes was the Quadruple Alliance of 1718, adding the Empire to the Triple Alliance, in virtue of which the Emperor compromised by pretending to recognise that Felipe V was King of Spain and that Don Carlos, his son by his second queen Isabel, would eventually succeed to the Duchies of Parma, Piacenza and Tuscany.

At first everyone cold-shouldered Savoy; but later France and Great Britain intervened in its favour. Spain was invited to adhere to the Quadruple Alliance, but Alberoni, more ambitious through having tasted some success, turned his attentions towards Naples, Sicily, the Tuscan Ports, the hereditary lands of the Grand Duke of Tuscany, and Parma, all of which seemed rightly Spain's. The United Provinces for the time being played a waiting game. For his part Alberoni tried by various tricks to gain time and hold off the pressure put upon him by Lord Stanhope, the British plenipotentiary, and the marquis de Nancré, the French envoy, while simultaneously attempting to fool the prudent Vittorio Amadeo of Savoy lest he should discover Spain's real intentions.

In the strictest secrecy Spain had prepared an expedition consisting of twenty-two ships of the line, three merchantmen, four galleys, two corvettes, a galleon and 340 transport ships, having aboard 30,000 picked troops under the command of the marqués de Lede. The fleet sailed from Barcelona on 18 June 1718,[65] and in Sardinia General Nuendáriz joined forces with them. On 1 July the expeditionary troops were landed on Cape Salento in Sicily. The expedition had been prepared by that great organiser José Patiño.

The Sicilians supported the Spanish who entered Palermo on 13 July. Soon all the principal cities of the island were in Spanish hands and the conte Maffei, in command of the troops of Savoy, was in full retreat without striking a blow. Baltasar de Guevara pursued the Sicilian squadron into the waters of Malta, where it was protected by the Grand Master, who declared the neutrality of his dominions. On 14 June a strong

III. Italy in the Eighteenth Century

fleet had set sail from England under the command of Admiral Byng who, on reaching Cádiz, warned Alberoni that he was going to guarantee the neutrality of Italy in fulfilment of the Treaty of Utrecht. An encounter between Britain and Spain was inevitable and took place at the battle of Cape Passaro, where Byng destroyed the squadron of Antonio Gastañeta on 11 August 1718.[66] The British were accused of perfidy, since they had attacked without warning, taking advantage of the state of the Spanish armada which at the time was dispersed in sections. The marqués de Mari's ships, separated from the main squadron, were destroyed off the coast of Aosta on 11 and 12 August. Alberoni answered with reprisals, expelling the British consuls from Spanish territory and sequestrating British property and ships sheltering in Spanish ports. Spanish land-forces, however, still dominated the island.

Alberoni now resorted to diplomacy to defend himself. At first he demanded the recognition of Spain's conquest of both Sicily and Sardinia; afterwards he sought only Sardinia and, for a moment, the French Regent Orléans favoured his single claim; but Vittorio Amadeo held firm to the Quadruple Alliance by a proclamation of 8 November, and a rupture between the Powers seemed imminent. Saint-Aignan now left Madrid and Nancré followed him soon afterwards, while Stanhope departed from Spain. Monteleón, Spanish ambassador in London, received orders to go to the United Provinces, and Villamayor withdrew from Turin. Great Britain declared war on Spain on 27 December 1718.[67]

Meanwhile in France a conspiracy against the Regent was discovered, directed by the Spanish ambassador, principe de Cellamare. Contemporary French writers exaggerated the dangers of this plot, and Dubois above all made the most of it, since he sought a pretext to join the British without gaining the odium of fighting against a grandson of Louis XIV. Baudrillart has carefully explained the situation, pointing out that this conspiracy was little more than a miserable intrigue, without a firm basis and conducted with absolute inefficiency. It is clear that, given the Regent's position, he found himself for some months at the mercy of mischance or of an accident.[68] Those involved in the conspiracy were the duchesse de Maine, an adventurer called Walef, the comte de Laval, the marquis de Pompadour, the abbé Brigault, and some military men. All counted on the support of Alberoni. The plot was discovered by Dubois and, on 13 December 1718, principe de Cellamare was arrested and sent to Blois.

On 9 January 1719 France declared war on Spain. In an extensive proclamation (20 February 1719) Felipe V explained his reasons for not joining the Quadruple Alliance. Meanwhile Alberoni during 1718 had intrigued with the northern Powers against Great Britain. Charles XII of Sweden[69] and Peter the Great of Russia were to aid Spain in bringing about a Jacobite landing in the British Isles. Alberoni also had been sharp enough to detect that the Regent Orléans had enemies in his own army, outstandingly maréchal Villars and maréchal Huxelles. He also counted on the revolt of Brittany against the French crown.

The Spanish troops in Sicily during the latter part of 1718 prepared to defend themselves against an Imperial army which increased from day to day; and in spite of their inferiority they were victorious in the bloody battle of Melazzo on 15 October 1718. In February 1719 the Old Pretender (James III) was set up in Madrid, and Alberoni sent off a naval expedition bound for the British Isles. The fleet, however, was caught in a storm off Cape Finisterre, and Admiral Baltasar de Guevara saved some ships only with the greatest of difficulty. In April 1719 no more than a thousand Irish exiles landed in Scotland. The revolt of Brittany was equally disastrous, since the Duke of Ormonde, who was to direct it, did not receive the reinforcements which would have allowed him to set out from the ports of Santander and Laredo. On 21 April 1719 a French army of 20,000, commanded by the marquis de Tilly, crossed the River Bidasoa into Spain, and soon Behovia, San Marcial, Santa Isabel and the port of Pasajes, whose shipyard was burnt, fell into his power. Spain's reply was to send a strong army to besiege Fuenterrabía, captured by the invaders. Felipe V took command of his army on 27 April and published a manifesto to the French troops in the hope that they would join him and at the same time remain faithful to the Regent. On 18 June Fuenterrabía capitulated, and the King, who learned of it *en marche*, returned to Madrid. In August an expedition of combined English and French forces burned several ships in the harbour of Santoña, and a short while afterwards San Sebastián surrendered to a Spanish army under Berwick.

Alberoni showed indomitable courage in adverse circumstances. He intrigued everywhere, promising aid to the Bretons, fomenting a revolt in Poitou, and seeking out enemies of France and Great Britain by all kinds of means invented by his fertile brain. The marqués de Lede did wonders to maintain the defensive in Sicily against far superior forces and, when driven to a battle on 20 June 1719 at Francavilla, fought indecisively but honourably against the Austrians. He could not, however, send help to Messina, which fell to the Imperialists on 28 October, and the Spanish retreated to Castelvetrano and Siaca, where they defended themselves for the rest of the winter.

The French now ventured into the Pyrenees, occupying the Valle de Arán and the whole of the plain of Tremp.[70] In October 1719, Seo de Urgel fell to Berwick, who could not, however, take Rosas, since a storm destroyed the small squadron which was going to blockade the fortress (27 November). Guerrillas, however, harrassed the French forces, which retired over the mountains. Already, on 10 October, 4,000 British troops had landed in Vigo and overcome resistance in the town. This was enough, and Felipe, losing his nerve, proposed absurd conditions of peace, while the Allies demanded the explusion of Alberoni from Spain as the first of their conditions. It was above all the letter of the marchese Scotti, the Duke of

Parma's envoy, which forced the hesitating Spanish King to make up his mind. Alberoni was ordered to leave the country, and the fallen Cardinal made for Genoa. On 26 January 1720 Felipe V announced his adhesion to the Quadruple Alliance. On 16 February the marqués de Beretti-Landi, the Spanish ambassador to the United Provinces, handed the Spanish document of peace to the plenipotentiaries of the Empire, of France and of Great Britain, while the following day it was delivered separately to the King of Sardinia. Between 26 February and 2 April peace was made, and between May and August Sicily and Sardinia were evacuated by the Spanish armies. By that time the marqués de Castel-Rodrigo had driven out the last of the French forces occupying Seo de Urgel and Tremp.

With the departure of Alberoni, writes Baudrillart,[71] there disappeared from the political scene a man of unquestionable talent, but not a man truly fitted for affairs of state, since one can hardly claim that for someone who had failed as he had done. All the same, Alberoni, even though he had failed, had roused Spain from her lethargy and had proved that he knew that she was capable of energy and resource granted that the country were well and intelligently administered.

If it had accomplished nothing else, Alberoni's rule had proved to the Powers that Spain was far from being a spent force and, above all, it had brought into relief Spain's relationship with France, the natural ally of the Spanish Bourbons. After a hostile beginning and despite stormy passages in the years to come, Spain and France were never to be far apart in the world's affairs, a diplomatic feature of the eighteenth century.

Felipe V,[72] embittered by the conduct of the Regent Orléans, sent the Irishman Patricio Laulés to France in April 1720. Laulés there found Dubois and Orléans well disposed to a reconciliation and, in order carry this into effect, the marquis de Maulevrier-Langeron went to Madrid, where he saw that conditions at court had changed with the years. Pro-French and anti-French parties were to be seen. Of those inclined to France the leading figures were the duque de Veragua, the conde de Peñaranda and the duque de Solferino; while of those opposed to France the outstanding were the marqués de Mejorada, the conde de Aguilar, the marqués de Santa Cruz and the duca de Popoli. Three men controlled affairs of state, José Rodrigo, Miguel Durán and the marqués de Grimaldo, the last of these, Minister of External Affairs, a man of most engaging character, who believed strongly in the importance of the union of the two Bourbon monarchies.

The Spanish plenipotentiaries, the conde de Santesteban de Puerto and Lorenzo Berrusio, marqués de Beretti-Landi, went to Cambrai, and at the end of 1720 José Patiño organised a naval expedition to Ceuta to chastise the Moors who had attacked the fortress. The Spanish squadron, under Carlos Grillo, sailed from Cádiz in October 1720 carrying 16,000 troops, commanded by the marqués de Lede, and by 12 December Spain had amply revenged herself on the Moors.

The most important clauses open to dispute in the Congress of Cambrai were those referring to the succession of the sons of Felipe V and Isabel Farnese to the Duchies of Parma, Piacenza and Tuscany.[73] From the first one can notice the enmity of the Emperor Charles VI to Spain, for he was only ready to concede the duchies on terms which would place the young princes under humiliating Imperial feudal control. In view of this attitude both France and Great Britain decided to conclude a separate peace with Spain, for both saw that it would be to their advantage—in the case of France to gain a friendly neighbour and in the case of Britain to guarantee its commerce. On 27 March 1721 the marquis de Maulevrier-Langeron and the marqués de Grimaldo concluded a treaty of alliance between France and Spain.

Among the basic clauses of the treaty were those concerning the restitution of the Spanish fortresses occupied by the French, France's engagement to defend Spain's pretensions to Parma, Piacenza and Tuscany and the abandonment of Gibraltar to Spain. On 13 June 1721 peace with Britain was confirmed and constituted a new Triple Alliance,[74] but this negotiation was not as easy with Britain as with France and Spain, since Felipe V demanded the return of Gibraltar. Stanhope promised that this would be done and King George I reiterated this promise in a private letter to Felipe.[75] Shortly afterwards, on the initiative of the Spanish monarchs, a proposal of marriage, which should result in the aggrandisement of the House of Orléans, was brought forward for the Regent Orléans's consideration. If implemented it would set a seal on the sincere reconciliation of Orléans and Felipe V. The proposal was to arrange a marriage between Don Luis, príncipe de las Asturias, elder son of Felipe V by his first marriage and heir to the Spanish throne, and Louise-Isabelle de Montpensier, fifth daughter of the Regent Orléans. In exchange the Regent was to agree that the Infanta María Ana Victoria should go to France to be educated there and, having reached a suitable age, should marry King Louis XV.

The French evacuated San Sebastián and Fuenterrabía on 22 August 1721, and there was an exchange of ambassadors-extraordinary between France and Spain, the duque de Osuna travelling to Paris and the duc de Saint-Simon to Madrid, the first on 29 October and the second on 21 November. On 20 January 1722 Luis de las Asturias and Louise-Isabelle de Montpensier were married at Lerma.[76]

The Congress of Cambrai had also as its objects the re-establishment of relations between Vienna and Madrid and the guarantee of the Treaties of Utrecht and Rastatt. From the beginning of the Congress the bad faith of the Emperor was evident from the position taken up by his representatives who joined the Congress in January 1722. Spain sought France's more decided support over the question of the Italian duchies and, to further this, a new marriage proposal was presented to the Regent, the marriage of another of his daughters, Philippa-Isabelle de Beaujolais to the Infante Don Carlos, eldest son of Felipe V and Isabel Farnese and pretendent to these duchies; but this marriage never did take place. Both this and the Asturias marriage were arranged by Père Daubenton, Felipe V's confessor.

Charles VI was ready to drive a hard bargain until the last moment on the question of the investitures of the Italian duchies, but the French and British plenipotentiaries made such strong representations to him that he finally assented on 3 December 1722. The Grand Duke of Tuscany Cosimo (III) de'Medici protested because he believed that he had the right to appoint to the succession and that what remained of the Medici family should succeed before the young Don Carlos. The court of Vienna found this a convenient argument for delaying Queen Isabel's dream; and when the Grand Duke himself died, on 16 November 1723, Felipe V agreed that the last of the line, Gian Gastone de'Medici should reign in Florence.[77]

On 2 December 1723 the duc d'Orléans died and was succeeded as Regent by the duc de Bourbon. A little while afterwards, on 10 January 1724, to the astonishment of the European courts Felipe V abdicated in favour of his eldest son Luis de las Asturias.[78] It was unknown that he had made a written statement to this effect as early as 27 July 1720 and had reiterated his intention twice more after that. The secret had been sedulously kept by the King and Queen. This vow was, in principle, to abdicate on 1 November 1723, but various circumstances, particularly the Congress of Cambrai which Felipe wished to see terminated before he abdicated, caused him to defer this decision. Much that is merely fanciful has been written about the causes of the abdication, but doubtless what influenced this decision was the King's realisation that his melancholy fits were a prelude to the madness which overtook him in his later years and that he might before long be incapacitated.[79]

On 19 January 1724 Luis I was proclaimed King of Spain with great solemnity, the beginning of a reign which was to last only eight months. With two children such as Luis and Luisa Isabel on the throne,[80] Felipe and Isabel, although they retired to San Ildefonso, continued to govern. Ministers and courtiers scrambled for places. Luis I's ministry was composed of Luis de Miraval, President of the Council of Castile, Diego de Astorga, Archbishop of Toledo, the Inquisitor-General Camargo, the marqués de Lede, the marqués de Aytona, the marqués de Valero, Blas de Orozco and Juan Bautista Orendain, who for a long time had been an obscure agent of Grimaldo. Orendain, whose papers are an important source for this period,[81] became Minister for External Affairs, while Antonio Sopeña was in charge of the Navy Department, Castelar the War Department, and Verdes Montenegro the Finance Department. In the background, supported by his own family, the Castelars, was the most able man in the kingdom, José Patiño.

The duc de Bourbon, the enemy of the Orléans family, sent maréchal de Tessé to Madrid as ambassador,[82] with instructions to approach the court of San Ildefonso and flatter Felipe and Isabel, at the same time undermining the influence of Grimaldo. Meanwhile young Luis I was behaving like a sixteen-year-old boy rather than a king, and Luisa Isabel, the child Queen,[83] wrote witty letters about Tessé, which delighted the duc de Bourbon. She had no consideration for her consort and showed off her bad manners towards Luis, turning her back on him in their coach or at table and, during meals, not eating a mouthful and running off afterwards to eat with her ladies-in-waiting. The antipathy of the King towards her was so great that it was generally held that their marriage had not been consummated. Annulment was considered—and a new marriage.[84]

Meanwhile the Congress of Cambrai continued. The Grand Duke of Tuscany, Gian Gastone de'Medici protested about the Bourbon-Parma demands for his duchy and brought forward the claims of his sister the Princess Palatine. In Parma, Duke Francesco Farnese favoured the pretensions of Isabel of Spain, but the Duke's brother Antonio could well marry and have offspring. The Papacy held Castro and Ronciglione, and the Emperor Charles VI pretended to sovereign rights in the states which were to be destined for Don Carlos. At the same time the British and Dutch, afraid of Imperial ambitions in the commericial field, opposed the growth of the Ostend Company and now supported Spain in its aspirations, which broke the Congress. Between 2 and 28 April 1724 the plenipotentiaries of Spain, the Empire, Sardinia and Parma declared their varying ambitions.

Queen Luisa Isabel was by now setting the court talking. She had acquired in Paris a certain boldness and independence which shocked severe Spanish etiquette. Jokes, of which the chief lady-in-waiting, the condesa de Altamira, was a victim, and laughing and horseplay with her girl companions at court constantly disgusted Luis I. Her light behaviour reached its height when she appeared nearly naked on the main staircase of the royal palace. Her excesses in eating and drinking alarmed the young king, who ordered that she should be placed under restraint for a few days. He soon pardoned her, taking into account how young she was and the education she had received. After all, he himself was said in an innocent caprice to have sallied forth from the palace at a very late hour with his companions to steal fruit from the royal orchards. His father had to take him to task for this infantile behaviour which ill-befitted a king.

All this, however, was to have a sudden ending, for Luis I caught smallpox and died shortly afterwards, on 31 August 1724,[85] declaring in his will that his father was his heir.[86] Luisa Isabel finally showed her best side and attended him faithfully to the end, running the risk of contagion.

Felipe V had many scruples about assuming power once more; but maréchal de Tessé, aided by the Papal nuncio, Aldobrandini, and Queen Isabel, influenced him about the efficacy of overcoming this repugnance. A council of theologians was divided into two camps, one favourable, one opposed; and the Council of Castile, at first vacillating, finally decided categorically that Felipe should reassume the kingship. On 7 September 1724 he became King again.[87]

Preoccupation with the future of Don Carlos, their eldest son, continued to exercise Felipe V and Isabel, and although príncipe Fernando, born of Felipe's first marriage, was on 25 November 1724 sworn in as heir to the crown, Felipe's sole thought, troubled as he was by the overbearing tantrums of the Queen, was to find a way to accommodate Don Carlos.

Isabel Farnese was not the simple and humble little princess that Alberoni had painted for his own convenience. She had talent and plenty of ambition; she was of lively character, astute and intrepid, and of a proud and aggressive temperament. Dissimulating and circumspect, she was firm and tenacious in her aims and followed an affair with constancy up to the very end. Knowing the uxoriousness of the King she never left him an instant, even accompanying him when hunting and bearing with his black fits of melancholy. Felipe could not sever himself from her, and she was the mistress of his will until the last day of his life.

The earnest desire of Isabel was to provide for her sons Carlos and Felipe and she did not miss an opportunity to bring this wish to fruition. One can affirm that the whole of Spanish politics during Felipe V's second reign revolved round this vehement desire of the Queen.

A change of ministers took place during the first months of Felipe V's return to the throne. The marqués de Miraval, successor of Francisco Ronquillo, lost the presidency of the Council of Castile, and his post was occupied by Juan de Herrera, Bishop of Sigüenza. Verdes Montenegro and the marqués de Lede retired, and Orendain and Grimaldo reached first place. The marqués de Campo-Florido became Financial Secretary. Soon, however, rising out of the shadows, there appeared a figure who was to eclipse all the rest and become the King's trusted adviser. This was Ripperdá who, for a moment, was master of Spain as the instrument of Queen Isabel's ambition for her sons.[88]

Johann Wilhelm, Baron de Ripperdá was Dutch, of a noble family of Groningen, once under Spanish rule. He was educated as a Catholic in a Jesuit College in Cologne, entered the army and fought in the War of the Spanish Succession. Later he became a Protestant and was a deputy in the Estates General of the Republic of the United Provinces. At Utrecht he showed his ability in commerce and in economic affairs, and later was appointed Dutch ambassador to Spain where he got to know Giudice and Alberoni, with whom he formed a friendship. Restless, ambitious, a fantast and a great liar, he liked Spain and, on the termination of his ambassadorship, settled there.[89] To please Felipe V he returned to Catholicism and was appointed superintendent of the factories of Guadalaraja, with lands and a palace. Then Alberoni deprived him of the superintendency; but when the cardinal fell from power, Ripperdá sent letters to the King and Queen, flattering them, condemning their ministers and telling them that he knew how to make Spain great, and was nominated superintendent-general of all the factories in the kingdom. He had an outstanding enemy in Père Daubenton, but the Jesuit's death removed that danger.

Ripperdá knew the inmost secrets of Queen Isabel and her desire that her son Carlos should inherit the Italian duchies. Felipe V's abdication upset his plans; but when Felipe reassumed the kingship, Ripperdá gained a renewed ascendency in the palace and proposed to Isabel a secret mission to Vienna, profiting from his supposed good friendship with the Emperor and Prince Eugène of Savoy. The adventurer had chosen a propitious time since the Congress of Cambrai was on the point of breaking up, in consequence of the proposals of the Spanish envoy-extraordinary, the Sicilian marqués de Monteleón. Neither Great Britain nor Cardinal de Bourbon, now Regent of France, upheld with any firmness the rights of the Infante Don Carlos, which they actually omitted from an article of the Quadruple Alliance. The Queen decided to seek in her husband's old enemy what she could not obtain from a useless friendship.

Feigned pretexts were brought forward for his journey, and Ripperdá went incognito to Vienna with ample instructions on 22 November 1724, having given up a high-sounding commercial project in Madrid. On arriving in Vienna he entered into negotiations with the Imperial Chancellor Zinzendorf, Prince Eugène and Count Stahremberg. The three accepted the Spanish proposals favourably and began conversations, but certain imprudences on the part of Ripperdá made them suspicious of the plenipotentiaries of Cambrai.

In March 1725 occurred something pleasing to Vienna—the breaking off of the arrangements for the marriage of Louis XV and María Ana Victoria, Infanta of Spain, at which Queen Isabel hardly concealed her fury. The author of this diplomatic rupture was the Cardinal de Bourbon who, alarmed by the young King's illness, wanted to marry him off at once so that there might be an heir, since he was afraid that if he died childless the crown of France might revert to the hated House of Orléans; and the little Infanta had not reached marriageable age. The abbé de Livry communicated this displeasing news to Felipe V. Louis XV was betrothed to Maria Leszczynska, daughter of the ex-king of Poland, now Duke of Lorraine. As a reprisal Felipe and Isabel ordered Philippa-Isabelle de Beaujolais, who was engaged to Don Carlos of Bourbon-Parma, and Luisa Isabel the widow of Luis I, to return to France. On 17 May 1725 María Ana Victoria returned to Spain, and, a few days afterwards, the two French princesses took their departure.

This act caused a break between Spain and France and smoothed the path for Ripperdá's negotiations with the Imperialists, desired too much by Queen Isabel who, with her dominant idea of gaining thrones for her two sons, wanted them to marry the duchesses of the House of Austria.[90] In conformity with the orders he had received, he made in Vienna between 30 April and 7 June 1725[91] three agreements between Spain and the Empire, one of alliance, one of commerce and navigation and a third of peace.

The First Treaty of Vienna was the result of spite, since seldom had Spain signed anything so disadvantageous to herself.[92] The Emperor acknowledged the King of Spain at last without reservation, but on the forseen condition of his renunication of the French throne. Felipe V, for his part, agreed to declare that Parma, Piacenza and Tuscany were fiefs of the Empire and promised not to set up Don Carlos in Italy or to send garrisons to the dukedoms. As to commercial affairs, Spain promised to protect the ships and commerce of the Imperial Ostend Company against the attacks of British and Dutch privateers. In exchange the Emperor promised his good offices and mediation to win over the British into restoring Gibraltar and Menorca to Spain.

The most gratifying of the agreements, and one which for a long time raised the hopes of Queen Isabel, was the promise, made on 5 November by the Emperor and Empress and confirmed in the letters of Ripperdá, of the marriage of the Infante Don Carlos of Bourbon-Parma to the heiress of the Empire, Maria Theresa. The crafty Ripperdá, however, told only half the truth, for in reality the Imperial pair had gone no further than considering the question. France's intended reconciliation with Spain had not taken place, and the Congress of Cambrai was dissolved on the announcement of the Treaty of Vienna. At the celebrations with which the news of the success of the negotiations at Vienna had been received at court, Orendain obtained the title of marqués de la Paz, and the fortunate negotiator Ripperdá was made a duke and a grandee of Spain. Great Britain and France were alarmed by the alliance between Spain the Emperor. In opposition to the Treaty of Vienna, the League of Hanover was set up; in the castle of Herrenhausen a defensive alliance was confirmed on 3 September 1725 between France, Prussia and Great Britain.

In order to contest this, a treaty[93] was concluded by Ripperdá on 5 November 1725 between the Empire and Spain; and this was not only a defensive alliance, for it presupposed that war with France at least and perhaps with Great Britain (if a stand was made about Gibraltar and Menorca) was probable, and the prickly business of marriages was clearly thrust to the front. The Emperor promised to give two of his three daughters (without designating which) in marriage to the Infantes Don Carlos and Don Felipe, but he did indicate that if he died before Maria Theresa was of marriageable age, she would be married to Don Carlos.[94] The allies of the Treaty of Hanover (Herrenhausen) understood that the union of the Empire and Spain was a threat to the peace of Europe. On 11 December Ripperdá arrived in Madrid, very satisfied with the success of his negotiations and in travelling dress asked for an interview with the

King and Queen, who received him with the utmost agreeableness. In spite of Felipe V's repugnance towards appointing a prime minister, believing the falsehoods and trickeries of Ripperdá, who pretended that the Emperor vehemently wished that he should be so appointed, the King felt obliged to give him first a patent of counsellor of state and later, on 27 December, the entire direction of the Department of Foreign Affairs; this rendered him in reality prime minister. Notwithstanding this, Ripperdá was not satisfied; with his cleverness and with his gift of tongue he finally obtained the position of universal minister, that is, the controller of all the ministries. He deprived Orendain (de la Paz) and Grimaldo of their posts, drove Castelar out of the country by appointing him Spanish ambassador in Venice, and afterwards broke the friendship between Sopeña and Patiño. His own son, Luis, a youth of twenty, took Ripperdá's place at the embassy at Vienna.

The attitude of Ripperdá was imprudent. He started by menacing France and Britain. His boasts about the return of Gibraltar and Menorca to Spain were ridiculous, and he went so far as to threaten George I of Great Britain with an invasion of Hanover by Germans, Russians and Poles, as if with an invasion of Vandals and Huns. He set about organising the army and navy and setting them on a warlike footing, but his steps in that direction failed. Even so, infatuated by his power, he did not give up his wild and ill-considered behaviour. What he feared was the arrival of the Imperialist ambassador, Count Koenigsegg, who knew a good deal too much about him and his lies. When in January 1726 Koenigsegg finally arrived in Spain, Ripperdá could not fulfil the promise that he had made of sending subsidies to the Emperor. Driven to these straits, he therefore developed another policy, sending a certain Marcellac to Versailles and another adventurer, the comte de Lamtilly, to Britain to join with the Jacobites in something that he called a decisive action. To this end he communicated with the French agents in Madrid, the abbé Montgon and Stalpart; and in April 1726 Lord Wharton, agent of the Chevalier de Saint-Georges (James, the Old Pretender), came to Madrid. In the capital there was a group of Jacobites, the leaders of which were the Duke of Ormonde and the duc de Berwick. Immediately, Ripperdá opened negotiations with Wharton, projecting nothing less than a landing in England with Imperialist auxiliaries.

Ripperdá at first publicly denied his plans, but in an excess of anger and petulance he referred to the 'treaty' in the presence of Stanhope and van der Meer, the ambassadors of Britain and the united Provinces respectively. Stanhope complained to Felipe V of the hostile intentions of Spain and the Empire. Felipe replied with vague words, and Ripperdá continued his Jacobite intrigues, which were discovered by Stanhope. When Ripperdá had finalised everything with Lamtilly and Wharton, he went to Koenigsegg to claim the collaboration of the Emperor; but Koenigsegg's cold and reserved attitude discouraged him. He then tried to sow discord between the representatives of the maritime powers, but the ruse had been discovered and he was placed in a disagreeable situation. War was imminent and so was Ripperdá's fall. Queen Isabel wanted war, and Emperor Charles VI began to want it too. Both might have continued to shield him; but such were the incoherences, falsehoods, indiscretions and boastfulness of Ripperdá that even Felipe V, usually so malleable, realised that there would be a public outcry against his favourite's blunders.

Koenigsegg persuaded the adventurer to renounce the direction of Finance, pointing out to him that he had not the resources to pay the promised subsidies to the Emperor. Ripperdá left the financial administration, being immediately replaced by la Paz (Orendain) and Arriaza, and gave up all his offices, and on 14 May 1726 this was accepted by the King. Angry though he was Felipe V gave him a good pension in recompense for his services, but with his troubled conscience Ripperdá lost his head and sought asylum with Lord Stanhope in the British embassy, declaring himself culpable. On 24 May bailiffs surrounded the building and the adventurer was conducted with a strong escort to the Alcázar of Segovia, whence he escaped some months afterwards. This was the end of Ripperdá's intervention in Spanish politics.

Ripperdá's fate was strange. He stayed for some time in Portugal and England, then went to The Hague, where he became a Protestant again. Afterwards he went to Morocco, became a Mohammedan and attacked the fortress of Ceuta, defeated a Spanish force, but was later himself defeated. He then founded a new Mohammedan sect, being known by the name of Osman. Next he left Morocco, went to Tunis and while there was asked by a revolutionary group of Corsicans to proclaim himself their king, but was refused permission to leave his territory by the Sultan. Finally he died of tuberculosis in Tetuan when he was about to go to Rome to beg pardon from the Pope for his past errors.[95]

Spanish politics continued to be vacillating, inclining on one side to the necessity of an understanding with France, and on the other to a treaty with the Empire to further the ambitions of Isabel in Italy where she wanted states for her sons. Don Carlos, the elder, seemed unlikely ever to gain the throne of Spain, which obviously was for Don Fernando, Felipe V's son by his consort, María Luisa of Savoy.

The leading spirit of this part of Felipe V's reign is José del Patiño, born in Milan in 1666,[96] but of a family from Galicia.[97] He was a Jesuit novice, but later left the Society and entered an administrative career, becoming superintendent of the army of Extremadura in 1711. In 1713 he was sent to Cataluña; the following year, on the fall of Barcelona, he became President of the Royal Council of Justice and Government and of the Council of Administration of the city of Barcelona. In 1717 he was made Intendant-General of the Navy in Sevilla, whence he was called by Alberoni to Barcelona to prepare the naval expeditions to Sardinia and Sicily. In the following years he was the stabilising force in state affairs. On the fall of Ripperdá, Patiño was nominated Minister of Marine and of the Indies. The marqués de Grimaldo was restored to the position of Secretary of State, but he was excluded from the negotiations with Vienna, which were entrusted to Orendain, marqués de la Paz. Francisco Arriaza was put in charge of the Finance Department and the marqués de Castelar, brother of Patiño, went to the Ministry of War.

Ripperdá's disappearance from the political scene had not destroyed his diplomatic work, and the alliance with Austria, for which Isabel had so much illusion, continued as before. This implied a total opposition to a French alliance to the great disgust of the duc de Bourbon. In such circumstances the abbé Montgon arrived at court. He had come to know the King and Queen through Domingo Valentín Guerra, Archbishop of Amida, the Queen's confessor, and through the conde de Salazar the príncipe de las Asturias's tutor. The abbé had established magnificent relations with Bourbon, but a party in Spain sought the fall of the duke at all costs as a just reprisal for the affront inflicted on the King and Queen of Spain, by his having finally refused to consider the marriage of the young Louis XV to the Infanta María Ana Victoria. The youthful Louis was now married to Maria Leszczynska, daughter of the whilom King of Poland. In this cabal figured the duquesa de San Pedro, sister of the marquís de Torcy, Pere Laubrussel, confessor to the duquesa, the marchese Scotti, and the old wet-nurse of the Queen, Laura Piscatori. Bourbon was forced from power by his opponents in France, being succeeded by Fleury, Bishop of Fréjus, preceptor of Louis XV.[98]

It seemed likely that with the advent of Fleury and his attitude of peace at all costs Spanish politics would vary or change; but the case was that the United Provinces adhered to the Treaty of Hanover, and Spain and the Empire were more closely united than ever. The Imperial ambassador Koenigsegg was aulic counsellor of Felipe V, and those Spaniards who had followed the Imperialist party in the War of the Spanish Succession recovered their honours and their confiscated goods. The Emperor sought and followed alliances with Russia and Poland, while on the other hand Denmark joined the allies of the Treaty of Hanover. Without doubt Charles VI's intentions were pacific, and now surprisingly enough Koenigsegg made it understood that he favoured a policy of friendship between France and Spain and was willing to act as mediator.

Koenigsegg advised the Spanish court not to provoke Great Britain, but his behaviour was so strange that he succeeded in embroiling the British and Spanish governments. The consequence was that the British navy became active. A squadron under Admiral Jennings patrolled the Mediterranean, Admiral Wager sailed with another to the Baltic, and Admiral Hosier made for the West Indies. All Spanish coasts were put in a state of defence: engineers repaired fortifications, the garrison of Cádiz was strengthened; and three small swift craft were despatched, one to La

Habana, one to Cartagena and one to Veracruz to give orders as to the defence of the Spanish Main and to prevent the British from establishing themselves in the Gulf of Mexico. These energetic measures were undertaken by Patiño.

Meanwhile it was discovered that Padre Bermúdez, King Felipe's confessor, had been in correspondence with Cardinal Fleury, with the result that he was disgraced. Another who was ruined was the marqués de Grimaldo, who because of his past relations with Stanhope was dismissed on 29 September 1726, his place being taken by Orendain, marqués de la Paz. Next, Koenigsegg obtained the dismissal of Arriaza, President of the Council of Finance, for his lack of activity; Patiño took his place. At the same time Jennings cruised along the northern coast of Spain and Hosier blockaded Porto Bello. A rupture between Britain and Spain appeared imminent.

Charles VI, besides allying himself with Catherine I of Russia, had obtained the semi-defection of Frederick William I, King of Prussia, from the Treaty of Hanover. Spain put its faith in a reconciliation with France, while Britain feared that a Catholic cardinal might break faith with her; but Fleury remained steadfast to the British alliance. In November 1726 the Spanish ambassador to London, Pozo-Bueno, demanded that Britain should withdraw her fleet from America and, shortly afterwards, on 12 December, Orendain presented to Stanhope a note which was the equivalent of a declaration of war. Neither the Emperor nor France wanted war, since they knew that this would play into the hands of the maritime powers, Great Britain and the United Provinces. George I's speech from the throne, delivered on 28 January 1727, threatened war with Spain and the Empire and complained that Spain was supporting the Ostend Company and so threatening her trade.

To avoid a European war, negotiations between Madrid and Versailles were started, the intermediary for Spain being the abbé Montgon.[99] Montgon's mission was extremely delicate, since he had to hold the balance between the opposing families of Bourbon and Orléans and beware of the astute Cardinal Fleury. At first it seemed that Montgon would succeed, and he followed up what seemed to be a reconciliation by secretly introducing the pretensions of Felipe V to the French throne; but in an interview with Fleury on 4 February 1727 Montgon was completely outwitted. In fact, Fleury triumphed over Montgon's intrigues with the rival families and never forgave the meddling abbé.

Meanwhile Spain was at war with Great Britain. At the blockade of Porto Bello in Panamá, Spain captured the *Prince Frederick*, a British ship belonging to the South Sea Company, and then turning to another theatre, on 30 January 1727, began to besiege Gibraltar with 12,000 men commanded by the conde de las Torres, Viceroy of Navarra. On 22 February, the first breach in the defence-lines took place, but the British, in an advantageous position, prevented the Spaniards from reaching the fortress. On 11 March Stanhope demanded his papers in order to leave Spain. Spain had more success in America, where the British squadron, rendered inactive by woodworm in the ships' hulls and by illness, retired to Jamaica, and the Spanish navy of the West Indies, laden with treasure, returned without intervention, some of it to Cádiz and the rest to La Coruña.

It was precisely to avoid a general war that the pacifistic Fleury in collaboration with the Emperor Charles VI proposed peace conversations, while the Ostend Company was to be suspended until a congress decided what was to be done about it. To obtain the acquiescence of Spain, Fleury, on 11 February 1727 wrote to Queen Isabel, who answered cordially enough and stated that 'the ice was broken'. There followed a *Mémoire*, very sharp in character, written by the Emperor, refuting George I's speech from the throne, which led to the expulsion from London of the Imperial Resident on 16 March 1727. Fleury, sometimes tranquil and sometimes energetic, gave the negotiations a turn for the better, and after various changes of fortune the preliminaries of peace were signed in Paris on 31 May. The signatories were Baron Fonseca, Horatio Walpole, brother of Sir Robert, the comte de Morville and Willem Boreel, for the Empire, Great Britain, France and the United Provinces respectively. The duc de Bournonville, representing Spain, and the other ambassadors accredited there, signed a duplicate because Spain had no diplomatic agent in France owing to the tense situation existing between the two countries.

The preliminaries to peace contained as basic clauses the immediate cessation of hostilities, the suspension of the Ostend Company for seven years, and the establishment of a congress within four months; and it was painful for Spain to abandon the idea of regaining Gibraltar and disagreeable to allow the British to win back their commercial privileges in America. Finally the Emperor gave in over the question of the Ostend Company and Queen Isabel submitted to the disappearance of her matrimonial project for the Infante Don Carlos and the Archduchess Maria Theresa. Felipe V, attacked by melancholia and terror,[100] had already dictated his will to Patiño, and on 10 June Queen Isabel took over the rule of Spain. The conde de las Torres received orders to suspend operations against Gibraltar and on 23 June the armistice was confirmed. In Spain the two most important political figures were now José Patiño and his brother, the marqués de Castelar. They advised the Queen not to be bound to an alliance as insecure as that with the Empire, and to strengthen the army and navy. The Imperial ambassador tried to bring about Patiño's fall, but the Queen supported him and gave him further proof of her regard.

Her relations with the Empire having cooled, Spain now inclined towards France, and the abbé Montgon went to Paris with demands from Felipe and Isabel that the comte de Morville, joint cause with the duc de Bourbon of the failure to marry Louis XV to the Infanta, should be dismissed. D'Armenonville, Postmaster-General, and his son Morville resigned, the two of them being replaced by Chauvelin. At length, on 25 July 1727, a son and heir was born to Louis XV, who wrote a dignified and affectionate letter to his uncle Felipe V. A reconciliation between France and Spain had been reached and the comte de Rottenbourg was appointed French ambassador-extraordinary to the Spanish court.

The death of George I of Great Britain on 22 June 1727, before ratifying the Treaty of Vienna, was a setback for the peace of Europe. Suspicions between Britain and Spain were renewed. Since Spanish operations against Gibraltar[101] had not been more than suspended, the British now demanded that the fortress should be entirely left alone and that Spain should hand over the captured ship, the *Prince Frederick*. Lord Portmore fired on Tessé's batteries facing Gibraltar, and Admiral Wager appeared in the Bay of Cádiz. Spain asked the British to evacuate Providence Island and to demolish the ports which they had built on the coast of Florida. The French ambassador Rottenbourg had full power to resolve these affairs with Sir Benjamin Keene, the British ambassador, and van der Meer, representing the United Provinces; but they were tripped up by the energetic Queen Isabel, who displayed a letter signed by George I promising the restoration of Gibraltar to Spain. Moreover, Orendain and the Imperial ambassador Koenigsegg secretly agreed to oppose French influence. The abbé Montgon left France as a result of Fleury's manipulations, and arrived in Spain completely discredited. Felipe V's mental illness reappeared and led to the snail's pace at which the negotiations were carried out; his lethargy, his vague look and his strange silence made Queen Isabel fear that he would want to abdicate once more.

Rottenbourg, using his ability and tact, was about to conclude a peace treaty; but Chauvelin and Fleury refused to accredit him. Queen Isabel, still governing owing to the King's illness, asked Patiño on 15 December 1727 whether Spain was in a position to face a war and, on his replying in the affirmative, she ordered a tax of 26 per cent to be levied on all foreign assets found on Spanish ships. In Paris and London opinion hardened against Spain, and Admiral Hopson was sent to the West Indies, while Admiral Wager continued to ply the Spanish coasts. Once more war seemed inevitable. The Emperor's behaviour had changed the course of Spanish politics.

At the beginning of 1728 Queen Isabel gave in. On the one hand she feared the King's death and on the other she mistrusted the Emperor. Charles VI advised and favoured the marriage of Antonio Farnese (who had finally succeeded his brother Francesco to the Duchy of Parma in 1727) and Princess Enriquetta of Modena. The marriage took place and naturally tended to frustrate the hope of the eventual succession of Don Carlos of Bourbon-Parma to the duchies of Parma and Piacenza, while Gian Gastone, Grand Duke of Tuscany, was certainly not well disposed towards Spain. Queen Isabel found it advisable to send the marqués de

Monteleón to Italy as ambassador in Venice and plenipotentiary to the Italian princes. Monteleón was badly received, and through the mediation of France the Emperor came to a secret understanding with the maritime powers. Both Don Fernando, príncipe de las Asturias, and Patiño told the Queen that it was necessary to end the sending of subsidies to the Emperor; yet Koenigsegg believed himself the arbiter, and the Queen maintained her illusion about the Austrian marriage. King Felipe's state of mind remained so bad that Isabel began to consider the future and after some changes of heart she agreed to the signing of the Convention of Pardo on 6 March 1728, by virtue of which the blockade of Gibraltar was ended, Spain returned the *Prince Frederick* to Great Britain and freed foreign assets on Spanish ships. Orendain, Rottenbourg, Keene, van der Meer and Koenigsegg were the signatories.[102]

On 14 June 1728 there opened the first session of the Congress of Soissons at which Spain was to be the victim of the egoism of the great powers. From this long congress, which it was hoped would bring about a secure European peace, nothing positive resulted. France, with much ability, pursued a policy of sitting on the fence, since it did not suit her to break with the maritime powers; the personal friendship and political accord of Fleury and Sir Robert Walpole confirmed her pacific attitude. Yet France speciously sought also to strengthen the alliance between the Empire and Spain and to have some part in it, and for this reason issued a pretended declaration of mediation, attempting on the sly to cause a rift between these self-same powers. Charles VI gave promises about matrimonial projects between his family and the Spanish royal house, which greatly pleased Queen Isabel; yet he again put obstacles in the way of her Italian dreams. The Spanish subsidies continued, at which the British and Dutch showed some disquiet, since, in spite of this, Patiño had found means to keep twenty-four men-of-war in West Indian waters. At Soissons Spain's claims had gone unheard, for the British plenipotentiaries had not wished to listen to anything about the restitution of Gibraltar. The refusal of the Emperor to allow Spanish garrisons in Tuscany to secure the rights of Don Carlos exasperated Queen Isabel, and it was at this moment that the mental crisis[103] of Felipe V passed through an acute state. At times he lost his head completely, biting his arms and hands; at night he screamed and shouted and afterwards sang; he believed that he had turned into a frog; and he was afraid of being poisoned by a shirt and would only put on a chemise which the Queen had worn. He ate immoderately and spent entire days in bed, without wanting to move, in the middle of his excretions. A possible abdication was mooted at court, and the prestige of Fernando, príncipe de las Asturias increased. The Queen went so far on one occasion as to tear up a document in which the King stated that he would again and this time irrevocably give up his throne. Meanwhile, Orendain, marqués de la Paz, wanting to know what was going on at Soissons, decided to recall the duc de Bournonville, to Madrid. He arrived in November 1728, precisely when the court, in view of the news of the sudden illness of Louis XV, renewed the pretensions of Felipe V to the French crown, without his knowledge, of course. The recovery of Louis dissolved these projects. It is, however, interesting to notice that Felipe V, the duc d'Anjou of happier days, had a following in France and that, if Louis XV had died, both Fleury and Bourbon would in all likelihood have declared themselves in his favour.[104]

João V of Portugal had made marriage proposals between his family and the Spanish one, which were accepted by the Spanish court. Fernando, príncipe de las Asturias was to marry the Portuguese Infanta María Bárbara de Bragança, while the Spanish Infanta María Ana Victoria was to marry the Prince of Brazil, heir to the Portuguese crown. The Spanish royal family travelled to Badajoz in Extremadura, while the Portuguese royal family went to Elvas; and on 19 January 1729 on a bridge over the little River Cara, which separated Spain and Portugal at this point, the two princesses exchanged countries. The Spanish royal family afterwards undertook a journey to Andalucía and, after spending a short time in Cádiz and the Isla de León, on 10 April 1729 settled in Sevilla.

The Congress of Soissons went languidly on. Great Britain was angered by the harm which the delay was causing to her commerce; the Spanish plenipotentiaries were intransigent in their attitude, some of them like Macanaz going so far as to advise Felipe V to take energetic and even warlike measures. Britain's stance was threatening, and Brancas, French ambassador in Spain, tried to conciliate both parties. In March 1729 Queen Isabel had received a final rebuff from the Empire about the Austrian marriages. Koenigsegg understood that the alliance between Spain and the Empire had ended and asked his government to recall him. The Queen thought that the moment to ally definitely with France had arrived. The Italian duchies had come to be a subject of prime importance; but one had to reckon with Fleury, and on 28 April the negotiators went to Compiègne where the Cardinal resided. The Spanish plenipotentiaries advised a French alliance. Then on 20 July Charles VI categorically refused the Spanish proposals, demanded that France and Great Britain should guarantee the articles of the Quadruple Alliance and warned the Grand Duke of Tuscany that he should put his fortresses in a state of defence to avoid their falling into the hands of the Spanish. That was the point of the rupture whose consequence was the Treaty of Sevilla.

Stanhope—for now Great Britain was determined to be diplomatically involved—arrived at Sevilla, where Felipe V and Isabel were celebrating the birth of the Dauphin of France, and on 9 November 1729 the famous *Treaty of peace, union and mutual defence between the Crowns of Great Britain, France and Spain* was concluded.[105] In its clauses the commerce of France and Britain in Europe and America was re-established as it had been before 1725, British and Spanish commissioners were to arrange questions regarding captures, abuses and claims, and 6,000 Spanish troops were to occupy the forts of Livorno, Porto Ferraio and Piacenza. The contracting powers promised to defend Don Carlos against whosoever attacked his rights, and three separate articles confirmed the commercial privileges of Great Britain and made references to the return to her of the *Prince Frederick*, which still had not been carried out. Those who signed the Treaty of Sevilla were Brancas, for France, Stanhope and Keene (representing Great Britain), and Patiño and Orendain (Spain). King Felipe had wished Patiño to sign in addition to Orendain as his reputation was so great.

Difficulties about fulfilling the conditions of the treaty were sure to arise. Fleury pursued a chimerical plan of a European balance of power, while the United Provinces and Great Britain did not wish the union between France and Spain to be very close. The behaviour of Charles VI, however, put Spain in the position of calling for the fulfilment of the promises laid down at Sevilla. The Emperor, putting his trust in the support of Russia, increased his army in Italy and resolutely refused to allow the Spanish garrisons into Tuscany and Parma. Lucas Spínola, conde de Valverde, was sent to Paris in May 1730, and with him Chauvelin and Fleury discussed war plans which they did not believe they could carry into effect. Valverde returned to Spain, leaving behind the Spanish plenipotentiaries Santa Cruz and Barrenechea, who became the political toys of Fleury. Meanwhile Great Britain, by means of Keene, came to a direct understanding with Spain, and in October 1730 Felipe V, now recovering, sent to Paris the marqués de Castelar who left the Ministry of War in the more deft grasp of his brother Patiño.

Felipe's mental health, however, was still precarious.[106] He was capriciously lazy, turned night into day, disrupting the court with his unbalanced behaviour. He could not walk because he believed that one of his feet was not the same size as the other, and did not want to have his hair cut, although it had grown so thick and long that he could hardly bear to wear a wig. In spite of his condition he was very jealous of his authority and mistrusted Patiño. Franco-Spanish affairs had reached a difficult phase. Castelar was not a man to be made a fool of and haughtily demanded the fulfilment of the Treaty of Sevilla, perceiving the ambiguous attitude of Fleury and Chauvelin; on 28 January 1731 he wrote a declaration by which Spain disengaged herself from the Treaty of Sevilla and withdrew her ambassador from further negotiations.

There arrived the moment when the deceiver of all diplomats, the astute Cardinal Fleury, was himself deceived. Great Britain and Spain came to a secret agreement with the court of Vienna on 23 January 1731. Robinson, the British minister, and the duque de Liria, Spanish ambassador to the court of Charles VI, were the negotiators. Great Britain finally signed an agreement with the Emperor, who was uncertain of Russia and afraid of being left out in the cold, on 16 March 1731, and with Spain separately on 22 July, by virtue of which Charles VI at last allowed Spain to garrison the fortresses of Parma and Tuscany, now that Antonio Farnese, Duke of

Parma was dead.[107] By the first of these accords the Ostend Company's commercial enterprises in America were abolished and in exchange Great Britain guaranteed the Pragmatic Sanction of Charles VI, so dear to him, since it assured the continuance of his dynasty. By the second the Emperor made a pact with Spain and agreed to recognise the rights of Don Carlos and the introduction of the Spanish garrisons.[108] Felipe V renewed and confirmed the treaty of the Quadruple Alliance and that of Vienna of 7 June 1725, Great Britain and the United Provinces pledging full support.[109] It was a triumph for Spanish diplomacy. Three days later, on 25 July 1731, Felipe V came to an agreement with Gian Gastone de'Medici, Grand Duke of Tuscany, by which the latter pledged himself, in default of his male descendants, to recognise the Infante Don Carlos as his successor.[110]

France was isolated thanks to the slowness of Fleury and the tortuous policy of Walpole. Rottenbourg, French ambassador to Spain, now attempted to unite the two branches of the House of Bourbon. Britain took advantage of the situation and a squadron under Admiral Wager arrived at Cádiz and joined the Spanish fleet to transport 6,000 soldiers under the command of the conde de Charny to Italy. The Spanish ships were commanded by Esteban de Marí, the galleys by Miguel Reggio.[111] On 17 October 1731 the combined navies weighed anchor at Barcelona, while Don Carlos journeyed by way of Valencia, Barcelona and Provence as far as Antibes, where he embarked for Livorno, arriving there on 27 December. By a decree of the Aulic Council of Tuscany, Don Carlos was placed under the tutelage of the Grand Duke of Tuscany and the Duchess of Parma. The Infante was received in Tuscany with great emotion, and the German troops having retired from Parma and Piacenza, the Duchess Dorothea of Parma took possession of the latter's fortress in the name of Don Carlos.

This was the moment chosen by Patiño to suggest to the comte de Rottenbourg the convenience of a Bourbon alliance; Rottenbourg, as French ambassador, suspected that Spain had not recognised and guaranteed the Pragmatic Sanction, which in fact she had at Sevilla on 6 June 1731. Thereupon there developed a campaign of intrigues, with Spain working to destroy Fleury and the French attempting to bring about the fall of Patiño, who was protected by the Queen. She revealed her full support of him by expelling the abbé Montgon, who had opposed Patiño, from the country. The state of Felipe V declined once more; he dressed in ragged clothing and went so far in his rages as to hit his consort.

In 1732 Oran, lost in 1708, was reconquered by Spain from the Moors.[112] A suspicious Europe at first did not know what was the destination of the powerful armadas which gathered principally in the harbours of Cádiz, Alicante and Barcelona, the fleets commanded by Francisco Cornejo and the armies by José Carrillo de Albornoz, conde de Montemar. On 6 June

1732 Felipe V published a manifesto declaring the object of the expedition, on the fifteenth a combined fleet weighed anchor and on the twenty-fifth appeared before Oran. Having disembarked, the army under the marqués de la Mina, second-in-command, attacked Monte del Santo and forced the Moors to abandon the castle of Mazalquivir and leave the city of Oran, which on 5 July Montemar entered with the army. On his return to Spain he received the Order of the Golden Fleece as did Patiño. In August, Bey Hacen attacked Oran with 12,000 men and, backed by the Algerians, advanced to the fort. Reinforcements arrived from Spain, and a bloody battle followed in November in which the Spaniards came off victors; but it cost the life of the governor of the fort, the marqués de Santa Cruz. Meanwhile the Moroccans, with Ripperdá at their head, had also laid siege to Ceuta; but they were repulsed by the city's garrison.

Spain vacillated between France and the Empire. Queen Isabel asked the Imperial court to dispense with the question of his minority in the case of Don Carlos, so that he could immediately rule his Italian territories on his own account and so that he could be invested forthwith in view of his eventual accession. The duque de Liria worked hard to that end in Vienna, and in Sevilla bankers negotiated for this in secret with both Orendain and Patiño. The Emperor, however, did not accede to this request, and Queen Isabel inclined more and more towards France. The moment to negotiate had arrived. Rottenbourg lent himself to further this change of heart, and Patiño sent Castelar, in Paris, precise instructions for a projected treaty with France in August 1732. The bad faith of Charles VI over the question of Don Carlos favoured the Franco-Spanish negotiations, but Felipe V's new mental crisis caused the deferment of diplomatic action. A new assault of melancholy overtook him with his consequent silences; he did not want his hair dressed nor to be shaved, and he remained in bed for days on end. He spoke only to his Gentleman of the Bedchamber, Brière, to whom he confided that he wanted to make an end of the relationship with the Queen's four 'evangelists', Patiño, Scotti, the Archbishop of Amida, and her lady-in-waiting, Pellegrina. He longed for France, speaking of it wistfully, and there is little doubt that all his life he felt himself an exile. The emotions roused by the War of the Spanish Succession prevented him from introspection in his early years. He was, after all, involved in a cause and was for the duration a pivotal point of Europe. After that he lived landlocked in a world of sierras, moving from palace to palace still heavy with the fevers, the fears and the gloom of the last of the Habsburgs whose crown he now awkwardly wore.

For a moment it was believed that the intervention of Great Britain, whose ambassador Robinson seemed to be having some success in Vienna, would end the Emperor's resistance to Isabel's claims for Don Carlos; but the death of Augustus II, King of Poland and Elector of Saxony, on 1 February

1733 completely changed the direction of European affairs.

It was necessary for France to have a Spanish alliance.[113] The Polish King's death obliged Chauvelin and Fleury, contrary to their wishes, to protect King Stanislas Leszczynski,[114] Louis XV's father-in-law. The pacific cardinal saw himself obliged to go to war, and for him union with Spain was now valuable. The negotiations took a very good turn, since Queen Isabel, delighted with the decided attitude of France, was disposed to support her; but Patiño, who understood Spain's privileged position, imposed firm conditions. Spain wanted the annulment of the former treaties and of the renunciations which she had made at Utrecht, and the French government acceded to all the Spanish demands; but there was a flaw. France was now treating with Carlo Emanuele of Savoy and Sardinia since she did not wish Felipe and Isabel to come to an agreement with him, supposing with reason that he was a Bourbon presence in Italy.

Rottenbourg carried out the negotiations with Patiño, already charged also with the Department of Foreign Affairs by Orendain; but in April 1733 Patiño was forced from power by Felipe V's dislike of him. Perhaps it was his carefulness which slowed down the course of events that exasperated the maniac and made him hate him; but the Queen, as time went by, confided more and more in the faithful minister, who was, even after his fall, in close communication with his brother Castelar in order to conclude the groundwork of the Franco-Spanish treaty.

Spain even yet showed herself to be distrustful of the intentions of France and wished to be convinced of her good faith. Events in Poland and French intervention were what was going to convince her. At length Felipe V recovered and was active again, simply as a result of the news about a coming war, and on 16 May 1733 the court left Sevilla for Madrid. On the way, at Bailén Felipe V wrote a personal letter to his nephew Louis XV and, on 12 June, he and Isabel reached Aranjuez, where the king gave up his extravagances and resumed his normal life. On 26 September France signed the Treaty of Turin with Savoy. Less than a month later, on 19 October 1733, Castelar, who had prepared the preliminaries of the Franco-Spanish alliance, died. Finally, on 7 November the Treaty of the Escorial, the First Family Compact between the French and Spanish Bourbons, was signed.[115]

The principle clauses of this treaty were: there was to be a close and perpetual friendship and alliance between the kings of Spain and France and their respective heirs; France promised to defend the rights of Don Carlos and to guarantee his possession of Parma, Piacenza and Tuscany, and also all territory gained by Spain in Italy during the war; if Great Britain attacked Spain, Louis XV would make common cause with Spain, and would also render his good offices to restore Gibraltar to Spain; neither of the two countries was to take diplomatic action without the agreement of the other, in particular with regard to the Pragmatic Sanction; on military and commercial questions they were to be united. It is noteworthy that in article 14 the treaty is referred to as a 'Family Pact, perpetual and irrevocable'.

The Empire, Prussia and Russia opposed the free election of Stanislas Leszczynski, and favoured the candidature of Augustus III, Elector of Saxony. Queen Isabel's maternal ambitions continued to play a leading part in Spanish politics, and as a result of the strange Spanish intervention in the War of Polish Succession, her dear 'Carlet' was to obtain the Kingdom of Naples and Sicily. Stanislas had had bad luck in Poland, but France sent an army to the Rhine, and the old veteran maréchal Villars entered Italy to take command of the Franco-Sardinian forces, subsidised by Spain with 100,000 doubloons. The conquests of the allies in Italy were quickly made; Villars entered Milan, and before long Spain was fully involved in the campaign.

The conde de Clavijo sailed from Barcelona with a fleet of sixteen ships-of-the-line and some frigates, while Montemar embarked at Antibes with twenty-five squadrons of cavalry. The Spanish forces arrived at Livorno and La Spezia, and at Siena they united under the command of Don Carlos, who on 26 October 1733 had been named generalissimo by his father Felipe V. Villars prudently advised the defence of the line of the River Po and the shutting off of the Germans from the Alpine passes; but a disagreement with Carlo Emanuele of Savoy and Villars occurred, and against the latter's advice Carlo and the Spaniards decided to conquer Naples.[116] The maritime powers vainly tried to mediate with France and Spain to seek peace. The behaviour of Carlo Emanuele became all the time more suspicious, and France tried to woo the Spanish court with the promise of the Duchy of Mantua to Don Carlos. The Infante began the campaign, by journeying from Florence to Arezzo, where he joined his army on 24 February 1734 and marched from Perugia to the Papal States, gaining from the Pope the permission to pass through his territory. The conde de Clavijo took the islands of Ischia and Procida, and Don Carlos entered the Kingdom of Naples.

His conquest was a triumph; the population declared itself in his favour, and the Imperialist General Traun fell back from Mignano to Gaeta and Capua. From Città-Castellana Don Carlos advanced, on 14 March 1734, without obstacle to Mignano and Aversa. The viceroy Visconti had taken refuge in the province of Bari, and a force of the Spanish army, under the marqués de la Mina and the duque de Castropiñano, moved against the viceroy, while the conde de Charny attacked Naples. The castles of Santelmo and Castel-Novo surrendered to the Spanish, and on 10 May 1734 Don Carlos entered Naples. A few days before Felipe V had signed a decree in Aranjuez declaring Don Carlos King of Naples. The French, however, seeing that the position of Spain was not yet secure and that there was a possibility that the Imperialists might receive reinforcements, forced on Felipe V his conditional adherence to the Treaty of Turin.

On 25 May 1734 at Bitonto, the Imperialists, who had advanced along the Adriatic coast to try to reconquer lost territory, were attacked and defeated by Montemar. It was a resounding victory for Spain, for the German infantry had to surrender, the cavalry was destroyed and Generals Radoski and Pignatelli were taken prisoner. Visconti with great difficulty retreated to Pescara and from there to Ancona.[117] So brilliant a day's work gained for Montemar the title of duke, the status of grandee, a large pension, and the vital post of Governor of Castel-Novo. Shortly afterwards Gaeta capitulated, and in October Traun laid down his arms at Capua.

The conquest of Sicily was easier still. Don Carlos, called on by the Sicilians to come and take possession of their island, ordered Montemar to undertake the conquest and he set out on 8 August 1734. While the latter was disembarking in Palermo on the twenty-first, Marcillac was doing the same in Messina, and both were splendidly received. Lobkowitz, the Imperialist commander, had taken refuge in the citadel of Messina, and only this port and those of Trapani and Syracuse, garrisoned by Imperialist troops, presented any resistance. On 1 September the Senate of Palermo rendered homage to Don Carlos.[118] Meanwhile the campaign continued in Lombardy, with great danger to the Allies owing to the presence of Imperialists along the Po. Maréchal Villars, in despair at the conduct of Carlo Emanuele, begged to be relieved of his command, but he died a few days later. His place was taken by Coigny, who defeated the Imperialist Mercy, at the battles of Colorno and Parma on 29 June, and Koenigsegg, at the battle of Guastalla on 19 September. In other theatres Philipsbourg surrendered in July, and in the same month Danzig capitulated, which spelt ruin for the cause of Stanislas Leszczynski.

Great Britain and the United Provinces mediated once again to end the war. Carlo Emanuele still dallied suspiciously, and in October 1734 the advance of the Imperialists obliged him to retreat to the Adda. This news annoyed the Spanish court, for it saw the Kingdom of Naples threatened, and Montemar was sent to Lombardy. Coigny was superseded in the French command by the duc de Noailles. Meanwhile Don Carlos, in January 1735, crossed to Sicily and in July was crowned in Palermo. In May the combined strategy of the allied armies of France and Spain had forced the Imperialists to retreat, and in June the siege of Mantua began. This siege was the point of departure for the Spanish and Sardinians, for Carlo Emanuele did not wish to contribute to the conquest of the city if it was to go to the Spanish Bourbons, and the Spanish refused afterwards to make over any subsidies to Savoy. Montemar had already taken La Mirandola and was awaiting events.

The maritime powers added threats to their mediation, and France, ignoring the terms of the Treaty of the Escorial, negotiated secretly with the Imperialists. Cardinal Fleury, that friend of peace, wanted to end his days and his ministry with a resounding deed, such as would be the acquisition of territory for his country, though at the cost of sacrificing her ally Spain who, not for the last time, was to learn how selfishly France was to interpret the terms of the Compact. Thus France compromised her alliance with Spain in order to guarantee the Pragmatic Sanction and so, she hoped, reap positive advantages. King Stanislas exchanged the Polish throne for the Dukedom of Lorraine, while keeping the title of King, but the territory of Lorraine was to be united to France on his death. Such was Fleury's great success. The present Duke of Lorraine had to be indemnified, and this was to be done by giving him Tuscany after the death of Gian Gastone de'Medici. Don Carlos was recognised as King of Naples and Sicily, and he renounced Parma, Piacenza and Tuscany. The Emperor Charles VI joined the Duchies of Parma and Piacenza to that of Milan, so uniting them to his territory, and the King of Savoy-Sardinia (Carlo Emanuele) obtained only the districts of Tesino, Longha, Novara and Tortona. These were the main articles discussed by France and the Empire at the preliminaries of the treaty held in Vienna (the Third Treaty of Vienna) on 3 October 1735. Spain learned of the disloyalty of her ally, but finding herself alone, and faced by the superior Imperial forces of Klevenhüller in northern Italy, had to accept the armistice in Italy in December. On 1 December the French ambassador Vaulgrenaut had given an official report to Felipe and Isabel of the Imperialist negotiations.

Patiño was indignant at the behaviour of France, and van der Meer and Keene worked on behalf of the United Provinces and Great Britain to present the proceedings of Fleury in as bad a light as possible. Looked at from any angle it was reasonable that the Spaniards should ask for securities against being attacked in Italy, seeing that peace with the Emperor had not been confirmed. On 30 January 1736 Charles VI declared that he considered himself to be at peace with Spain; and on the same day the marriage contract between Francis of Lorraine, now Grand Duke of Tuscany, and Maria Theresa of Austria, the bride so much desired by Queen Isabel for Don Carlos, was signed. Montemar with the Spanish army had already recrossed the Po and retreated from Bologna to Tuscany. On 11 April a *Contract of Execution* was made between France and the Empire, and on the fifteenth Felipe V published a manifesto by means of which he declared himself to be in a state of peace with the Emperor, on condition that all clauses of the preliminary peace of Vienna were fulfilled. After some changes of heart, Charles VI fell in with this, and Schmerling, for the Empire, on 4 August 1736 signed at Compiègne a declaration to maintain a solid and stable friendship with Felipe V. Finally, after vexatious negotiations the instruments of cession were made by Montemar (Spain) and Klevenhüller (the Empire) at Pontremoli on 5 January 1737. The Emperor recognised Don Carlos as King of Naples and Sicily, while Don Carlos ceded Parma and Piacenza to the Empire, and the Grand Duchy of Tuscany eventually to the House of Lorraine. The evacuation of Tuscany began on 10 January 1737, and Montemar, taking the route by Genoa and Montpellier, returned to Spain.

The last months of 1735 had been taxing ones for the reinstated Patiño, but he continued to show his amazing worth; war, diplomacy, finance, naval affairs and commerce weighed on him and proved a superhuman task. This did not prevent his bitter enemies from developing an able, subtle and cruel opposition to him. On 8 December 1735 there began to appear a clandestine and anonymous news-sheet, written by hand and called *El Duende Político*, which continued until 7 June 1736. It was a rough satire directed against Patiño and his secretaries, and its object was to discredit the policy of Queen Isabel and her minister. The police finally discovered that its author was a Portuguese barefoot Carmelite, Fr. Manuel da Soão João, of the monastery of San Hermenegildo, Madrid, who was in the service of the Portuguese ambassador Cabral de Belmonte and was avenging certain injuries suffered by the ambassador in a riot, which a political incident in Portugal had occasioned. In the spring of 1736 it was discovered that Patiño's signature had been forged on some documents by a certain Artalejos, who had sent letters to the West Indies asking for money. Artalejos was executed in Madrid on 29 August 1736. To these difficulties which he had to bear was added Felipe's antipathy to Patiño. It was so great that Felipe discussed matters of state with him hidden from him by a curtain!

Patiño, worn out with work, fell ill with bronchitis on 12 September and the King, convinced at last of the skill and hard work of his minister, created him a grandee of Spain on 15 October. It was too late, for on 3 November 1736 Patiño died. According to a saying of Sir Robert Walpole, for Spain the death of Patiño was an irreparable loss. He had governed for ten years as a prime minister without holding that title, and was of the same calibre as his contemporaries, Walpole, Fleury and Koenigsegg, the most skilful politicians of the age. Patiño was a good economist and concerned himself, moreover, with the future of Spain as a naval power, creating the arsenals of El Ferrol, Cádiz and Cartagena; and he founded a school of marines, and another for engineers and the artillery in Barcelona. He launched twenty-two ships-of-the-line and 340 transport ships. He increased the size of the army with Swiss regiments, raising it to 80,000 men. In imitation of France he set up intendancies, and created a corps of 'Invalides'. He was a great supporter of commerce and navigation, suppressed various tax abuses, and inclined to a protectionist system, with the result that the cloth industry of Guadalajara flourished with 24,000 workmen, as did the glass industry of Llana and Olmedo and that of tapestry in Madrid. He put an end to interior customs except in Andalucía, although they were re-established in the Basque provinces. Finally he established trading companies for America and the Philippines. Patiño is with justice called the Spanish Colbert, and thanks to him Spain could sustain with honour a war against that Colossus, Great Britain.

The death of Patiño brought about a change in the ministry. The most important post, that of Secretary of State for Foreign Affairs, was given to a Basque, Sebastián de la Quadra, who had been page to Grimaldo and Orendain. The Treasurer-General, the marqués de Torrenueva, took over the Financial Department, and Francisco de Varas and the duque de Montemar became Secretaries of the Navy and of War respectively. In France, Chauvelin was disgraced and fell from power.

Spain now appeared to be inaugurating a pacific policy in order to consolidate the kingdom of Don Carlos. The prickly question was to be the marriage of Carlos, King of Naples. The conde de Fuenclara negotiated in Vienna his marriage to the second Archduchess, a sister of Maria Theresa, but in spite of the insistence of Felipe V, the Emperor refused this also. Marriage with the eldest daughter of Louis XV could not be considered because of her tender age, and on 1 January 1738 the choice finally fell on Marie Amalie, daughter of the Elector of Saxony, Augustus III King of Poland, the rival of Stanislas Leszczynski, a decision which could not have been more disagreeable for France.

The Grand Duke of Tuscany, Gian Gastone de'Medici, had died on 9 July 1737, and the dukedom, according to the arrangement, went to Francis of Lorraine. As a result of the Italian triumphs the court of Spain appeared to recover its normality; Felipe V was more master of himself and his faculties; his physical state was good, although in a crisis he suffered slight attacks of melancholy. The Queen held him in her power and preserved all the presence of mind of her youth. Passion dictated her resolutions, but she could be compassionate and she was pleasant and even delightful when nothing disturbed her; but she was jealous, suspicious, inquisitive and on occasion credulous, and she could be unbearably violent at the least opposition to her wishes. The only preoccupation which she had was with the aggrandisement of the power of Don Carlos in Italy, and with gaining positions for her other two sons Don Felipe and Don Luis, the latter Archbishop of Toledo and a cardinal since 1735.[119]

The ministry was composed of Navarrese and Basques of whom Sebastián de la Quadra was the most important. He was to be created marqués de Villadarias in 1739 and, slow, shy and upright, was held in high confidence by Felipe V and Isabel. Quintana took over the Departments of the Navy and the Indies, Ustáriz was Secretary of War, and Iturralde had taken the place of Torrenueva in the Department of Finance. The duque de Montemar was President of the Council of War, but was out of favour with the King and Queen. Some Frenchmen surprisingly enough held posts of importance, such as Sartine, Intendant of Cataluña, and the comte de Caylus and the comte de Marcillac, both provincial governors.

A conflict of importance blew up in 1738. Spanish trade with America was envied by Great Britain, and the British intended to extend their trade routes either legally or if necessary by contraband. Patiño's activity in increasing national trade, the navy, and merchant marine and manufactures, with the exclusion of foreigners, had caused great disgust in Great

Britain. British trade in Spanish America, in spite of the privileges enjoyed by the British, the *navío de permiso* and the *asiento de negros*, was continually suffering vexations, such as inspection, capture and confiscation. The progress made by the British planters on the coasts of the Gulf of Mexico, the clandestine commerce and the opposing pretensions of Spain and Britain in Carolina and Florida and the foundation of the new British colony of Georgia were other reasons for a break in relations. Sir Robert Walpole, Sir Benjamin Keene, the British ambassador, and Felipe V all wanted peace, but the Duke of Newcastle, Minister of Foreign Affairs, and British public opinion were eager for war.

Thus in April, 1738 the situation was very strained. Geraldino, Spanish representative in London, proclaimed Spain's right to board British ships in American waters.[120] Momentarily it was believed that a war could be avoided thanks to the promise made by the Spanish government to pay Great Britain £140,000 for indemnification. On 14 January 1739 the Convention of Pardo was signed, by virtue of which two plenipotentiaries representing each nation were to resolve in the space of eight months all unsettled litigation. These referred to the boundaries of Carolina and of Florida, and to trade and navigation in America and Europe. Further, Felipe V agreed to pay £95,000 to British subjects affected by any resultant changes. Shortly the conflict was to break out and was now held back only by the Convention of Pardo. The same day as the signing of the Convention, the marqués de la Mina, the Spanish ambassador in Paris, officially asked for the hand of Madame, eldest daughter of Louis XV, for the Infante Don Felipe, but the French court temporised. Peace was proclaimed with the Empire at the Fourth Treaty of Vienna on 28 June 1739. Spain did not recognise the Pragmatic Sanction, to which Fleury had yielded.

The French ambassador La Marck declared that the Spanish had too easily accepted the Convention with Britain. Certainly Spain had actually paid large sums of money to Britain, a country which ever since the Treaty of Utrecht had been profiting at Spain's expense from the *Asiento*. The Convention of Pardo was surely a sell-out! The *Asiento* contract would, however, end within three or four years, and it was known that the Spanish government did not wish to renew it. Anglo-Spanish relations grew more bitter every minute; British opinion, inflamed by Walpole's opponents among the younger politicians and the merchants, was for war, and a squadron commanded by Admiral Haddock appeared off Gibraltar to support British claims at which the minister la Quadra, marqués de Villadarias, protested. Diplomatic meetings in Madrid between the two powers made no progress, and Felipe V threatened to seize all British property in the New World that he could lay hands on. In July the Madrid discussions were broken off, and George II gave the order to make reprisals by taking Spanish ships and goods wherever found. On 23 October 1739 Great Britain declared war on Spain.

Walpole, in spite of his true pacifism, had been unable to avoid a war which the British Parliament and nation demanded. Between them they went to absurd lengths, and Parliament had the weakness to allow the smuggler Jenkins to stand at the bar of the House of Commons and to recount a trumped up story of how the chief of the Spanish coastguards had made him suffer horrible tortures. The war began on both sides with animosity and jubilation.[121] Mallorquín, Catalan and Biscayan ship-owners promised themselves excellent prizes, while France offered no longer mediation, but alliance. Fleury, however, wanted, in return for aid, to make a commercial treaty with Spain which should be advantageous for his country. Spain did not accept this proposition, and instead the Spanish ambassador, the marqués de la Mina, asked Louis XV himself with a certain asperity for French support without strings attached. Fleury, in indignation, asked Spain to send another ambassador to replace la Mina, and Luis Reggio Branciforte, príncipe de Campo-Florido, went to Paris. Felipe V seemed ready to yield to new negotiations about a commercial treaty, when unexpectedly and without any compromise French naval squadrons were sent to America to oppose the unjust British aggression.

Felipe V had gathered together all his resources for war, and the conflict began with good auguries for Spain. The Spanish American fleet sailed without delay to Spanish waters and took numerous prizes, eighteen being towed into the port of San Sebastián in the first months. Great Britain, for the first time in her modern history, was, like a great sea-monster, powerless in its own element. A great relief it was then when Admiral Vernon took Porto Bello on 22 November 1739; but in 1741 he came to disaster at Cartagena de las Indias. In the Pacific, however, Commodore Anson defeated Payta and took the galleon *Nuestra Señora de Covadonga*.[122] The exploits of the Spanish captains continued, however, and Great Britain lost 20,000 men and 407 trading vessels.

Felipe V prepared three areas in Spain in which to concentrate his forces in 1740; one opposite Gibraltar, commanded by Montemar, another in Cataluña, commanded by Esteban de Marí, ready to move against Mahón, and the third in Galicia under the Duke of Ormonde, from which an expedition to Ireland was to be made. Admiral Norris and the Duke of Cumberland, because of adverse winds, could not disembark troops at El Ferrol, and a Spanish fleet was able to set out for America.

The death of Charles VI on 20 October 1740 involved Spain in another warlike contest without her having ended the conflict with Great Britain. This was the celebrated War of the Austrian Succession over the succession to the Empire and the rights of the Archduchess Maria Theresa, married to Francis of Lorraine, Grand Duke of Tuscany. Queen Isabel of Spain considered an invasion of Italy to procure a good position for Don Felipe, while Felipe V made absurd allegations about his right to the Imperial crown and argued that Francis of Lorraine should not be Grand Master of the Golden Fleece.

Fleury did not want war, but there was a war party, led by the comte de Belle-Isle, which was gaining influence in France, especially after the recent invasion of Silesia by Frederick II of Prussia. On 5 January 1741, France made an alliance with Prussia in spite of having guaranteed the Pragmatic Sanction. Already Fleury was softening towards Queen Isabel's Italian projects, but he demanded an alliance with King Carlo Emanuele of Savoy-Sardinia, and this, as always, was repugnant to Spain. With respect to the election to the Empire, Spanish inclinations were towards Augustus III of Poland and Saxony, father-in-law of Don Carlos; but when France supported Charles Albert, Elector of Bavaria, Spain followed suit, hoping thereby to gain French backing for her Italian aims.

The preparations for the coming war brought a great minister, José del Campillo[123] to power. He was born of a poor family in Alles in Asturias on 6 January 1692. Soon left an orphan, he was taken to Córdoba, and protected there by Canónigo Antonio Maldonado, began his first studies. Not having any vocation for the Church, when he was eighteen he went into the service of the Intendant-General of Andalucía, Francisco Ocio, and in 1717 worked in Patiño's office. Patiño appointed him Paymaster of Marines in Cádiz. On an Atlantic voyage he escaped from the shipwreck of the *San Luis* on the coast of Campeche. In 1726 he was in charge of the shipyard at Guarnizo (Santander) when the relations of Britain and Spain were strained. Later, in 1734, he was Commissary-General of Montemar's army in Italy, and contributed to his victories. In March 1741 he was appointed Financial Secretary. Fleury understood that he was the true successor of Patiño, and asked Felipe to make him head of the War Department.

On 28 May 1741 the conde de Montijo signed a treaty of alliance between Spain and the Elector of Bavaria in Nymphenburg.[124] A few days before, on 20 May, Louis-Guy Guérapin de Vauréal, Bishop of Rennes, had arrived in Madrid as French ambassador, and he used all his powerful influence to bring the two courts together. The war with Great Britain continued. By October 1741 Campillo held the secretaryships of Finance, War, and the Navy and the Indies, and besides him only Villadarias occupied an important position, that of Minister of Foreign Affairs. Campillo was in reality the prime minister, and was responsible for preparing the Italian campaign. The news from Germany was not very consoling; Charles Albert of Bavaria, now Emperor Charles VII, having been crowned in Prague in 1742, saw Munich, the capital of his Electorate, occupied by foreign troops, and soon Parisian satirists called him 'John without land'. Walpole fell from power that year, his place being taken by Lord Carteret, who supported an anti-French policy.

Montemar took command of the Spanish army, which was to join forces with the Neapolitans at Orbitello. It appears that the duque's plan of campaign was modified at the last moment by Campillo, or perhaps by the Queen herself. The squadron weighed anchor at Barcelona on 4 November 1741 with nineteen battalions, and although the presence of the British under Admiral Haddock had made transport difficult, the troops were landed at Orbitello the following month. The Spanish cavalry under Jaime de Silva was in Genoa, but the infantry, badly fitted out and lodged, was not in a condition for brilliant feats of arms. The second shipment of troops, which arrived on 13 January 1742, had worse fortune, for the ships which brought them were surprised by a storm as they were sailing from the islands of Hyères to La Spezia, and there remained for a month. Montemar meanwhile had advanced with culpable slowness from Orbitello to Pesaro, and to add to the heap of ills, Carlo Emanuele of Savoy on 1 February 1742 made a pact with Maria Theresa so that the Imperialists, after their victories in Germany, were able to send an army to Italy.

The Infante Don Felipe, accompanied by his secretary the marqués de la Ensenada, crossed the Pyrenees and made for Italy; but Carlo Emanuele placed his army in a position to prevent his advance by land, while Admiral Haddock's squadron intercepted his supporting naval force along the Italian seaboard. Don Felipe, obliged to hold back at Antibes, awaited events. The aggression of Frederick II of Prussia contributed to increase the natural pusillanimity of Fleury, and the aid promised to the Infante did not arrive. The Spanish ambassador Campo-Florido, irritated by the cardinal's proceedings, found an ally in the minister Maurepas, who condemned Fleury's policy, and finally, to the great delight of Felipe V, Maillebois was sent with 30,000 men to aid the Bohemian army.

The situation of the Spanish army in Italy was becoming very difficult. The troops of the marqués de Castelar had joined those of Montemar at Pesaro, but the latter, old now, no longer had the vigour which he had shown in the campaigns of Oran and Naples, and contrary to all we otherwise know of him, Campillo allowed himself to be moved by personal spite, for what reason we cannot tell, and took a perverse pleasure in the blunders committed by his old chief. At the moment the Savoyards were advancing by way of Modena and Piacenza, and the Imperialist General Traun occupied the Duchy of Modena. Pressing orders from Madrid obliged Montemar to move, but he was already late. In June 1742 he directed his army of 35,000 men towards Bologna, and occupied Modena and La Mirandola, but feeling himself to be weak against superior forces, he fell back to Foligno, in spite of further despatches from Madrid, and in the end retired much farther than that, for in July the enemy pursued him as far as Rimini.

Meanwhile King Carlos in Naples was met by a British ultimatum. A British squadron arrived before the city in August 1742, and an officer, disembarking, informed him that he was either to be neutral and declare his Kingdom to be such, or else Naples would be bombarded. Carlos, wishing to save Naples from this, signed a document confirming his neutrality on 18 August, and the duca of Foligno led the Neapolitan army to barracks.[125] A few days afterwards on 9 September Montemar was relieved of his command, his place being taken by Juan de Gages.

Don Felipe now decided to take the offensive and advanced with his troops commanded by the conde de Glimes into Savoy; but almost immediately, on 29 September, Carlo Emanuele, who had defeated Montemar, arrived to defend his territory. The Spaniards, surprised by the Savoy-Sardinian troops and the Imperialists of Schulemburg, fell back on Montmélian and on 16 October left Savoy. At the same time maréchal Maillebois came to disaster in his expedition to Prague and returned to Egra on 22 October with an exhausted army. The marqués de la Mina, nominated commander of Don Felipe's army in place of Glimes, invaded Savoy and on 18 December took the castle of Apremont, and as a result Carlo Emanuele abandoned Chambéry. By 6 January 1743 there was not one Savoyard, Sardinian or Piedmontese soldier in Savoy, and Don Felipe entered Turin. Meanwhile maréchal Belle-Isle, taking over from Maillebois, brought the French army home.

Gages attemped an advance on Modena and finally retired to winter quarters; but on 8 February 1743 the Imperialists, under Traun, came up with him; the bloody and indecisive battle of Campo Santo followed, and the Spanish retreated to their encampment at San Michele, near Bologna. In March, Traun advanced with reinforcements and Gages once more retreated, while just before this an Imperialist force under Lobkowitz had obliged a Spanish army to find refuge in the Kingdom of Naples. Don Felipe, however, remained in Savoy, and the marqués de la Ensenada organised the complete conquest of the Duchy. As to French politics, Amelot, son of the former great French civil servant in Spain, maintained the same policy as Fleury, who had died on 29 January 1743, by attempting to attract perfidious Savoy with advantageous promises. Spain suffered a government crisis as a result of the sudden death of Campillo on 11 April 1743. His severity and rigidity had gained him many enemies up to the point of there being some suspicion that he had been poisoned.

José del Campillo, apart from his unreasonable aversion to Montemar, was an intelligent and upright administrator and a good Minister of Finance, notwithstanding that his ideas on the economics of trade between Spain and America, such as free trade between the various colonies and the allowing of Indians to take part in that trade which before had been the exclusive right of Creoles, were hotly opposed, although he stubbornly persisted until he succeeded in forcing them through.

Campillo carried out the registering and controlling of all Spanish ships trading with the West Indies and was able to reduce customs on merchandise destined for the New World. He also created the Cádiz and Guipúzcoa companies. Many of the measures attributed to Patiño were Campillo's or were the result of the collaboration of the two.[126]

It was now that Ensenada made his first important appearance. Cenón de Somodevilla y Bengoechea, marqués de la Ensenada, who had been private secretary to the Infante Don Felipe, was in Lisbon when he received an order from Felipe V to go immediately to Madrid to take over the departments held by Campillo at his death. The King's choice could not have been more happy, for Ensenada had been a collaborator of the dead minister, and both had been disciplies of Patiño. Ensenada[127] was born in Alesanco (Logroño) in 1702 of a noble but impoverished family of the Rioja. In 1720 at the age of eighteen he became an official in the Navy Department under Patiño, and in 1726 he served under Campillo, who noticed and recognised his exceptional abilities. In 1728 he became Commissary of the Navy, discharging this office successively in Cartagena, in El Ferrol and during the Oran expedition. Later he served as Commissary-Commander during the Neapolitan campaign (1734–35), and so greatly distinguished himself that King Carlos made him marqués de la Ensenada. A few years afterwards Felipe V nominated him Secretary of the Council of the Admiralty (1737), in which capacity he had during the next two years a great deal to do with Naval Ordinances. As Secretary to Don Felipe he took a leading part in diplomatic actions against the King of Sardinia. Although he did not want to become a member of the Spanish government he did so out of a sense of loyalty.

Amelot the younger, the French minister, believed in the deceitful promises of Carlo Emanuele of Savoy, who was secretly negotiating with Great Britain, and when Maria Theresa succeeded her father in 1740 she also fell under the spell of Savoy. Finally, however, the French minister was disenchanted, when, at the Treaty of Worms in September 1743, Carlo Emanuele made a formal alliance with the Empire and Great Britain, the effect of which was to irritate Louis XV, strengthen his attachment to Spain, and bring about the Treaty of Fontainebleau, known as the Second Family Compact on 25 October 1743. The articles of the Treaty of Fontainebleau were very explicit. France and Spain were to consider that the injury done to one pertained to both, and that the friends and enemies of one were those of the other. If either of the two nations were attacked, the other was obliged to provide armed aid. By article 4[128] Louis undertook to declare war on Sardinia and equip to that end thirty battalions of regular troops, five of militiamen, thirty naval squadrons and siege artillery. Spain was to place on a war-footing forty-eight battalions and thirty-eight squadrons. The allies were to set up the Infante Don Felipe in Milan, Parma and Piacenza. As to Great Britain, Felipe V and Louis XV were to take measures together to choose the right moment and circumstances for France to declare war on her, the object of which above all would be to destroy the British colony of Georgia and win back Gibraltar and Menorca. In October, 1743 the marqués de la Mina made an ill-starred attack on Savoy with Spanish troops, while the Prince de Conti commanded Don Felipe's forces.

France, having decided to declare war on Great Britain, put naval squadrons in a state of readiness, and encouraged the Chevalier de Saint-Georges (James, the Old Pretender) to send his son Charles Stuart, supported by a French squadron, to invade Britain. On 22 February 1744, a battle took place between the combined Franco-Spanish navy and the British off Cape Sicié.[129] The Spanish marines fought bravely and bore the brunt of the battle, and although the French Admiral Court manoeuvred with ability he came late to the assistance of the Spanish fleet and his delay resulted in much damage to the Spanish ships. Admiral Matthews sailed back unmolested to Mahón. Admiral Juan Navarro, in command of the Spanish fleet, was created marqués de la Victoria, but nothing could disguise the fact that the battle had been little short of a disaster for the Franco-Spanish allies. In the first place, a source of trouble for the future right down to Trafalgar, it was noticeable at this battle that the Spanish sailors did not wish to fight side by side with the French, for whom they showed an antipathy. In the second place, Britain had regained the mastery of the sea, and the expedition of Prince Charles Edward, the Young Pretender, to Scotland was postponed because of the presence of Admiral Norris in the Channel; nor did affairs go better in Germany where the conde de Bena had been sent by Spain to observe the behaviour of the French, in whom, in spite of the recent pact, the Spaniards had already lost confidence.

The lack of accord about war-plans resulted in inefficiency and slowness in the campaign on the part of the Franco-Spanish allies, who were nominally under the command of Don Felipe. Notwithstanding this, in April 1744 the Franco-Spaniards had conquered the county of Nice, and the King of Savoy-Sardinia retreated to Piedmont. In the interval King Carlos had ended his enforced neutrality and in March had advanced with his Neapolitan troops to join forces with the Spanish under Gages. The Imperialist General Lobkowitz came out to meet Gages, and the armies drew up against one another at Valletri. On the night of 11/12 August Lobkowitz attempted a surprise attack, but Gages realised this and was able to stand up to him. Great losses were sustained on both sides. It could be called a Spanish victory since the Imperialists retired northwards. A few days before, the Franco-Spanish had entered Piedmont by the valleys of Viarta and Stura, and afterwards Demont fell into their hands; but on 22 October the allies were obliged to raise the siege of Coni and retreat through the Alps to France.

To the dissatisfaction of Spain the marquis d'Argenson[130] was now made French Minister of Foreign Affairs, for he was a decided partisan of Savoy-Sardinia and was very opposed to Spanish aspirations, particularly to the dynastic plans of Queen Isabel. In spite of this, on 23 February, 1745 the French Dauphin and the Infanta Maria Teresa were married.

The death of the Emperor Charles VII on 21 February changed the aspect of European politics. Spain, or rather Queen Isabel, feared that France would make a pact with the Empress Maria Theresa. In April, the Elector Maximilian, son of Charles VII, accepted the Treaty of Fuessen, by which he was assured of the Electorate of Bavaria, which had been occupied by Imperialist troops. The French and Spanish decided to make a joint effort to finish the Italian campaign.

On 1 March in Aranjuez Felipe V signed a treaty of alliance with the Republic of Genoa, disgusted as he was by the conduct of Carlo Emanuele of Savoy-Sardinia, who was eager to gain Ligurian territory. The alliance with Genoa applied also to France and Naples. In March Gages began his remarkable march to Viterbo and, on 18 March 1745, he crossed the Apennines, outwitting the watchfulness of Lobkowitz, and in April pursued the Austrians as far as Secchia. Having received orders to join the main Franco-Spanish armies in Genoan territory, he made his way with amazing speed by the route of Gordano to the pass of Monte San Pellegrino, crossing the Apennines to arrive with his weary troops in the duchy of Lucca. From there without meeting with any obstacle he advanced to Sarzana on the Genoese frontier, where on 6 May he joined the duke of Modena. Having reached Genoa he took the famous Bochetta Pass which guarded the northern approaches to the city. On 11 May Louis XV won the battle of Fontenoy in Flanders.

The forces of the Infante Don Felipe and the French army of maréchal Maillebois moved more slowly. On 29 June they advanced on Albenga and took Arqui, and at Fregarolo the Infante and Gages joined forces. For his part Carlo Emanuele had united his army with that of the Imperialists under Schulemburg, but on 14 August they could not prevent Tortona from passing into French hands. The Genoese ably seconded their Franco-Spanish allies. The Spanish did not trouble themselves about Montferrat, and it was the Genoese who surprised Piacenza, taking it by assault on 9 September. France had no interest in this part of the campaign, but nonetheless the Spanish continued to gain brilliant triumphs, and on 22 September Pavia surrendered. On 27 September Carlo Emanuele was defeated by Gages and Maillebois at Bassignano, and on 12 October the victorious armies entered Alessandria, while Valenza, Casale and Asti surrendered to the *galíspanos*, as they were then called. The Infante Felipe wanted to advance to Milan but Maillebois did not follow him. The troops of Gages, however, advanced from Pavia and entered Milan on 19 December 1745. The campaign had ended. It only remained to conquer Mantua and reduce the citadel of Milan and a few other fortresses still held by Imperialist or Sardinian garrisons.

D'Argenson held to his original point of view and wanted to ally France with Genoa applied also to France and Naples. In March Gages began his moved to Dresden to stir up support for the King of Poland as candidate for the Imperial title, thereby making an enemy of Maria Theresa and certain German courts; but on 13 September 1745 Francis of Lorraine, Grand Duke of Tuscany, husband of Maria Theresa, was elected Emperor. D'Argenson's desire for peace was increasing, and he was disposed to sacrifice to it Spain's immoderate ambitions. The pretender Charles Stuart seemed to be triumphing in Scotland, and d'Argenson demanded of

Spain positive help for him. Bena was carrying out negotiations in Dresden; but Frederick II of Prussia's victory at Kesselsdorf on 15 December filled the Imperialists with fear, with the result that the latter made peace proposals to France and Spain, Maria Theresa offering Parma and Pavia to the Infante Felipe. These propositions were refused. The worst was that d'Argenson, without consulting Spain, initiated talks with Carlo Emanuele, and official notice of these negotiations was presented to Spain by the French ambassador Vauréal. Felipe V, angered by the conduct of d'Argenson, sent the duque de Huéscar to France as ambassador extraordinary,[131] so that he and the ordinary ambassador Campo-Florido might at all cost bring about d'Argenson's fall. The two ambassadors also did all they could to prevent Louis XV from signing a treaty with Savoy-Sardinia. Intrigues began to ruin d'Argenson, who counted among his enemies such powerful ones as Noailles and Maurepas. From now on relations between France and Spain were by no means cordial, and the correspondence of both Louis XV and Felipe V reveals suspicion and disquiet. Felipe V yielded to French demands. Meanwhile Carlo Emanuele began his tricks with Louis XV once more, and yet again France and Spain were reminded of the Savoyard King's bad faith.

The arrival of Imperialist reinforcements enabled Carlo Emanuele to begin the offensive on 5 March 1746, and soon Asti and Alessandria were abandoned by the *galíspanos*. Disagreements arose between Don Felipe and Maillebois, and all the fruits of the splendid campaign of 1745 were lost as a result of d'Argenson's torpidity. On 18 March 1746 the Duke of Modena and the Infante Don Felipe suddenly left Milan. D'Argenson still obstinately carried on negotiations with Savoy-Sardinia and ended by directly threatening Spain. On the other hand, Louis XV, now desirous of giving complete satisfaction to Spain, on 30 March sent Noailles to Madrid to try to bring about renewed confidence between the two courts.[132] Meanwhile in Italy, one disaster for Spain after another followed in quick succession: in April the Spanish evacuated Parma; on 2 May Carlo Emanuele entered Valenza; and in spite of the victory of Codogno gained by Pignatelli over the Imperialists on 6 May, the troops of Gages fell back on Nura. Piacenza passed into the power of the Imperialists, and the Infante Felipe asked Maillebois for help, which was accorded; but the Imperialist Liechtenstein defeated the Franco-Spanish armies in the bloody battles of the River Trebbia and Piacenza on 15 June.[133] It has been said[134] that it was the Spanish who bore the brunt of the fighting, which is uncertain; but what is sure is that 4,000 French soldiers remained disengaged and 1,000 prisoners, seventeen flags and ten cannon were taken by the Imperialists. It was not just a defeat, but a real disaster. A short time afterwards, on 9 July, just after writing to Louis XV, Felipe V died suddenly in the palace of Buen Retiro. His last thoughts were centred on Italy and he had agreed with Noailles that Don Felipe should rest contented with Parma and Piacenza.[135]

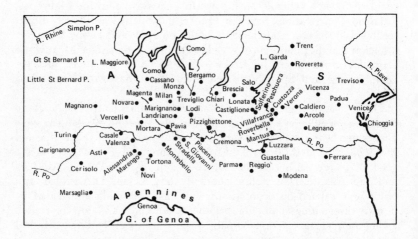

IV. Battlefields of Northern Italy in the Eighteenth Century

PART TWO

The Reign of Fernando VI (1746–59)

Fernando VI,[1] only surviving son of Felipe V by his first marriage with María Luisa of Savoy, good natured but very limited in mind, succeeded at the age of thirty-five. The British ambassador Sir Benjamin Keene had said of the newcomer that he would love peace as much as his father had loved war. Since 1734 Fernando and his wife Bárbara of Bragança had lived completely outside the course of public events, and some of that time even in disgrace, thanks to the machinations of Isabel Farnese. In consequence, although naturally generous, he had developed a suspicious and absolutely reserved character, which made him enigmatic. If for the diplomats who surrounded him he was an unknown quantity, for the nation as a whole he represented a hope for the future, and it awaited with enthusiasm the coming of a new king born on Spanish soil.

The French ambassador Vauréal looked forward to a closer alliance between the French and Spanish Bourbons, but he was wrong. On the contrary as d'Argenson wrote: 'King Ferdinand assumes the reins of government at the most difficult moment which has existed for a long time. During the time of Louis XIV the Spanish government was French, for the rest of Felipe V's reign it was Italian; now it will be Castilian and nationalist'.

Fernando VI showed his generosity by not repaying his stepmother Isabel Farnese in the same coin but permitting her to live at court—a situation of which the astute, ageing Italian took full advantage. Indeed her behaviour soon threatened the peace of the court, and as a result Fernando was forced to order her to retire to the palace of San Ildefonso; when she asked the reason, he replied officially: 'What I determine in my Kingdom is to be carried out and obeyed without being questioned beforehand by anyone'. The King certainly had very good reason for these strong words since the Queen-Mother Isabel was a restless and dangerous enemy, who until her enforced retirement had had her eye on the smallest movement of the young King and Queen, and who even afterwards maintained an active correspondence with her hidden confidants, who gave her minute accounts of them, even to their slightest illnesses. The fretting widow awaited the moment when her stepson should die so that her beloved son Carlos, King of Naples, could succeed to the Spanish throne; it was for this reason that she was so vitally interested that Fernando and Bárbara should not have offspring.

Fernando, with his vacant and pasty face, his stocky and short body, was of timid character; but the firmness of Queen Bárbara ably supported him. María Teresa Bárbara de Bragança, daughter of the epicurean Jão V of Portugal, was ugly. Her skin was sprinkled with pockmarks, her mouth was large, her lips thick, her eyes small and her cheekbones projecting, although in her young days she had had a certain grace of body which was afterwards destroyed by an obesity that was remarkable. At the time of her becoming Queen she yet preserved a regal appearance which chimed in well with her love of ostentation and luxury, a defect inherited from her father. These deficiencies, however, were palliated by great kindness, sweetness of temper and a cultivated intelligence. Husband and wife loved one another passionately. Very sympathetic towards Spain, Queen Bárbara looked always to the good of the nation and, being on every occasion encouraged by her husband to take part in politics, her influence in this field, though dissembled, was very real. Both Fernando and Bárbara were what one would call neurotics, both subject to melancholia, he terrified of being assassinated and she obsessed with the idea that after his death she would be left in financial distress, or even misery. After her death it was discovered that the locked chests in her private suite were crammed with money.[2] He, however, was by far the mentally weaker and more unstable of the two, he was sexually abnormal,[3] and his strange mental condition degenerated into madness, no doubt hereditary, before his early death.[4]

During the first months of the reign nothing appeared to have changed. Fernando confirmed Villadarias as Secretary of State, while Ensenada was in charge of the other departments. Nor did the new King wish to change his international politics; having inherited a war he continued it, believing that Spain's honour was compromised and that he must support his half-brother Don Felipe in his beleaguered Italian duchies. Cordial relations were maintained with France; but the King did not approve of the diplomacy of Campo-Florido, and the duque de Huéscar became Spanish ambassador at Versailles. As commander-in-chief of the army the marqués de la Mina took the place of Gages.

A fortnight after Felipe V's death the Dauphine Marie Thérèse (María Teresa of Spain), died in Versailles, and Fernando made propositions through the Spanish ambassador that the now widowed Dauphin should marry his dead wife's sister María Antonia, but Louis XV, for reasons of conscience (or so it was put out), did not wish his son to marry his sister-in-law. He seems to have been influenced by Gallican doctrine, for any problem about such a matter would not have occurred to an Ultra-montane. Fernando and Bárbara, offended by the rebuff, began to turn away from France, a situation which the pertinacious d'Argenson had already nearly brought about in secret. In December 1746 José de Carvajal was nominated minister.

In the war the Austro-Sardinians gained the advantage, and Franco-Spanish forces were defeated at San Giovanni and Rottofreddo, near Piacenza. The retreat was disastrous, the worsted armies falling back to the boundaries of Nice, Mina escaping to Savoy where he set up winter quarters and Maillebois placing his contingents behind the River Var. Spain had abandoned Genoa to the fury of the Imperialists, and Traun, at the head of 30,000 Austro-Sardinians, invaded Provence up to the gates of Toulon. General Botta-Adorno, with more Austro-Sardinians and supported at sea by the British, entered Genoa, his native city, and returned it to Carlo Emanuele of Savoy, although an Austrian army remained there.

While this was going on, France began negotiations in Breda with the Maritime Powers, and d'Argenson double-crossed Spain by coming to a secret agreement with the United Provinces and Savoy-Sardinia. Noailles, Conti and Vauréal all tried to drag d'Argenson from power and they finally succeeded. First his favourite general Maillebois was dismissed from his command, being replaced by Belle-Isle, and the minister himself fell on 12 January 1747, Puyzieulx taking his place.

In war the tables had apparently turned; the Austro-Sardinians were successful everywhere, and were going on from strength to strength, ready it seemed to annihilate the French and Spanish armies, when everything was suddenly changed by the rebellion of Genoa. A stone thrown at the Austrians by a boy was the signal for it, and on 5 December 1746 the Genoese, after a series of street fights, drove the Imperialists out of the city. With this disaster at their backs the Austrians were compelled to leave French territory, with the result that in February 1747 the Franco-Spanish armies were able to re-cross the Var. Disagreements, however, arose between Mina and Belle-Isle, which led to the Austrians under Schulemburg once more threatening Genoa; but later the French were able, in June 1747, to take Nice, Montealbano and Villafranca, and the Spanish advanced to Oneglia. In view of this the Austrians raised the siege of Genoa, and although Carlo Emanuele went to the defence of his territory, Ventimiglia surrendered to the French on 2 July. Belle-Isle, ill supported by Mina, attempted the pass of Colle de l'Assietta on 19 July, with the loss of his brother and 4,000 men. This misfortune only increased the growing disunity between the French and Spanish.

The combatants wanted peace, and their plenipotentiaries came to Breda to try to secure it. Queen Bárbara showed more ability than Queen Isabel had done, or at least more secrecy, and negotiated with Great Britain by means of Portugal. Horatio Walpole, Sir Robert's brother, was partial to an Anglo-Spanish alliance.

Spain was represented at Breda by old Melchor de Macanaz, an extraordinary character, who had not lost with his years his audacious and extravagant ideas, asking for Sardinia, Gibraltar, certain rights to the sovereignty of the Low Countries, and Tuscany besides for Don Felipe. When the time came for negotiation, he declared that he had no power to treat, which brought ridicule on him and other foreign diplomats. Macanaz paid for his folly by being recalled to Spain and imprisoned in the castle of Pamplona. The Congress of Breda was dissolved without positive result in May 1747. It was the French victories of maréchal Maurice Saxe in the Low Countries which obliged the Austrians to turn to ideas of peace. Le Esclusa, Sas-de-Gant, Hulst and Axel capitulated, and on 2 July Saxe won the battle of Lawfelt. In September the French under Lowendal sacked Bergen-op-Zoom, and on 10 November 1747 George II of Great Britain announced the opening of a congress at Aix-la-Chapelle.[5]

The Allies had fallen out with one another: Maria Theresa mistrusted Carlo Emanuele and France suspected Spain, while Great Britain was discontended with the United Provinces. In Italy, Carlo Emanuele recovered Ventimiglia, only to lose it once more, and for the rest of the winter the belligerents remained practically stationary in their positions: the Bourbons in the Duchy of Piacenza and the Austro-Sardinians in Lombardy. The Spanish representative at Aix-la-Chapelle was Jaime Masones de Lima, duque de Sotomayor; he was the reverse of the coin of Macanaz and his timid attitude made him the plaything of the intrigues of the comte de Saint-Severin d'Aragon who, behind the Spanish envoy's back, negotiated with Kaunitz, the Imperialist plenipotentiary, Lord Sandwich, representing Great Britain, and F. H. van Wassenaar and G. A. Hasselaar representing the Netherlands.

Meanwhile the British and Dutch armies, under the Duke of Cumberland and Batthiany respectively, were still being punished and forced to retreat in the Low Countries by Saxe and the French, and it was this which hastened the negotiations of the Treaty of Aix-la-Chapelle, the preliminary signing of which by Saint-Severin, Sandwich and the two Netherlands representatives took place on 30 April 1748.[6]

The main clauses of the peace were: Don Felipe was to rest contented with the Duchies of Parma, Piacenza and Guastalla, territories to which his male heirs were to succeed; but if he left no male descendants and if his brother Carlos became King of Spain these territories were to be returned to the present possessors or their descendants. Carlo Emanuele of Savoy received everything promised him except the Duchy of Piacenza. The Republic of Genoa recovered the Marquisate of Finale. As to France, she gave up her conquests in the Alps and the Low Countries. The Duke of Modena regained his territory. As regards Spain, the validity of the British demands was recognised. These were that she should enjoy the *Asiento* again for four years to indemnify her for the years during which she had not enjoyed this privilege. If the astonishment of the other plenipotentiaries was great, the irritation of the Spanish representative and of Fernando VI had no limit, since France, without letting Spain know anything of it had been responsible for making a treaty so hurtful to Spanish interests. On 18 October 1748 the definitive treaty between France, Great Britain and the United Provinces was signed. Maria Theresa did not sign until 8 November, and Sardinia not until 20 November. Fernando VI asked Louis XV to modify the clauses of the *Asiento* but, meeting with no response, signed the treaty resignedly, though greatly offended, on 20 October.

Gossips, and among them the British ambassador Keene, said that the man who exercised the greatest influence on the King was his confessor, Padre Rávago, a keen-minded Jesuit; but it is also said that he only interfered in ecclesiastical matters. Until April 1747 Père Jacques Lefevre, a Jesuit from Alsace, had been Fernando's confessor, but something that he said in the Palacio de los Afligidos, in which at that time Isabel Farnese was resident, caused his dismissal. His position was taken by Padre Francisco Rávago, who came from Potes in the Province of Santander, and was presented to Fernando VI by the new minister Carvajal.

Another favourite at the court was the renowned Neapolitan singer Carlo Broschi, known by the name of Farinelli. In 1737 Isabel Farnese had asked him to come to distract Felipe V from his melancholy. Farinelli's magnificent voice had been heard at the Imperial, French and British courts and at nearly all those of Italy, and at the age of thirty-two he had reached the peak of his fame. It is curious that, according to the famous singer's own confession, the man who had given him the most practical advice on his art was the Emperor Charles VI, Felipe V's rival, who would never have suspected that his words would go to help the singer to perfect himself and to sweeten the last days of his old enemy.

Fernando and Bárbara were extremely fond of good music and Farinelli was their intimate friend, the organiser of opera in the Buen Retiro and the person in whom they had the most confidence; but in spite of his positive influence, Farinelli never meddled in political affairs and did not use his influence except in charitable works and in the protection of the unfortunate, as in the case of the family of the painter Amigoni, whom he supported after the artist's death. Isabel Farnese, with her viper's tongue, said that Spain was governed by Portuguese intriguers and by musicians and flung at Queen Bárbara the disgraceful calumny that she maintained with Farinelli not friendship, but intimacy of another kind. The court composer, the great Domenico Scarlatti who had settled in Madrid in 1729, had before that been master of the Chapel Royal in Lisbon and music master to Bárbara, composing for her his famous sonatas. Now that she was Queen his position at the Spanish court became secure and pleasant.[7]

It is worth at this point considering the two famous ministers of this reign. José de Carvajal y Láncaster,[8] born in Cáceres in 1698, was the son of Bernadino de Carvajal Montezuma y Vivero and Josefa María de Alencastre y Noreña. He was not Portuguese, as has been stated; but as her names indicate, his mother was of mixed Portuguese and English descent. He was of noble family being connected with the duque de Abrantes. Educated at the University of Salamanca, he pursued a diplomatic career, and accompanied the conde de Montijo on several missions. He became the friend of Campillo and, on Ensenada's recommendation, entered the office of the Secretary of State. He was a very skilful, cunning, sutble and reserved diplomatist, severe in appearance and at times brusque, who hid his thoughts and spoke little. Justice has not been done to Carvajal, because historians have been accustomed to judge him by means of the calumnies heaped upon him by the ministers of the 'enlightened' reign of Carlos III, for his whole political standpoint was opposed to theirs. He was an absolute counterbalance to Ensenada and held completely different views, especially on international affairs.

Carvajal was inclined towards coming to an understanding with Great Britain, bringing forward two weighty reasons for this attitude: first, the British, at this very time, on the eve of events decisive for them needed the friendship of Spain and wanted to detach Spain from France; while secondly—so thought Carvajal—this attitude of Great Britain could lead to a mutually beneficial alliance, since Spain needed time to set her affairs in order and to leave her free from attacks on her overseas empire, which still miraculously defended itself with skeleton forces. Carvajal's ideas are expressed in his *Testamento político*[9] and in his *Pensamientos*, written before 1753, in both of which he set down the idea of the balance of Europe as being based on a firm alliance between Spain, Portugal and Britain. His attitude towards Britain as declared in these two statements was also founded on the belief that not only were the present needs of Spain and Britain the same, but that their aspirations need not clash. Great Britain wanted supremacy at sea and in commerce, while Spain would concentrate on her land power by guarding herself from France, counting on British naval power to defend her wide-ranging dominions. In order to bring about this alliance, and as a pre-requisite, Carvajal demanded the return of Mahón and Gibraltar. One might, however, argue that the very fact that Britain aimed at maritime and commercial pre-eminence would threaten Spain's New World Empire, which Britain could hardly be expected not to covet in the end.

Zenón de Somodevilla y Bengoechea, marqués de la Ensenada[10] was as a man and politician just the opposite of Carvajal. An able courtier, he succeeded in keeping his post on the death of Felipe V and soon gained the confidence of the new King and Queen, in particular Bárbara, who nominated him her secretary. Ensenada was an ostentatious person, magnificently dressed and generous to a fault. He lived in such pomp that the gossip about him reached the King's ears. Fernando asked him the reason for all that luxury, to which Ensenada in courtly manner replied: 'Sire, by the livery of the servant the master's greatness is known'.

Ensenada was no Englishman, as his enemies said of Carvajal; on the contrary, he had an excessive inclination towards France. He knew the defects of that nation, but he preferred French to British friendship, not so much out of affection for France as out of hatred for Great Britain, which he saw as the effective cause of Spain's decline. These were the two perfectly logical points of view of the two ministers, both keen, even aggressive, Spaniards who in their schemes were bridled by Fernando VI, who discreetly defended the maintenance of peace, which would certainly be disturbed if Spain were to make alliance with either France or Great Britain. Spain had been exhausted in serving the selfish policy of Isabel Farnese which had involved the country in diplomatic complications and burdensome wars.

Ensenada, having, for the time being, the upper hand, improved the army and navy, created new regiments, some of them foreign ones, set up horse-studs and increased the artillery, and built arsenals in Barcelona, Mallorca, Cádiz, on the Portuguese frontier and in El Ferrol. He sent Jorge Juan, the marine engineer, to London to study ship-building. French engineers, such as Briant and Godin were brought to Spain. Above all he bent his efforts to setting up a proper merchant marine, which Spain had lacked before, and it was this part of Ensenada's plans which alarmed the British cabinet. He also concerned himself with roads and with irrigation. Mining engineers such as Bowles came to Spain, financed by Ensenada. Finally he reorganised state finances with such success that taxes, which before his time amounted to 53,000,000 ducats, under his administration rose to 90,000,000 and Fernando left at his death a reserve of 60,000,000. He began a sinking fund for the national debt and considered an income tax.

Thanks to Ensenada, Spain was converted into a considerable naval power, and the famous Bernardo de Ulloa was put in charge of the building of the great arsenal at Cartagena. To Ensenada was due the setting up of public granaries (*pósitos*). Industries, laid low by the war, revived, and the silk one gained great prosperity. He gave new life to trade, permitting the export of metals on payment of an insignificant duty. The canal of Old Castile was projected, and a highway was opened through the Guadarrama mountains.

Sir Benjamin Keene, the British ambassador, reported that he heard Ensenada say: 'If at any time you see me preferring the French flag to the Spanish one, have me arrested and hanged as the greatest malefactor on earth'. This is one of the proofs of Ensenada's patriotism, and of the falsity of the reports circulated by his enemies to the effect that he was sold to France. As to Carvajal, Keene wrote to the duc de Belfort: 'I cannot make him as English as I should like, but I am ready to guarantee that he will never be French'.

Fernando remained faithful to his original position, turning neither to

Great Britain nor to France, but he did not allow himself to lose the advantages of a family connexion with the French royal family. In fact, he and Louis XV were first cousins twice over, since they were sons of two brothers, the Dukes of Anjou and Burgundy, and two sisters, the Princesses of Savoy, and he was thus ready to remain personally friendly towards the French royal family in spite of the Treaty of Aix-la-Chapelle and a matrimonial rebuff. Meanwhile, the duc de Duras, a light character who displeased both Fernando and Bárbara, became French ambassador to Madrid. Fernando arranged the marriage of the Infanta María Antonia and Prince Vittorio Amadeo, heir to the throne of Savoy-Sardinia. Celebrated on 12 April 1750, it distinctly influenced the direction of Spanish politics.

In his diplomatic attitudes Fernando VI differed absolutely from his half-brothers, Felipe Duke of Parma and Carlos King of Naples, and this was clearly shown in his move towards the House of Austria, the eternal rival of the Bourbons. Count Esterházy, Maria Theresa's ambassador in Madrid, began to plan a defensive alliance in Italy. As wife of the Grand Duke of Tuscany, Francis of Lorraine, and as ruler herself of the Milanese, Maria Theresa sought to bring about the settlement and pacification of Italy. Spain agreed, and in spite of the opposition of France and of Ensenada, the defensive treaty concerning Italy, called the Treaty of Aranjuez, was signed by Carvajal, Count Migazzy, successor of Esterházy, and the marqués de Marsan on 14 June 1752. Naples and Parma could have joined in, but did not do so, and Don Carlos as King of Naples protested, as he had done already at Aix-la-Chapelle, because he believed that by still further strengthening Austria's interests in Italy Bourbon interests, his own territory and that of his brother Don Felipe, would be imperilled in the end. His criticisms went unheeded, and Spain, Savoy-Sardinia and Austria guaranteed each others' sovereign rights in Europe.

The British government sought to join the Treaty of Aranjuez, but Carvajal was careful not to be encouraging, arguing with Keene that it would not be to Britain's advantage. While Fernando, in spite of his personal attachment to his cousin, remained distant to France, his step-brothers Carlos and Felipe, in particular the latter, very French at heart and married to a daughter of Louis XV, moved diplomatically closer to the court of Versailles and tried to make a treaty with France, opposed to that of Aranjuez. Indeed Fernando suffered further annoyances from these step-brothers, Don Felipe, Duke of Parma because of his exorbitant expenditures, which Fernando good-naturedly paid off, and Don Carlos, King of Naples, because, without letting him know anything about it, he was, contrary to his usual attitude, parleying with the British and considering giving them trade preferences in Naples.

There now began a battle of intrigue between the courts of St James and Versailles to win Fernando for one side or the other. The pro-French party in Spain wanted to make Ricardo Wall, who unknown to it then was pro-British and a strong opponent of Ensenada, the Spanish ambassador in London. Wall was an Irish Catholic in Spanish service and had fought in the Spanish army in Sicily, under Montemar in Naples, and in Don Felipe's army against the Sardinians. Wall went to Madrid and, with the support of Carvajal, was able to destroy French machinations in October 1752. Carvajal, now Secretary of State, learned how to withstand French offers of a new Family Compact, for when Louis XV offered him the Grand Cross of the Order of the Saint Esprit, he refused it with ability and diplomatically, declaring that he had not accepted that of Santo Gennaro of Naples either; the Golden Fleece, which his own king had given him was enough for him, he said.

Meanwhile there had come about a diplomatic wrangle with singular consequences. The two ministers, Carvajal and Ensenada—as was likely to happen sooner or later—came to blows over the signing of a treaty which was negotiated by the former and in which Ensenada afterwards intervened in an altogether strange manner. The independent, brusque and haughty Carvajal had prepared at Madrid in 1749 a treaty with Portugal that resolved the long-debated question about the colony of Sacramento,[11] by which Portugal was to cede it to Spain in exchange for certain territories in the intérior of Paraguay, where there were Jesuit missions. It cost a great deal to convince the King of Portugal, João V of the advantages of the treaty, and at his death soon afterwards his son and successor José I, influenced by his minister José de Carvalho, did not wish to continue the negotiations. Carvajal, however, won over Queen Bárbara to persuade her brother the King of Portugal and the stubborn Carvalho to agree to the Treaty of Madrid as it was named, which they finally accepted on 13 January 1750.[12]

Carvajal's enemies led by Ensenada immediately began to accuse him of selling out to Portugal, which was false.[13] In fact, his idea was to liberate the mouth of the Río de la Plata from the Portuguese for Spain's benefit; but it is all the same true that the treaty was too vague, and there were many difficulties surrounding his Río de la Plata plan, especially due to the bad will of the Portuguese and the opposition of the Spanish Jesuits in the Paraguay territory; so the treaty was held in abeyance and negotiations continued. They were still continuing when on 8 April 1754 Carvajal died without having solved the question, and it was then that Ensenada intervened.

The protests of the inhabitants of the territories along the Río Paraguay which were to be ceded, the report of the Jesuits, and the work on the boundaries appeared to show that perhaps Carvajal had made a mistake. The death of Carvajal had given a new spirit to Ensenada and the French party, but soon the duque de Huéscar and the conde de Valparaíso contested Ensenada's influence. Ricardo Wall left his embassy in London and became Minister of State. Ensenada sought to hold up the realisation of the Treaty of Madrid and looked for a way to reduce the evil that he believed had been done or if possible scrap the treaty altogether. Not finding any means of doing so, he told Carlos, King of Naples, heir presumptive to the Spanish throne, what had happened. This was unpardonable, and led to Carlos's protest at the signing of a treaty in which he had had no chance of taking part. While Carlos made his official complaints, Ensenada discussed with the French government a plan of attack on the British settlements on the Gulf of Mexico. The British ambassador Keene, a good friend of Wall, found out about these discussions,[14] and joined with the leaders of the anti-French party, Wall and Huéscar, to bring about the political ruin of Ensenada;[15] on 20 July 1754 'the Mogul', as Wall dubbed him, was banished to Granada. The King's order for his banishment arrived at night when he was asleep, but on being wakened he rose at once and said: 'We are going to obey the king'. In his wardrobe they found forty suits of the richest kind, 180 pairs of breeches, 1170 pairs of silk stockings and elsewhere forty watches and a collection of porcelain and pictures of great value.

Here should be mentioned a piece of work carried out by Ensenada which was to have long-lasting consequences and was to result in a workable settlement between Spain and the Papacy. The problem which he solved had existed since 1709, when Pope Clement XI had recognised the Archduke Charles as King of Spain. After the fall of Alberoni, who had intended to reach a solution, Innocent XIII in 1723 in the bull *Apostolici ministerii* attempted to heal the differences between the Vatican and Madrid, which in time led to the concordat of 1737. This did nothing, however, to deal with such vexed questions as royal patronage and the nomination to vacant bishoprics and abbacies. It satisfied no one and soon became a dead letter. At last in 1753 Pope Benedict XIV with Ensenada as intermediary came to full terms with Fernando VI in a concordat which was more advantageous to Spain than anyone could have dared to hope. It seems to have satisfied both parties by a compromise on nomination and patronage, the division between those in the Pope's hands and those in the crown's being founded on tradition, although the Papacy had the right to oppose any irregularity on the crown's part.[16]

So pleased was Benedict XIV with Ensenada for having resolved the difficulty that he offered him a cardinalate, which the statesman wisely refused.[17]

The fall of Ensenada who had been in charge of the Ministries of War, Navy, the Indies, Finance and State, caused general consternation, even among the very people responsible for it. Great Britain, on the other hand, was delighted. It was not necessary to have the eye of a lynx to divine Ensenada's intentions, and the British ambassador Keene could understand them well. Ensenada's secretary, Agustín Pablo de Ordeñana was also exiled, followed by the Abate Facundo Mogrobejo, confidant of both; and finally, not long afterwards, in January 1756, Keene obtained the removal of Padre Rávago, the King's confessor, because of the understanding he had reached with the Jesuits of Paraguay.[18] For some time it was believed that Rávago was innocent, but after the publication[19] of the documents concerning the matter, no doubt remains about Padre Rávago's political intervention. Influenced by Carvajal, he approved in principle of the treaty of 1750, but realising the discontent of the Jesuits in Buenos Aires, Tucumán and Paraguay, he intervened with Fernando VI to avoid the carrying out of the treaty and encouraged the Spanish Jesuits to resist it.

The members of the pro-British party in Spain were more than pleased at the disappearance of the francophile Ensenada, and Wall, Huéscar (Alba) and Valparaíso believed that Fernando VI would agree to the British proposals. Ricardo Wall, who replaced Ensenada as Secretary of State, had been raised to that position by Huéscar, the King's gentleman-in-waiting, and by the conde de Valparaíso. These drove Wall on and supported him, but Wall hesitated from showing Fernando his British inclinations, since he realised how these—Irish though he was—could be interpreted. On the other hand, there were many who regretted the fallen Ensenada. Julián de Arriaga, Secretary of the Indies, blindly obeyed Wall's orders; but being the creation of Ensenada he felt gratitude to his former protector. Valparaíso, Secretary of Finance, but little fitted for his charge, confided in the officials of his department, nearly all of whom had been nominated by Ensenada. Sebastián de Eslava, the Minister of War, supported Fernando's ideas of neutrality, although the British ambassador Keene perceived in him some inclination towards France. The majority of the chief administrative and judicial positions were held by friends of Ensenada, and others who had been displaced on Ensenada's fall were later given back their posts. Among them was Gordillo, Royal Accountant, who in 1755 was appointed chief official of the War Ministry.

The struggle between France and Great Britain seemed about to begin in earnest. The two Powers had already come into collision in India, in Nova Scotia and on the banks of the River Ohio. The French ambassador Duras, having sought in vain to win over Farinelli, began to ingratiate himself with Queen Bárbara, who received a letter from Louis XV inviting her to take part in a secret and confidential correspondence with him. She immediately informed Fernando of what had happened, and being thus foiled, Duras attempted to speak to the King officially of the offences inflicted upon Spain by Britain in America. Disgusted by the imprudent behaviour of the French ambassador, Fernando VI asked for his recall, and in October 1755 Duras left Spain. In the meantime France tried a new diplomatic tack by asking Spain to mediate in the quarrel between her and Great Britain; but Fernando VI stated that such mediation was impossible, since Spain herself had many litigious questions to settle with her.

The Seven Years' War now took shape with Austria and France, the age-old enemies, as allies against Great Britain, Prussia and Portugal. Sweden and Russia joined the Austrian camp, while Spain, the United Provinces and Denmark remained neutral. On 18 May 1756 in London, Great Britain officially declared war, although in reality it had already begun. The British Admiral Byng with the Mediterranean fleet went to the assistance of Menorca, on which the French had landed an army of 12,000 men under the duc de Richelieu; but he was defeated in a naval battle on 20 May 1756, and on 28 June the British garrison of Menorca surrendered to the French.[20] France now redoubled her efforts to attract Spain to her side, promising to negotiate the Polish throne for Don Felipe, and offering Spain Menorca and support for the reconquest of Gibraltar. Maria Theresa intervened and made tempting offers to the Spanish through the marqués de la Mina, Captain-General of Cataluña, but Fernando VI remained obdurate and maintained his political neutrality.

Keene did not neglect opportunities to oppose French machinations, but public opinion was greatly incensed because of outrages committed by British privateers on Spanish trade, British contraband in America and the extension of British holdings of redwood, so necessary for British industry, in the Gulf of Honduras and on the Mosquito Coast during 1757. The moment had arrived when Britain's disadvantageous position in the contest made the possibility of an alliance with Spain very precious for her; and this is how a politician of the stature of the elder Pitt saw the situation, as can be understood from his letter to Keene in which he unfolded a plan to obtain Spanish support. Pitt, in exchange for an alliance, offered Gibraltar to Spain on the condition that Spain should help to recover Menorca from the French.[21] Considering the way in which the offer was made, Keene realised that Pitt would fail to win Spain over; but all the same the ambassador carried out his orders, hearing from Wall's very lips hard words and bitter complaints about Great Britain, which was no surprise for such an experienced diplomat and one who knew Spain so well as Keene. On 6 September 1757 he answered Pitt, and twenty days later the zealous representative of Britain's interests in Spain died there.

Queen Bárbara, corpulent and asthmatic, was nearing the end of her life. On 25 September 1757 she attended the consecration of the magnificent church and convent of the Salesians, where she considered spending her retirement if she survived the King, which she had always expected to do. Soon afterwards she took to her bed suffering terrible pain. As the months passed boils broke out over her whole body, and she at last died on 27 August 1758. The opening of her will destroyed the popularity which she had enjoyed during her lifetime, since it was found that she had been a miser who had accumulated a respectable fortune of 7,000,000 *reales*—which she left to her brother the Infante Dom Pedro of Portugal, who became her universal heir.[22]

Immediately the question of succession arose and marriage proposals for

Fernando VI were set afoot; but the King's health cut short the initial plans, and it is unlikely that he would even have countenanced them. No sooner was the Queen dead than he fell victim to profound melancholy, hiding himself away in the palace of Villaviciosa, where he began to show signs, each day more pronounced, of a progressive madness,[23] inherited from his father, and according to others, due to a blood infection, resulting from contagion with Queen Bárbara, from whom he had refused to be separated even during the last stages of her illness. The King's symptoms were soon alarming; he wanted to be alone, hating the company of the very people who before had enjoyed his full confidence. During the last months of his life he hardly ate, taking only soup; he beat his servants and did unending extraordinary things.

The Council of Castile and the ministers did not know what part to take. Fernando's step-brother the Infante Don Luis, Archbishop of Toledo and Sevilla, at first kept his mother Isabel Farnese informed of the progress of the King's illness, but later, terrified by Fernando's sudden paroxysms of rage, he left Villaviciosa and went to San Ildefonso. In Naples King Carlos[24] maintained the height of circumspection, not wanting to be mixed up in the affairs of the government until the King's death; but after some months he saw himself forced to give urgently needed advice to the bewildered government, in particular after the death of the only strong figure in the ministry, Sebastián de Eslava, Minister of War. Finally, Fernando, wildly mad, tried to commit suicide with a pair of scissors, begged for poison with loud cries and, with a few lucid intervals, was completely extenuated with a high fever, dying on 10 August 1759.

One cannot deny that this reign, apart from the qualities or defects of the royal pair, has a certain grandeur, both attractive and sympathetic.[25] Spain had thrown off her slavery to France, the political norm during the greater part of Felipe V's reign, and was not hard pressed, as in the period of the Spanish Habsburgs, but was on the contrary admired and desired, although with an interested love, since friendship with Spain, both on account of her diplomatic situation and her mercantile wealth, was valuable for all the greater European powers: the balance of power could pass into the hands of whichever one of them gained her alliance. As was said at the time: 'Spain was a lady whom all wished to please only for the advantages of her favour and of her society'.

Fernando VI has been called 'the Discreet' (*el Discreto*), although this may be qualified by considering his indolence and hypochondria, inherited not only from his father Felipe V, but from his grandfather, the Grand Dauphin, son of Louis XIV, whom Saint-Simon had once described as 'drowning in gloom'.[26] The second Bourbon was a prudent and well-meaning king—so loyal in his proceedings that his great defect was said to be that he never failed to keep his word. Very apathetic, uxorious like his father, a collector of watches and fond of hunting, he paid great attention to government affairs and was upright and just. His detractors say that he was of mediocre intelligence. He had no patience with high-flying intellectuals and chose hard-working and reasonable ministers. He showed himself firm in resisting the approaches of France and Great Britain who with their sirens' songs sought to draw Spain out of the benefits of her neutrality.

PART THREE

The Reign of Carlos III (1759–88)

On 22 August 1759, twelve days after Fernando VI's death, the news of it arrived in Naples. Carlos, King of Naples and half-brother of the dead king, before renouncing his Italian kingdom for that of Spain, had to resolve a question of succession of the utmost importance, since his brother Felipe, Duke of Parma, was ambitious to gain the vacant Neapolitan throne. Besides, Maria Theresa of Austria and Carlo Emanuele III of Savoy-Sardinia had interests which were involved; the former wanting to win back Parma and Guastalla, and the latter desirous of recovering Piacenza. It was necessary to remove these dangers. The French minister Choiseul undertook to do this by holding back Savoy with promises and by quietening Maria Theresa's efforts to bring about the marriage of her eldest son Joseph, heir-apparent to the Empire, to the Infanta Isabel, daughter of Don Felipe, Duke of Parma. Of the sons of Carlos of Naples and Maria Amalie of Saxony, the eldest, Felipe was a cretin, the second, Carlos was designated heir-presumptive of Spain, and to the third, Fernando, fell the Kingdom of Naples. Carlos III succeeded to the Spanish throne thanks to the will of Fernando VI and by natural right.[1]

The new King embarked on 7 October 1759 on the *Fénix* and ten days later disembarked at Barcelona, where he was splendidly received. He was forty-three, of medium height, broad-shouldered, of ruddy complexion, with small eyes and an enormous nose which jutted out over a toothless mouth. He was affable and hated ceremony. From the first he made an agreeable impression on the Catalans, to whom he gave privileges and compensations for what they had been deprived of by Felipe V after 1715, although in 1768 he was to make an end of the teaching of Catalan in schools,[2] something accepted by the people with equanimity, surprising unless one realises that they were satisfied by a benevolent policy which favoured their mercantile interests.

Queen Marie Amalie had a masculine look, the sharpness of her face accentuated by wrinkles and thick lips. Her voice was grating and was all of a piece with her impatient and haughty nature, which could not brook any contradiction whatsoever.

From Barcelona the new King and Queen travelled by way of Zaragoza and Alcalá to Madrid, coming to court incognito; they settled in the palace of Buen Retiro, where the Queen-Mother Isabel Farnese, who had acted as regent during her son's absence, came to meet them. The very day after his arrival Carlos III adopted a way of life which he observed ever after, public affairs and hunting taking up the greater part of his time. Assiduous in fulfilling his duties as sovereign, he also dedicated himself to the chase in order to avoid by this exercise and distraction his tendency to melancholy, a perpetual threat to all the members of his family. Constant in his affections he never failed to have at his side José Fernández de Miranda, duque de Losada, a member of his bodyguard who had accompanied him to Italy and who until his death enjoyed the King's friendship.

Carlos liked Spain, which he associated with the best years of his infancy and youth; not so Queen Marie Amalie who, accustomed to her delightful residence in Naples, found Madrid cold and gloomy. She was of bright intelligence and of simple ways and, in spite of her angular manners, always sought the well-being of her new kingdom, giving the king wise advice on both international and national affairs. In her letters to Tanucci, the honoured Neapolitan minister, who more than anyone else had trained Carlos in an enlightened outlook, Amalie spoke of Isabel Farnese with a certain disdain, saying that the old Queen's talent had no depth, but was only superficial. In this she was unjust, since she knew her only in her old age when she was paralytic, half-blind and decayed, and she forgot that it was thanks to her that her husband had gained the Kingdom of Naples. Amalie's main failing was that she allowed herself to be dominated by the covetous and avaricious duquesa de Castropignano.

Carlos disliked new faces, and to begin with hardly altered the ministry which existed at the death of Fernando VI, his only appointments being that of Juan de Gaona y Portocarrero, conde de Valparaíso, who was made ambassador to Poland, and the Italian Leopoldo de Gregorio, marqués de Esquilache, whom he presented to the vacant position of Minister of Finance. Ricardo Wall was Minister of State, Alfonso Muñiz, conde de Campo Villar, a mediocre magistrate, was Secretary of Grace and Justice, and the old and incorruptible Julián Arriaga was head of the Secretariats of the Navy and the Indies. The most outstanding personage was Wall. The new King soon made it clear that he was jealous of his authority and wished to have complete control of the opinions and designs of his ministers. He himself took in hand the reorganisation of Finance and the Armed Forces.[3] The chief diplomatic figure was Gerónimo Grimaldi.

In the first months of the reign royal bounties had been responsible for wiping out part of the economies accumulated by Fernando VI, for Carlos III pardoned the arrears of the Provinces of Castile, Valencia and Mallorca outstanding since 1758, and commanded that his father, Felipe V's debts should be paid. He and Amalie had put off their solemn entry into Madrid until 13 July 1760, when much against his inclination it was held with great pomp; but shortly afterwards on 27 September Amalie died of a 'putrid infection' at the age of thirty-six, and Carlos held her memory so dear that he remained unmarried for the remainder of his life. She, it appears, shortly before her death had advised the King to maintain a policy of neutrality, and this had much bearing on his future stance.

Choiseul knew that Carlos III had been resentful towards the British ever since the humiliation inflicted on him as King of Naples in 1742, when the French ambassador of that time had not lost the opportunity of proposing a French alliance to him; but such proposals had always been countered by Queen Amalie's firmness and by the ability of the Neapolitan minister Tanucci to avoid diplomatic encumbrances. For a moment in 1759 it was feared that the British would disembark in the French part of Santo Domingo, since this action would place Spanish control of Spanish markets there in danger; but the British cabinet gave securities that they would not do this. In September 1759, Albertini, the Neapolitan ambassador in London, offered Pitt the mediation of the Kingdom of Naples in bringing Britain and France together, while in Madrid the anglophile Wall was parleying with the British ambassador Lord Bristol. On 21 September 1759, Carlos III promised his assistance to Louis XV as a mediator, influenced thereto by the French ambassador to Spain the marquis de Ossun, whom he had known and liked in Naples. The King sent instructions to the Spanish ambassador in London, Abreu,[4] to court Britain. Pitt replied courteously and prolonged the negotiations, saying that a congress would soon be convoked in The Hague. Meanwhile Choiseul continued his labours to win Spain over to an active partnership with France, pointing out the piratical behaviour of Britain in the West Indies. The fears of Choiseul, however, had no effect on Wall, who defended the opinion that in Europe Prussia constituted an indispensable brake on Austrian ambitions, and it was Frederick II who far more than Britain was the opponent of France in the Seven Years' War. The conduct of Britain, however, finally impelled Carlos III towards France. The Spanish ambassador in London, Abreu, continually complained to Pitt of the capture of Spanish ships by British privateers, of their activities in Honduras, in Campeche Bay, and round Lake Términos. They cut redwood and carried out contraband, introducing prohibited goods from Jamaica.[5] Carlos III wanted Great Britain to concede fishing rights on the Grand Banks of Newfoundland to Spain, which would have annulled one of the articles of the Treaty of Utrecht. Pitt's reply was: 'I would as soon give the Spaniards the Tower of London'.[6]

Joaquín Pignatelli, conde de Fuentes, had meanwhile succeeded Abreu at the Spanish Embassy in London. He promised himself complete success in these negotiations, dazzled by the splendid manner in which he had been received; but he was of mediocre intelligence and was easily fooled by Pitt, who temporised, saying that he must lay Spain's claims before Parliament.

Carlos, by now impatient and no longer restrained by his pro-British consort, for Queen Amalie had recently died, sent Grimaldi to The Hague to see how the land lay from a place of vantage. It was there that the contest between Choiseul and Pitt to win Spain's friendship began and where negotiations were being initiated in which France treated with Great Britain, now that the Seven Years' War seemed to be nearing its end, to make a separate peace and abandon their allies. Having thus briefed himself, Grimaldi was posted as Spanish ambassador to Paris on 11 February 1761 to replace Sotomayor and further to propose an offensive and defensive treaty between France and Spain,[7] but only in principle and with great care, for Carlos had no wish that Spain, having all this time avoided the great War, should at the eleventh hour become involved in it.

The position of France was delicate, since her negotiations with Great Britain obliged her not to press ahead with her friendship with Spain lest it awakened suspicions in London; later, if the peace proposed by Britain were acceptable, then the offensive alliance with Spain would have no place, whereas if on the contrary the attitude of the British cabinet were intransigent, it would be considered that the moment had arrived to unite French and Spanish forces in order to press hard on British pre-eminence. The collapse of the Franco-British negotiations made Choiseul rather unwillingly decide to accept Grimaldi's proposals.[8]

Early in 1761 projects for an alliance between France and Spain began, first with Spain's demand that there should be a naval guarantee to strengthen Spanish demands on Britain; but Choiseul did not accede to this, and the conversations continued at a snail's pace. Finally, however, Choiseul and Grimaldi brought about two treaties, one the Third Family Compact,[9] signed on 4 February 1762, resembling the former ones of Fontainebleau and El Escorial, but perhaps even more forceful than they, and the other, signed in secret six months earlier,[10] an agreement to bring Spain into the Seven Years' War at France's side. Choiseul was still half-hearted about such an alliance; it was Louis XV who had taken the initiative.

The sagacious Pitt had conjectured the existence of this secret treaty between France and Spain and wished to declare war on the latter; but as he had nothing to support his surmise beyond the sudden and unwontedly aggressive attitude which he had noticed in the Spanish ambassador Fuentes, he could not win over his colleagues to vote for war. Shortly afterwards Pitt fell from power, and his place as chief minister was taken by the Earl of Egremont, although the Marquess of Bute was the true head of the government. The retirement of Pitt did not change the march of events, but retarded hostilities, which gave Spain a breathing-space which she used to free her West Indian fleet from danger. When the Earl of Bristol, British ambassador to Spain, asked point-blank whether a secret treaty did exist, threatening to leave Spain, thereby breaking diplomatic relations, if he did not receive 'an unequivocal answer', he was informed that he might leave. In reply Fuentes left London.[11]

What had been signed in both treaties was the union of the two Bourbon families and their subsidiaries, the Kingdom of Naples and the north Italian duchies. Their principal object was once and for all to unite permanently and indissolubly the French and Spanish Bourbons and their descendants, which earlier Compacts had failed to do. Whichever nation attacked one of the two crowns would be considered to have attacked the other; Spain and France mutually guaranteed to one another their territories and empires overseas, and this guarantee extended to the King of Naples and to the Duke of Parma, both of whom adhered to the Compact. France guaranteed to assist Spain, if she were attacked, with an army of 24,000, while Spain was obliged in return to support France with one of 12,000. Each was obliged to have twelve men-o'-war and six frigates ready within three months of their being required by the other. Thus both were offensive-defensive dynastic alliances.[12]

The terms of the treaties comprehended the following extreme possibilities: France would support the pretensions of Spain relative to Honduras and Newfoundland; war would be undertaken jointly and on mutual agreement, peace would only be made by both countries together and the terms only be reached with the assent of both. In the same way they were to concur on territorial concessions, which were to be that Spain would yield to France the West Indian islands of Dominica, Saint Vincent, Saint Lucia and Tobago, while France would hand over Menorca to Spain, and the two countries agreed to force Portugal to close her ports to Great Britain. As to commerce, France and Spain were to administer the commerce in cloth and hardware jointly, and British goods, especially woollens and hardware, were not to be allowed into either French or Spanish territory. There was an article in the Compact referring to the Duke of Parma, and another dealing with the compensation to be paid to the King of Savoy-Sardinia in return for the Duchy of Piacenza.

The French said that the Third Family Compact had been an *affaire du cœur*, and in truth it came to be much more for them than for the Spanish; it was in fact a very great convenience for France and a bad business for Spain, who very soon suffered the immediate consequences of her lack of foresight. The French were on the way to realising the dictum of Louis XIV's court about there being no Pyrenees, and the advantages of the moment were positive; but Spain had compromised herself into being involved in a war for which she was not prepared. The disorganisation of land and sea forces and the decline in the quality of the administration of the American Empire placed Spain in a situation of inferiority in the face of a Britain formidable, warlike, experienced, scarcely scathed, and invested with the peculiar haughtiness produced by her recent triumphs over France in India and in North America. One should consider, however, both the King's and popular resentment against Great Britain, who for fifty years had plundered her shipping, sacked her Caribbean ports and boldly undercut her trade; and Carlos III harboured old resentments against her, such as Gibraltar and memories of British insults which he had suffered as King of Naples. It was then an emotional force which drove the Spanish King and people (though not the more reflective aristocracy and professional classes who opposed it) to an unequal war with Great Britain.

As a result of the Third Family Compact, Portugal was advised to close her ports to Great Britain; and to force this on them the French diplomat Jacques O'Dunna went to Lisbon, where he joined the Spanish ambassador José Torrero in demanding that the Portuguese minister, Luis Acunha, should do this within four days. Portugal faced a serious difficulty, but before the time was up the British General Tirawley landed with a number of officers and promised a prompt reinforcement of 10,000 men. Thus supported, on 26 May 1762 Acunha replied that King José I of Portugal wanted to maintain good relations with France and Spain, but was bound to Britain by treaties of friendship; and since she had no grounds for repudiating them, it was regretted that he could not accede to Carlos III's wishes. In reply O'Dunna announced that the allied Franco-Spanish armies would cross the frontier, not to conquer the territory, but to prevent its being occupied by the British; the Portuguese King was free to receive them as allies or regard them as enemies. Franco-Spanish detachments had already entered Portugal, but the French, believing that the British were arriving with the large force that Tirawley had mentioned, left immediately while the going was good, leaving their allies to their fate, a pointer to the future. The small Spanish force was detained at Estremez by Portuguese troops until the Portuguese representative in Madrid returned to Portugal.[13] Already, on 15 December 1761, Great Britain had declared war on Spain, and Spain had replied in like coin; but it was an inopportune, indeed a fatal, moment for the latter.

The old and gouty marqués de Sarriá was to invade Portugal with a well-equipped army of 40,000 men. The original plan was to capture Almeida and march down the Tagus valley to Lisbon, there to deliver a definite and swift blow which would make an end of Portuguese resistance. But the strategy of a Catalan engineer called Gaber was adopted in conformity with Carlos III's wish that the horrors of war in Lisbon, the residence of his favourite sister María Victoria, Queen-Mother of Portugal, might be avoided. Gaber's proposal was to besiege Miranda and Bragança, to occupy the region of Tras-os-Montes and the district between the Douro and the Minho, and to take Oporto, thus cutting off the north from the rest of Portugal.

Shielded by the artillery, Sarriá made his headquarters in Siete-Iglesias, whence he issued a manifesto in which he repeated the ideas expressed by the Franco-Spanish diplomats. The Portuguese, disorganised and unprepared, could not make any resistance; all they could do was to gather together some guerrilla units commanded by British officers. Great Britain, in spite of Tirawley's promise, at last sent only 6,000 men hastily recruited and badly trained, armed and clad; and Pombal, the chief minister of Portugal, fearing the possibility that a Franco-Spanish invasion would reach Lisbon, had twelve ships ready and waiting to take the Portuguese royal family and its retinue to Brazil. What saved the Portuguese was the timely arrival of Graf von Lippe, a German officer, who in a short time reorganised the Portuguese army, concentrating troops on the plain of Abrantes to defend Lisbon.

Meanwhile Spain lost precious time, which if it had been used to profit from its enemies' lack of cohesion to strike at once, would have made victory certain. At length Spanish armies were on the move, one entering Portugal by Galicia and taking Chaves, another, under the conde de Maceda, taking up its quarters in Ciudad Rodrigo, and a third, commanded by Gregorio Muniain, covering Extremadura. The marqués de Ceballos conquered Bragança, the marqués de Castremañes entered Moncorvo, but at Villaflor 5,000 Portuguese presented a brave resistance, obliging the invaders to retreat. Francisco Lascy, however, attacked Miranda, and the towns between the Douro and Minho were very easily taken. In Madrid it was confidently expected that Oporto would fall at any minute, but the bad condition of the troops, due to a disgraceful lack of organisation, held up the operation. One glaring and shameful example is to be seen in the case of a detachment under Alejandro O'Reilly which had to break off its advance on Villareal owing to hunger.

Old Sarriá, who had not moved from Siete-Iglesias, began once more to favour the original plan of attacking Portugal through the Tagus valley. It was already late. Nonetheless, he moved to Junca, and in front of Almeida 8,000 French, under Prince Beauvan, joined the Spanish. On 15 August trenches were dug, and on the twenty-fifth Almeida capitulated in spite of its garrison of 4,000 men commanded by British officers. It is true, though, that the defenders were raw recruits, and the civil part of the population had much to do with the surrender. Sarriá gave up his command and was replaced by the conde de Aranda, before long to become famous as a statesman.

The undertaking confided to Aranda in this stage of the campaign was very difficult, since Lippe had had time to fortify his position, and besides, the mountainous route made the operations for advancing very hard. The conde de Ricola occupied the defiles of Pinel and La Guardia, and the bulk of the Franco-Spanish army followed by way of Aldea Nueva and Castello Branco. In Las Talladas the French and Spanish came up against the troops of Lippe, which were defeated, although afterwards before Vilavelha the British surprised and overwhelmed a Spanish detachment. Aranda did not move from Vilavelha, and his troops, wearied by continual skirmishes and the autumn rains, retreated to Badajoz and later to the fortress of Albuquerque.[14]

This fruitless campaign can, however, be considered fortunate for Spain if one compares it with the war waged against the formidable naval power of Great Britain, who had at her disposal 372 warships, to which Spain could oppose only fifty-eight ships-of-the-line, twenty-seven frigates and sixteen xebecs (small, swift craft). Already, a short while before the declaration of hostilities, the Spanish ambassador Fuentes had given reports of British preparations for war.[15] Admiral Pocock took command of a strong fleet with 6,000 soldiers aboard and sailed for the Caribbean. If he were to attack Cuba he would find that La Habana was in a very bad condition to defend itself, as Juan de Prado, Governor of Cuba, realised only too well. Two engineers, Francisco and Baltasar Ricaud, hastily looked over the fortifications, and the marqués del Real-Transporte raised in Cuba some reinforcements which proved useless, the greater part of thirteen companies being laid low by the 'black vomit'. Juan de Prado, not knowing this, decided to throw himself on the British if they dared to land on Cuba.

On 6 June 1762 Admiral Pocock appeared in front of La Habana with twenty-four ships-of-the-line, ten frigates and 140 transport ships, manned by 10,000 soldiers and 2,000 negro workmen from Jamaica. Having destroyed by cannonades the maritime quarters of Coximar and Bacuranao, the British disembarked on 7 and 8 June, and 8,000 men advanced on Guanabacoa, while the Spanish troops under Carlos de Caro retreated to the south of La Habana. The British now moved up from La Cabaña and on 11 June attacked the castle of Morro, which was so well defended by Luis Velasco, the commander, that he was able to keep up a resistance until the end of July, when he died of wounds. It was Prado who capitulated to the British on 13 August on honourable terms, thanks to Velasco's heroic defence, but La Habana was lost. At the end of the war Prado and Real-Transporte were brought to trial and condemned to be deprived of their titles and employments and to be fined a considerable sum.[16]

A new and deplorable reverse in another part of the world was the loss of Manila, in the Philippines, surprised by a fleet of thirteen British warships, which landed 6,000 British soldiers under Brigadier Draper. Here was another example of the dèterioration of Spanish colonial rule in the later eighteenth century. The garrison of Manila[17] was reduced to 550 trained soldiers and 4,000 new recruits who were more of a nuisance than a help. The town was bombarded and, since the majority of the houses were wooden, fires soon spread, thanks to the 20,000 cannon balls and the 5,000 bombs which fell. The defence committee decided that it was useless to prolong resistance, and the Archbishop of Manila, Antonio Rojo, went to see the British commanders. He asked that the Catholic religion should be respected, that property should be guaranteed, and that the law courts, as then existing, should be maintained; and when these requests were granted British sovereignty over Manila was recognised on 22 September 1762.

After three days of sacking, the British demanded the payment of 4,000,000 *pesos*, and two of these millions were paid cash down, towards which the Archbishop contributed his jewels and the church plate, the rest being paid by Carlos III himself.

While the British were occupying Manila, the Chief Justice, Simón de Anda y Salazar, organised resistance in the interior of the island, finding much support in the formation of guerrillas from the Augustinian monks and farm servants. Ambuscades and attacks on them only three or four miles out of Manila kept the British in a state of insecurity. Anda was able to destroy various British detachments, but above all he kept alive the spirits both of the Spanish and of the natives and was able to hand over the command to the new Governor of the Philippines, Francisco de la Torre, after the Peace.

The only slight compensation for the loss of both La Habana and Manila came in November 1762 when Pedro de Ceballos occupied the Portuguese town of Colonia del Sacramento in the Banda Oriental of South America.[18]

Spain had done badly in war, but in the peace which followed she was much more favourably treated than might have been expected after all her defeats. The reason for this was the political situation within Great Britain. At the very beginning of the hostilities Choiseul had had occasion to establish relations with London on account of the imprisonment of comte d'Estaing there, and the negotiations were handled very well indeed through Viry, ambassador of Savoy-Sardinia. Choiseul was soon in communication with Lord Egremont, who pointed out the peaceful intentions of the British government. Choiseul informed Grimaldi of this, and Jacques O'Dunna[19] came to Spain as French representative. Carlos III agreed to talk the matter over, and the duc de Nivernais went to London, while the Duke of Bedford moved to Paris.

The death in early 1762 of the Czarina Elisabeth brought to the Russian throne Peter III, the enthusiastic supporter of Frederick II of Prussia. A continental war in which northern Germany would be involved pre-occupied George III, who after all was Elector of Hanover, and worried the British ministers, who were afraid of the return to power of the great war-minister Pitt. In truth George III and the Marquess of Bute wanted peace, but they had to contend with the parliamentary opposition of Pitt and the Duke of Newcastle. Another party, that of the pure militarists and the Duke of Cumberland, friend of Prussia, sought the prolongation of the war. The taking of La Habana warmed British spirits, but the King and Bute hated Pitt and would not listen to his proposals to the cabinet, which appeared to them excessive. These were[20] that the Spaniards, in return for Britain's handing back La Habana and Manila, should make over to her Puerto Rico, Florida, Providence Island and the factories of Honduras, and accede to Britain's exclusive right of trade in the West Indies which would be controlled by an English company; thus George III in his eagerness for peace let it be known that he might not be so exacting.

Carlos III had received the news of the fall of La Habana with serenity, and peace preliminaries collapsed before his firmness, for he refused to hear anything about Spain giving away any other territories. The opening of the British Parliament had been fixed for 8 November 1762, and what was feared was an explosion of patriotic British pride, which would drive the country on to continue a war so advantageous in its results to the honour and profit of the nation; but the ability of the French negotiator, the duc de Nivernais, resulted in its being postponed until 25 November. Choiseul, however, had already, on 3 November, convinced Spain to agree to British conditions, and at the Treaty of Fontainebleau Carlos III accepted Louisiana, ceded by France, and agreed to the revised British demands. These were: Spain's recovery of La Habana and Manila in exchange for Florida, the fort of San Agustín and Pensacola[21] Bay, which went to Britain; the evacuation of Portugal by the French and Spanish, the return of the colony of Sacramento to the Portuguese, and the right of the British to cut campeachy wood in Honduras on the condition of their destroying their fortifications there.[22] Carlos III also gave up pretentions to fishing rights on the Grand Banks. Naval prizes were discussed in the courts of the British Admiralty, and Menorca was surrendered to Britain by France.

This was the preliminary treaty; the definitive treaty with the same conditions incorporated with the other peace arrangements in all theatres, the famous Treaty of Paris,[23] was signed by Grimaldi (Spain), Choiseul (France) and Bedford (Great Britain) on 10 February 1763 and ended the bloody Seven Years' War. As a result of the struggle Prussia was reborn like a phoenix from the ashes, Austria had been proved to have been unable to carry out her ambitions, while France, humiliated on the Continent, lost both India and Canada to her implacable enemy Great Britain. Spain came out of the conflict far better than her foolhardy entrance into it had deserved; but all the same Spanish national pride had diminished, her self-respect been damaged, and contemporaries placed at France's door the bitter fruits of the Family Compact which she had gathered.

Gerónimo Grimaldi, marqués de Grimaldi, was an insinuating Genoese of great loquacity but dignified presence, who had first been Spanish ambassador in The Hague and had later returned from France with the brilliant reputation of an able diplomat for having brought the Family Compact to a successful conclusion. Carlos III nominated him Minister of State in the place of Wall, who had become unfit to continue in high office on account of health and had retired. Pignatelli, conde de Fuentes, succeeded Grimaldi as Spanish ambassador to France in October 1763, and Grimaldi formally became Minister of State in February1764, holding that post until 1776. At once satires against him and his Italian retinue began, one of the most wounding, ridiculing Grimaldi, being the witty ballad entitled: *El marqués más conturbado*.[24] Throughout his ministry, particularly in its early years, Carlos showed Grimaldi particular favour. There seemed now to a critical public to be almost an Italian government in Spain. Other Italians most in evidence politically were the princes La Cattolicà, Bonavia, Imperiali, Colonna and, in particular, the Abbate Alessandro Pico de la Mirandola, one of the heads of the Italian party which for a time was allied with that of the *golillas*, lawyers and intellectuals, so called because of the ruff which the legalists wore as part of their official attire.

A companion of Grimaldi, an Italian also, was Leopoldo de Gregorio, a *parvenu* and former business employee who in Naples had won Carlos III's favour when he was King there. Carlos had placed him at the head of the financial administration of the Kingdom of Naples, and pleased with his services gave him the title of marchese de Squillacce, which became Esquilache when dressed in Castilian style. Grimaldi and Gregorio were opposed in character, since Grimaldi, a member of a great family, enjoyed society and a certain ostentation and was inclined towards France, while the Sicilian Esquilache, born in Messina of humble family, of careful habits, very hard-working and of rough manners, did not like the French. Esquilache discharged the functions of Minister both of Finance and of War, his experience for the second position being that he had once served under Montemar as provisioner of the army.

After the Peace of Paris these two personages directed Spanish political affairs, Carlos III having total confidence in them, in spite of the warnings of his mentor Tanucci, who had no sympathy for Esquilache, and said that when the Spanish populace grew to hate him he would fall and damage the crown.

Important questions now occupied Spain's attention, the first of them being that of maintaining Louisiana, the other the commercial advantages which Choiseul, jealous now of the privileges surreptitiously gained by Great Britain in her trade with Spain, sought to win for France. To this end Choiseul made use of a talented agent, the intriguing Abbate Beliardi, an Italian and native of Sinigaglia (Ancona), whom he had known when he was French ambassador to the Holy See. Grimaldi, as a foreigner, was able to defend his position among his Spanish colleagues because of his prudence and circumspection. Although his affection for France was well known, he was timid in his foreign policy, and Choiseul could not hope for much from him. Indeed, Grimaldi allowed himself to appear to the British ambassador Lord Rochford as the loyal fulfiller of the treaties which Spain had made with his country, permitting himself at times to go so far as to make jests at French pretensions. On the other hand Esquilache was much more explicit with Rochford and with great smiles of triumph confided to the British ambassador what he represented to be the true feelings of Carlos III, which were, he said, to avoid the deceits of France, and which were wholly favourable to Great Britain. Notwithstanding this, Rochford realised how little he could believe him, since the gossip was that

Esquilache, apart from his financial projects, knew nothing, and that such was his ignorance of international affairs that, in order not to appear ridiculous in the eyes of the Council of State, he had to rely for his information in this area on the Sardinian ambassador.

On 11 February 1764 Francisco Orsini, Graf Rosenberg, arrived in Madrid to ask for the hand of the Spanish Infanta María Luisa for Leopold, heir to the Tuscan dukedom, second son of Maria Theresa of Austria, to which Carlos III agreed, stipulating that all the wealth of the House of Medici should go to the young pair. At the same time the betrothal of Carlos III's son Carlos, príncipe de las Asturias, (afterwards Carlos IV of Spain) and María Luisa, daughter of Felipe Duke of Parma was announced. This Princess[25] was only thirteen, but already gave signs of an imperious character, and everything pointed to the fact that she would dominate her husband, a youth of seventeen, strong and muscular, keen on athletics and a voracious eater, who had hardly cultivated his mind at all, although he had been given some scanty education amounting to small doses of geography, mathematics, music and drawing by his German Jesuit tutors.[26]

In June 1765, the Cartagena squadron was engaged in taking royal ballast backwards and forwards, first depositing Archduke Leopold's intended in Genoa, and then returning to Spain with the new princesa de las Asturias and her suite. On 3 September Carlos III left San Ildefonso and fifteen miles from there met his daughter-in-law. Soon afterwards came the formal marriage, the witnesses being Grimaldi, the marqués de Montealegre, and Ossun, the French ambassador.

Esquilache's commercial negotiations, which had been interrupted, were not renewed; but in January 1766 he had a meeting with the Abbate Beliardi, Choiseul's agent, who complained to him about his treatment at the hands of Spanish customs officials, to which the Minister of Finance replied ill-humouredly that everyone was treated the same, and that his complaints were fanciful. Esquilache's power, however, was nearing its end, for the people of Madrid hated him and accused him of making ruinous reforms. His wife Doña Pastora was joined in his discredit, the malcontents accusing her of aiding him in amassing a fortune; but basically there was general discontent in Spain as a result of the presence in the government of so many foreigners, as if there were no Spaniards capable of dealing with national affairs.

Esquilache angered the Church by prohibiting clergy without certificates of residence from living in Madrid. He had already restricted the power of ecclesiastical judges and had obliged them to pay taxes, as laid down in the concordat of 1753. He had also alienated the populace by making a monopoly of bread and oil and putting up the price of both.

In 1764, on the occasion of the marriage of the Infantes Carlos and María Luisa, this resentment against Esquilache increased, for it was popularly believed that it was he who had given the order to the Walloon

Guard to charge the crowd, which had gathered in the Plaza del Buen Retiro to see the festivities, killing about twenty innocent spectators. What, however, brought people's patience to an end was the order of 10 and 11 March 1766, drawn up by Esquilache, which forbade the wearing of wide-brimmed hats and ample capes which could be used to muffle the face, greatly affected by the Madrileños, and ordered that instead they should wear a short cape and a three-cornered hat.[27]

The punishment for the first infraction of the rule was a fine of six ducats or twelve days in prison, for the second offence the double of this, and for the third four years of imprisonment. The notices of the edict were torn down at night and in their place appeared broadsheets inciting the population to disobedience. In the working-class quarters there was a great stir, officers of the law were received with scoffs and sneers, and the commissaries who accompanied the police to see that the new laws were carried out heard the first menacing murmurs of revolt. People provoked the Walloon Guards by walking up and down in front of their barracks with their faces half-covered by their cloaks and with wide-brimmed hats. On 13 March two civilians ran into the calle de la Paloma each holding up a pair of blue bands[28] and an enormous wig whitened with flour, shouting: '¡Esto no ha de prohibirlo el marqués de Esquilache!'[29] Small riots followed on the 15[30] and 18 March, but from the twentieth to the twenty-second threatening larger groups walked about the streets.

At length, on 23 March 1766, came Palm Sunday and, as two men muffled by their cloaks walked in front of the barracks of the Invalides in the Plaza de Anton Martín, a soldier approached one of them, who was wearing a large white hat, and said to him:'¿Por qué no observa Vd lo mandado y no apunta su sombrero?'[31] The cloaked figure replied with a rough refusal, and the soldier tried to arrest him; but he, seizing the soldier's sword, threw him to the ground. At that a whistle called many cloaked individuals together, and an officer ordered the troops back. Rioters now ran to the calle de Atocha yelling: '¡Viva el Rey!¡ Viva Espana! ¡Muera Esquilache!'

The mobs reached the Plaza Mayor, where they were joined by others who had come by way of the calle de Toledo and from the Plaza de la Cebada, and advanced to the Royal Palace, where the duque de los Arcos, Captain of the Royal Bodyguard, told them in the name of the King to quieten themselves so that their petition could be considered. The crowd afterwards went to the calle de las Infantas, to the House of the Seven Chimneys (*casa de las Siete Chimineas*), where Esquilache lived. Luckily for him he was absent from home, for they broke into the house and sacked it, burning his furniture, and went to the neighbouring calle de San Miguel, where Grimaldi lived, but they contented themselves with only breaking his windows.

On the following day, the twenty-fourth, the riot assumed alarming proportions, and several members of the much-hated Walloon Guard were killed. The duque de Medinaceli and the duque de los Arcos tried in vain to appease the rioters. A council was held in the palace, at which the duque de los Arcos and the condes de Priego and Gazzola were of the opinion that the riot should be stamped out with the utmost rigour, while the marqués de Sarriá and the condes de Revillagigedo and Oñate were inclined to clemency. The King appeared to be of the latter opinion. The monks of San Felipe de Neri and those of San Gil exhorted the crowd, and a member of the latter brotherhood, Padre Cuenca, brought the King the propositions of the rioters. Carlos III, appearing on a balcony of the palace, listened to the proposals which Padre Cuenca read to him, nodding in assent, and he also heard the speech of a ringleader in a short jacket and a white hat.

The people celebrated their triumph with rejoicings, but on the twenty-fifth the Madrileños became suspicious that the King had secretly left Madrid for Aranjuez, accompanied by Esquilache, who until then had remained hidden in the palace. At this the disturbances were renewed and street lamps were broken. Next the rioters sent as their representative to the King, now indeed at Aranjuez, a certain Diego de Avendaño, a native of Toboso, who returned with the royal promise that their desires would be met. On the twenty-seventh Esquilache, under escort, travelled to Cartagena where he embarked for Italy.[32]

The riot in Madrid was not an isolated incident, for the same thing happened in several other places including Barcelona, Zaragoza,[33] Cuenca, Guadalajara, San Ildefonso, Murcia, Sanlucar, Huesca, Ciudad Real and La Coruña, and the cause of them all was the dearness of goods. In Zaragoza the riot reached violent proportions and the marqués de Castelar, Captain-General, was at the point of despair when some armed civilians came to his aid and re-established order. The King had no wish to leave Aranjuez, being in reality disturbed by what had happened.[34]

Everything seemed to point to a change of ministry, and the party led by the old magnate the duque de Alba gained power in the event. Miguel Muzquiz, afterwards conde de Gausa, was appointed Secretary of Finance, and Gregorio Muniain, Commander-in-Chief of Extremadura, obtained the portfolio of War. Some cliques of Alba's party were discomfited by the appointment of the conde de Aranda to the post of President of the Council of Castile in the place of Diego de Rojas, whose conduct had been very suspicious during the Madrid riots.

Alba did all he could to prevent Aranda's rise to power; but the latter had supporters in his friends Roda, Muzquiz, Muniain and Grimaldi himself, who wanted his position to be assured, and finally Aranda triumphed.[35] On Aranda fell the task of re-establishing normality in Madrid and in the whole kingdom as well. The high position which he held as President of the Council of Castile gave him sufficient strength and prestige to make headway against this prickly problem. Carlos III felt repugnance about re-entering Madrid at the cost of carrying out his promises, but Aranda resolved the conflict by getting the guilds, the nobility and the municipal council to declare that they were unwilling to carry out demands forced on them by violence, and further that Carlos should be asked to return to Madrid. The King, pleased with the resolution of the Council of Castile, now stated through his fiscals that whatever had taken place during the Esquilache riots was to be considered null and void. On 6 July the Walloon Guards marched back to Madrid, and Carlos was about to return to his capital when the death of his mother Isabel Farnese on 16 July 1766 obliged him to go to San Ildefonso.

It was felt in official circles that the riot was not spontaneous, but had been carefully prepared. There was general dissatisfaction at the rise in food prices; yet as so often has been the case in history the general discontent was thought to have been engineered by politically inspired groups, above all by Ensenada who, just freed from his exile at Medina del Campo, was hoping to take Esquilache's place when he fell; for Ensenada hated the power of the Italians who had flourished since Carlos III's accession.[36] And what could be more understandable than that the Jesuits, so much beloved by Ensenada, had supported him? Certainly their part in the *Motín* had been underground, but nevertheless it had existed, although it seems likely that only certain members of the Society had been involved, at any rate according to Francisco Javier de Idiáquez, the Provincial, who disclaimed any part in it.[37] It has also been regarded as originating in the upsurge of the bourgeoisie[38] who, beginning to feel their potential power and impatient to see their equivalent in neighbouring countries gaining recognition, stirred up a dissatisfied populace which was quick to react to a word in the ear about the cost of living and the country being ruled by foreigners, and was ready to act for a handful of money. Certainly someone was paying—it was noticeable that during the riots the ringleaders ate and drank well in the taverns and, what was even more remarkable, from under their ragged outer dress emerged fine holland shirts and silk stockings.

Legal proceedings, carried out by the Council of Castile, began, Aranda choosing as his colleagues Miguel María de Nava and the fiscal, Pedro Rodrígues Campomanes, who were later joined by Pedro Ric and Luis del Valle Salazar, and later still in October by the conde de Villanueva, Andrés de Moraver y Vera and Bernardo Caballero.

On 8 June 1766 Campomanes presented his report and later drew up a memorandum in which he put the blame on the Jesuits, but the Chief Magistrate of Madrid, Alonso Pérez Delgado, refused to believe in their culpability. Notwithstanding this, suspicions were laid at the door of Padre Isidro López, Procurator of the Society of Jesus in the Province of Castile,[39] and proceedings were opened against Miguel Antonio de la Gándara, the Abbate Hermoso and Benito Navarro. It was also stated as almost a certainty that the marqués de Valdeflores and Ensenada had participated in the events.

The conde de Aranda,[40] the true author of the expulsion of the Jesuits,[41] was born in the castle of Siétamo (Huesca) on 1 August 1719, his name being Pedro Pablo de Abarca y Bolea. Educated at Bologna and at the Military Academy of Parma, in 1740 he was appointed Captain of Grenadiers of the Regiment of Castile, and two years afterwards he became colonel, serving under Montemar, Gages and Felipe of Parma. In 1749 he married his cousin, Ana María del Pilar Fernández de Híjar, and had two sons, Luis and Augusto, and a daughter, who afterwards became the wife of the marqués de Mora. He paid a visit to Frederick the Great of Prussia, resided in Paris, and on his return to Spain in 1755 was promoted to be Lieutenant-General. He took the place of the conde de Perelada as ambassador to Lisbon, quarrelled with Pombal, the Portuguese chief minister, and returned to Madrid, where, on the recommendation of Wall, Fernando VI in 1756 invested him with the Order of the Golden Fleece. Appointed Director-General of Artillery and Engineers, he discovered cases of embezzlement and asked to be relieved of his post, which was allowed; but he was banished to his estate for two years, owing to the influence at court of those who were afraid of being unmasked. In 1760, however, his fortune changed when he was named Spanish ambassador to Poland, after which he took part in the war with Portugal in the closing stages of the Seven Years' War. On 3 April 1763 Aranda received the title of Captain-General; he was forty-four, and his career could not have been more rapid. He was Governor of Valencia when Carlos III, after the Esquilache riots, appointed him President of the Council of Castile.

Aranda was in reality a great Aragonese gentleman, very Spanish in his sentiments, but at the same time in love with French Encyclopaedism and French anticlerical ideas. His physical appearance was strange: his complexion was dark, his hair, before it thinned and he took to a wig, dark chestnut, his nose, always stained with snuff, thick and curved; he had large grey eyes, the right one squinting, a toothless mouth and a hoarse voice; and yet there was nothing vulgar about him. Morally he was a strange mixture of qualities and defects. Incredulous, a philosopher, obstinate, a discreet epicurean, a gallant sensualist, a proud aristocrat, moody, irascible, quarrelsome and something of a crank. He lacked tact, but was very well-educated, although his ideas were ill-disciplined. As a contemporary put it, he was 'a well with a narrow entrance'. He was generous in spirit, rough and of open manners, and was beloved by the common people, whose wishes he listened to with patience; in a word, he was a man of great intelligence with an iron will, active and unwearied in work. The King said of him that he was 'more stubborn than an Aragonese mule'.

King Carlos III, a fervent Catholic, was very jealous of his authority and of his prerogatives and resented any interference of the Church in temporal matters. In this he had been from the first supported by the attitude of his minister Wall, an anticlerical royalist, and was still influenced by the unbelieving Tanucci. The publication of a pontifical brief of 14 June 1761, signed by Clement XIII,[42] in which the catechism of the French theologian Mésenguy was condemned, gave place to a conflict.[43] Carlos ordered that publication of this brief should be suspended. Manuel Quintano y Bonifaz, Archbishop of Pharsalia and Inquisitor-General, who had published it, was punished with exile. On 18 January 1762 there appeared a pragmatic sanction which empowered the Council of Castile to consider all bulls, briefs, rescripts and pontifical letters before their publication. The intervention of the King's confessor, Joaquín Eleta, to whom the Pope wrote, ended in the suspension of the pragmatic sanction, and this led to Wall's resignation. There followed a kind of truce, but no more than that, since the King continued to follow a policy hostile to Rome, and attacked the Jesuits, whom he considered the principal influence on Clement XIII and indeed the chief support of the Papacy. The Jesuits were powerful in America, and in Spain all pre-university education was in their hands, as a result of which they were increasingly unpopular with laymen intellectuals and upholders of enlightened despotism. In the middle of the seventeenth century the Jesuits had kept up a very acrimonious controversy with the Augustinians concerning the opinions of St Augustine and in 1732 they had attacked the works of the Augustinian Cardinal Enrique Noris, whom they accused of Jansenism. This last question was prolonged, thanks to the interference of Padre Rávago, who seems to have manipulated the then Inquisitor-General Francisco Pérez de Prado. The Spanish Inquisition in 1732 and 1748 had included in its Indexes various works which defended Noris, and in the latter year works by the Cardinal himself in spite of Papal ordinances in his favour. The publication by Padre Isla, a Jesuit, of his clever satire *Fray Gerundio*[44] against bad preachers led to new hostilities. The fulfilment of the treaty of 1750 concerning Colonia del Sacramento and the consequent limits set on the activities of the Jesuits angered the Society and made it realise how its enemies were stealthily working against them. When Carlos III recalled Ensenada to court from his exile, the Jesuits, who had a friend in him, hoped for an improvement in their lot; but this was no more than a flash in the pan when it was seen that there was no chance of the fallen minister's being asked to take part in the government. On the contrary, on the death of Muñiz, conde de Campo Villar, Manuel de Roda y Arrieta, a Jansenist and a fierce enemy of the Jesuits,[45] became Secretary of Justice. In fact, Roda had formerly been in Rome where he had struck up a friendship with Padre Vázquez, General of the Augustinians and a declared opponent of the Jesuits.

Carlos III, in company with other enlightened despots of the time, was not at all well-disposed to the Society of Jesus, and for this reason it was not very difficult to turn him decidedly against it. The King loved the Franciscans, was a tertiary of the Order, and venerated the memory of Palafox y Mendoza, Bishop of Puebla de los Angeles, who had maintained bitter and violent controversies with the Jesuits. Carlos's ardent desire was to press the Pope for the canonisation of Palafox. Some have regarded the attitude of the Freemasons as one of the factors leading to the ruin of the Jesuits in Spain; but this has never been conclusively proved.[46] Royalism and the ideas of the *golillas*, the anticlerical party, which had its influence in the council of Castile, played its part; but it was above all Encyclopaedism[47] which brought about the climate of opinion which destroyed the Jesuits in Spain. Such Encyclopaedist aristrocrats as Fernán-Nuñez, duque de Villahermosa, and the marqués de Mora knew Diderot, D'Alembert and Condorcet, took part in the gatherings at the Paris salons of Madame du Deffand, Madame Geoffrin and Mademoiselle de Lespinasse, and visited Voltaire at Ferney. Finally, so unreligious a man as Aranda, who in 1780 was to become Master of the Grand Orient Lodge of Freemasons, took a leading part in driving the Jesuits from Spain.

The expulsion of the Jesuits was general in the Latin countries. They were expelled from France by Choiseul and Madame de Pompadour in 1764, from Portugal by Pombal in 1759, from Naples by the marchese de Campo-Florido in 1767, and from Parma by Duke Ferdinand, the disciple of Condillac and Mably, who had succeeded his father Felipe in 1765, on the pressing advice of the French adventurer Tillot, in 1768. In Spain the question was more complicated. Wall, Grimaldi, Esquilache and Roda, united in their opposition to the Jesuits, had prepared a hostile climate for them. Yet Carlos III did not allow himself to be influenced by the example of other countries, and went so far as to give refuge to the Jesuits expelled from France. However, in Madrid the bull *Apostolicum pascendi*, published by Clement XIII[48] in favour of the Society on 17 March 1765, had left a bad impression. Padre Lorenzo Ricci, General of the Society, feared new calamities, and some far-seeing Jesuits had already forecast the coming danger in Spain itself.

The storm began with the investigations into the causes of the Esquilache riots, when the fiscal, Campomanes, openly accused the Jesuits of fomenting them. It was also affirmed that in Paraguay they held unlimited power and, further, that at the taking of Manila by the British they had been in communication with Brigadier Draper. It is certain that Carlos III, influenced by the duque de Alba and by Aranda, had become convinced that the Jesuits aspired to universal power. The first decree, signed by the fiscal, Campomanes, and his adviser Nava on 8 June 1766, condemned the Jesuits, and this was confirmed at an extraordinary meeting of the Council of Castile, Campomanes and Nava also being present, by Aranda, as President, Pedro Ric and Luis del Valle on 11 September. Finally, on 29 January 1767 the Tribunal Extraordinary of the Council of Castile formulated its opinion in documentary form which was presented to Çarlos III. It was divided into two parts: in the first the motives for the necessity of expelling the Society of Jesus were set out; the second part contained the details of how this was to be done. The first part has disappeared, and had already vanished by 1815.

On 20 February 1767 a commission sat, being composed of Alba, Jaime Masones, Grimaldi, Padre Eleta, Miguel Muzquiz, Gregorio Muniain and Manuel Roda. To blacken the Jesuits still more, a letter, supposed, without foundation, to have been written by the Jesuit General Padre Ricci, was circulated, in which it was stated that Carlos III was the son of Isabel Farnese and Alberoni. Carlos now decided to act: on 27 February 1767 the Royal Decree was composed; it was despatched to Aranda on 1 April, and was carried out on 2 April.[49]

Aranda[50] was invested with unlimited power and threw himself into his task with all his accustomed zeal. Functionaries throughout Spain and the New World received precise orders about fulfilling the King's will. In Spain the expulsion was carried out on 2 April, except in Madrid, where it was brought about a few days earlier. With scarcely any opposition the houses of the Jesuits in Spain and America[51] were closed, and the Fathers were taken to the ports, entailing great hardship always, and sometimes real suffering, where they were obliged to embark in ships which eventually took them to Corsica. On 31 March Carlos III communicated his resolution to the Pope, in which he said he was placing the Jesuits under his immediate, holy and wise direction. Clement XIII, greatly upset, contested this on 16 April with his brief *Inter acerbissima*. The Council, influenced by Roda, made on 30 April a celebrated reply, in which were enumerated charges against the Society of Jesus. The main points made against the Society were the despotic behaviour of the new General Padre Acquaviva, its defence of probabilism, molinism, the doctrine of regicide, its Malabar rites, its opposition to the reduction of its powers in Paraguay, and even the constitution of the Society itself.

According to trustworthy calculations the number of Jesuits now expelled was five or six thousand. There were in Spain 146 houses with 2,641 Fathers. In the number of houses one includes the colleges, hospitals and residences of the Society. From Spanish America were driven 2,267, to which number one must add the novices of the four Jesuit Provinces of the Spanish Empire.[52]

On 2 May Carlos III replied courteously to the Pope, and the energetic Venetian Cardinal Carlos Rezzonico, the Pope's nephew, said he would not receive the Jesuits in the Papal States, since he feared that Carlos would not pay them their promised pension; but in view of what these poor disowned Fathers from other states in Europe besides Spain were suffering in Corsica, at that time in the grip of a civil war, the Pope allowed 10,000 of them into the Legations of Bologna and Ferrara, the Duchy of Urbino, the March of Ancona, Imola, Forlì, Rimini and Bagnacavallo.[53]

In November 1767 the expulsion of the Jesuits from Naples caused Pope Clement XIII further bitter sorrow. The situation grew worse every minute and soon the Papacy found itself opposed by all the reigning members of the House of Bourbon. The Jesuits of Parma had been ordered to leave by Tillot, but, owing to various complications they were still on Parmesan territory when on 30 January 1768 the Pope published a warning to Parma, in which he contrasted the anticlerical decree of the Duke with the rights of the Papal Curia. Indeed, the Holy See had never recognised the Treaty of Aix-la-Chapelle by which Don Felipe had gained his duchies, and which had led to complete erastianism in them.

Choiseul directed the coalition, and the Kings of France, Spain and Naples complained to the Pope about his proceedings with the Duke of Parma. The French Parlement prohibited the publication of the Papal monitorium on the 26 February 1768, and the Council of Castile declared itself against the Papal brief during the same month. Orsini, the Neapolitan ambassador to the Holy See, d'Aubeterre, the French ambassador, and the Spanish one there, Azpuru, protested to Clement XIII, but his reply was energetic and his decision to abide by his brief irrevocable. Reprisals then began. Carlos III put in vigour the pragmatic sanction according to which the bulls and briefs were submitted to *regium exequatur*. Padre Eleta, who had years before been opposed to this form of retaliation, thereby bringing about Wall's fall, now supported Carlos III's action and changed attitude. The fiscal, Campomanes,[54] published his *Juicio imparcial* against the power which the Holy See sought to exercise over the Duchy of Parma, and laid down other royalist doctrines, which were very much in accordance with the taste of the time, although they were heavily censored by the extraordinary committee of the Council of Castile. José Moñino y Redondo, the other fiscal of the Council, later to become famous as the conde de Floridablanca, revised his colleague's work, cutting out certain propositions which were too harsh, to meet the complaints of the clerical members of the Council. Finally Carlos III decreed that the possessions of the Society of Jesus were confiscated.

Clement XIII opposed these actions with all his might and in the bull *In coena domini* he condemned those responsible for the decrees of expulsion. As a reprisal in June 1768 the French occupied Avignon and the Neapolitans Benevento and Pontecorvo. The Papal court was favourable to the Jesuits; Cardinals Rezzonico[55] and Torregiani, the first the Pope's nephew and the second Secretary of State, did not in the end desert them in their hour of expulsion. There is no doubt that the Bourbon courts, by mutual accord, had decided to force from the Pope the suppression of the Society of Jesus. Clement, however, took vigorous measures to oppose this and set out his arguments in what could well have proved to be a paper war; but his death on 2 February 1769 brought new hopes to the House of Bourbon of being able speedily to have their way and gain Papal assent.

Preparations for a conclave to elect a new Pope were immediately set afoot, while d'Aubeterre, Orsini and Azpuru followed the instructions of their respective courts to bring about the election of a candidate favourable to the Bourbons and, if possible, of one who was ready to suppress the hated Society. The result of the election was surprising, for no one before May

1769 could have thought of the possibility of Cardinal Ganganelli's triumph. It was early in the month that Cardinal Rezzonico's party, which was the most powerful, began to speak of the Franciscan Ganganelli and finally obtained through the good offices of Cardinal Albani the aquiescence of the Bourbon courts. Finally Ganganelli was elected Pope on 19 May 1769, taking the name of Clement XIV.[56] The question as to whether Clement XIV promised as one of the terms of his election to bring about the suppression of the Jesuits is doubtful in view of the support which Rezzonico gave him. Some[57] have defended Clement's memory, saying that he gave no such promise, but others[58] are inclined to take the view that Ganganelli, ambitious and timid at the same time, had given securities both to the friends and the enemies of the Jesuits, and this will satisfactorily explain the unanimity with which he was elected.

The energetic Cardinal Carlos Rezzonico, supporter of the Jesuits, now gave place, as the influential figure at the Papal court, to the Franciscan party surrounding the new Pope, who had already revealed himself as a weak and irresolute man, faced with the diplomatic abilities and pressures, amounting to menaces, of France, Spain and Naples. Clement XIV inaugurated his pontificate with the most attractive promises of concord and ordered a medal commemorating his elevation with the legend FIAT PAX IN VIRTUTE TUA to be struck. He promised to concern himself with the question of the canonisation of Palafox, and afterwards sought to define the dogma of the Immaculate Conception, so dear to Carlos III of Spain, to whom he wrote on 30 May 1769 an affectionate letter. For his part, Carlos by the Royal Edict of 9 June 1769 abolished the pragmatic sanction and ordered the re-opening of the nuncio's tribunal in Spain.

The French Cardinal Bernis, politician and courtier, took the place of d'Aubeterre at the Roman embassy, and his appearance there marked the beginning of intrigues and meetings between the diplomatic representatives interested in the extinction of the Society. Clement XIV had great confidence in Bernis and deferred to him, but this led to the amplification of the matter in which the three Bourbon courts were interested. Bernis and his colleagues presented to the Pope three successive memorials in which the wishes of their governments were set down. In answer, by his letter of 30 November 1769 the Pope promised Carlos III that he would disband the Jesuits; but since Bernis did not show signs of pressing on fast with the negotiations, it was decided to entrust them to the Spanish ambassador Azpuru, recently appointed Archbishop of Valencia. Azpuru was, however, not in good health, and this forced him into inaction. Meanwhile fifty (the great majority) of the Spanish prelates declared themselves in favour of making an end of the Society, among them those of Barcelona, Salamanca, Ávila, Segovia, Tarragona, Burgos, Sevilla and Zaragoza.

Azpuru made no headway with the Pope, and on 9 June 1770 a memorial was drawn up begging him to publish a brief. Clement XIV answered with fair words, but no resolution was forthcoming. Meanwhile the Jesuits were reposing some hope on the attitude of Maria Theresa and above all on the fall of Choiseul and the influence of the clerical party in France. The new French minister, Aiguillon, let time slip away, Bernis took no action and Clement XIV maintained a guarded attitude. Weary of this temporising Carlos III sent to Rome as ambassador José Moñino y Redondo, fiscal of the Council of Castile,[59] the son of a notary and trained as a lawyer, being thus a natural member of the *golilla* party and so an opponent of the Aragonese party led by Aranda.

Senior members of the civil service disapproved of his nomination, and Moñino soon gained the nickname of 'Don Quijote', disparaging remarks being made about his *erudición murciana* (Murcian learning), in other words his provincialism, for he was born in Murcia; but in the end all were bound to acknowledge his capacity.

Neither Aranda nor Roda were consulted about Moñino's nomination; it was the doing of Carlos III and Grimaldi alone to pick him out from among the *golilla* party as the man with the very ability needed to lead the ticklish mission to extract the longed-for brief from Clement XIV. Moñino arrived in Rome on 4 July 1772 and from the very first moment encountered an atmosphere of suspicion on the part of his colleagues who were with him to carry out negotiations. In spite of this Moñino began to work untiringly on the confidants of the Pope, ceaselessly intriguing, talking and investigating. In his audiences with Clement he was decisive and firm, expressing his unswerving resolution to go on to the very end, bearing at hand the attractive inducement of the return of Avignon and Benevento, seized by France in 1768, to the Papacy. Having done this, he went to Naples to confer with the Bourbon court there and to arrange a definitive settlement.

Moñino's constant pressure did not leave the Pope any way out and, frightened by the more or less veiled menaces of Spain, Clement decided to publish a brief, although not a bull, for the suppression of the Society of Jesus. Cardinal Zelada and the Spanish Generals of the Dominicans and Franciscans collaborated with Moñino and, on 21 July 1773, the Pope published the brief *Dominus ac redemptor*, by which the Jesuits were suppressed. Moñino was repaid with the title of conde de Floridablanca; the agent Azara, who at the start of the mission had disliked Floridablanca and is supposed to have been the first to dub him 'Don Quijote', was nominated Member of the Council of Finance, and Buontempi, the Pope's secretary, received a pension of 1,500 Roman *escudos*. A few months later the health of the Pope, shattered by the chagrin which his suppression of the Jesuits caused him, failed, and he died on 22 September 1773,[60] not without suspicion of poison.

Floridablanca now became worried about a possible change of front on the part of the conclave, which he feared might react by choosing a Pope from one of Rezzonico's party, which let it be known that it wished to re-

establish the Society of Jesus. With this in mind he spoke to the Dean of the
Sacred College, Giovanni Francesco Albani, a cardinal with a great deal of
influence, laying before him the present situation, which he called one of
conciliation and harmony, and comparing it with the state of affairs on the
election of Clement XIV in 1769, when there had been a rupture with
Portugal, when the nuncio had left Spain, when France had occupied
Avignon, Naples had seized Benevento, Tuscany was in an uproar, and
German pens had been busy drawing up denunciations of the pretensions
of the Roman court. If, he argued, the cardinals elected a pontiff with ideas
different from those of the dead Pope, all these calamities would again fall
on the Church. Floridablanca not only tackled Albani but all the cardinals
he could possibly meet, finding able support among the foreign ministers at
the Papal court, especially Bernis and Orsini, the Neapolitan ambassador.
Bernis, in particular, managed the foreign cardinals with such ability that
his candidate, Cardinal Braschi, obtained a unanimity of votes on 15
February 1775, taking the name of Pius VI. He maintained a complete
silence about the extinction of the Sociey of Jesus.[61]

The courtly, spirited and flexible marqués de Grimaldi with the manners
of a *grand seigneur* was for a great part of Carlos III's reign in charge of
foreign affairs, and was just the man to be so in such an age of elegance and
nicely balanced diplomacy. Albeit internationally minded, he was an
intense upholder of the Family Compact, and as such showed himself
favourable to the commercial pretences of France. Supported by Muzquiz,
on 2 January 1768 he signed with France the treaty by which the French
obtained the same mercantile rights in Spain as Great Britain enjoyed,
although not in the American Empire, any more than did the English. This
was followed on 15 May 1769 by another treaty with France about her
consuls.

Relations with Great Britain were not very cordial, since she claimed
through her representative Lord Rochford the Spanish abandonment of
Manila.[62] Grimaldi refused to recognise the promise of the Archbishop of
Manila,[63] and his haughty language led one to suppose that a break
between the two powers was near. The príncipe de Masserano, Spanish
ambassador in London, had a forthright conversation with the British
Secretary of State, Conway. Nonetheless, the Marquess of Rockingham,
head of the ministry, in June 1766 renounced the claim that Spain should
give up Manila. The bone of contention now became the Falkland Islands
(Malvinas). Some years before, in 1764, the Frenchman Bougainville had
built on one of the islands, the East, the fort of Saint Louis and had
established a small colony; but before its official reclamation by Spain, the
Falklands were occupied by Captain Felipe Ruiz Puente, and in 1766 the
French left. Already on 23 January 1765 Captain Byron, 'foul weather
Jack', the father of the poet, had momentarily taken possession of the
archipelago, hoisting the British flag in the strait between Saunders and

Keppel Islands, and calling the site Port Egmont in honour of the First Lord of the Admiralty. In January 1766 Commander MacBride arrived at the Falklands in the *Jason* and disembarked on Saunders Island, ordering plans to be made for a meteorological station to be set up, which ended with the British building a blockhouse. The news produced confusion in London and Lord Egmont resigned. But the bellicose attitude of Lord Chatham led to a convoy being sent to the Falklands with provisions for the British garrison at fort Egmont in August 1766.[64]

Spain protested and alleged the violation of article 8 of the Treaty of Utrecht. The French minister Choiseul intervened timidly in Spain's favour. Masserano and Lord Shelburne, the British Secretary of State, held frequent conversations. On 20 January 1767 Grimaldi counselled the Spanish ambassador in London to temporise, insinuating that he would submit the question of the British recovering Manila to a tribunal. Events, however, hastened to a climax, for Arriaga wrote to Bucarelli, Governor of Buenos Aires on 25 February 1768, giving him instructions to occupy the Falklands, which he accordingly did, driving the British out of Port Egmont on 10 June 1770. The case entered a critical period. Spain said that Bucarelli's action had been provoked by the insults of Commander Hunt, head of the British colony. All this coincided with Carlos III's actions which were always hostile to the interests of British commerce. Great was the indignation in London, where 'Junius' penned a libellous insult against the Spanish King. Grimaldi feared that war would break out at any moment. He now turned to France and reminded Choiseul of his obligations towards Spain; but Choiseul had no wish to comply, and reproached Grimaldi for his warlike letters. Meanwhile Weymouth, Secretary of State for the Southern Department, in his exchanges with Masserano became more and more arrogant. George III, however, did not want war since if that occurred his hated Chatham would return to power; and Lord North, recently become chief minister and the King's 'humble servant', wanted peace. In Spain, on the other hand, Aranda advised war; and Spain could count on other allies if not France—Austria, Tuscany and Naples, for example—but none of them could have formed a navy between them to match the British, and so, for all Aranda's bravado, prudence was necessary.

Nor was this all, for Britain let it be known that only after the action of Bucarelli had been disowned by the Spanish government, and after the return of the British settlers and the re-establishment of the *status quo* would the question of who owned the Islands be discussed. Britain prepared for war, and it seemed that it was on the point of erupting. If Chatham had been given rein he would with one of his fiery speeches have demolished North and his followers; but George III was not going to allow this and, stepping in, saved the ministry, substituting Lord Rochford, who had been ambassador at Madrid from 1763 to 1766 and was a flexible person with a knowledge of Spanish attitudes, for the warlike Lord Weymouth as

Secretary of State on 19 December 1770. He brought the Earl of Sandwich into the government to fill the post that Rochford had left, the Secretaryship of the Northern Department. Sandwich, however, was only to remain in that post just over Christmas, becoming in the New Year First Lord of the Admiralty. Thanks to King George, North remained unshaken.

Worse still was in store for Spain when the same month (December 1770) Choiseul,[65] the creator of the Third Family Compact fell from power. France now no longer wanted to have any obligations towards her partner, and Louis XV wrote a letter to Carlos III which crossed one of Carlos's to him. Carlos asked for help in the likely struggle, while Louis wrote that he could hope to give him no more than good advice—it was peace that he was after. In Spain, Aranda kept up his warlike attitude, supported by O'Reilly, Gálvez and the King of Naples; but, stubborn Aragonese that he was, he quarrelled with O'Reilly over his war plans, and since he did not mince words in his references to Grimaldi and even to the King, to whom they were immediately reported, Carlos III did not pardon the insult.[66]

Meanwhile Harris was recalled by the British government and Masserano from London by the Spanish; but Masserano did not leave at once. He was too circumspect, and thanks to his attitude a catastrophe was avoided, for he temporised by first asking for confirmation of the order, and in the interim Carlos III, abandoned by his allies, accepted George III's conditions. On 25 January 1771 North laid before the cabinet Masserano's statement. In spite of the opposition's attacks, it was decided that a formal declaration of the disarmament of the two powers should be carried out on 10 April. As a result the British were once more put in possession of Port Egmont, but North promised to remove the garrison when public opinion had quietened.

The Falklands question had shown the weakness of the Family Compact and the feebleness of a France incapable of fulfilling its obligations. It had obliged the King of Spain to excuse himself to Great Britain and the world.

Carlos III was wounded by Aranda's insulting letter, which Grimaldi, seeking an opportunity to detach Aranda from him, had shown him. Indeed Aranda's difficult, intractable character and his language, which was not always that of a subject, led to his disgrace and to his being sent from court to France as ambassador there. He was to take the place of the conde de Fuentes who was on the point of resigning. In August 1773 he set out for Paris, where the Encyclopaedists were awaiting his arrival with delight as 'the Spanish Hercules who had cleansed the Augean stables', the stables being the institution of Jesuitism. On seeing him, however, longing turned to disappointment, then to irony as they beheld this yellow-complexioned courtier, squinting and toothless, who nearly always remained silent in the salons and who when he did speak vouchsafed no more than the odd phrase gracelessly spoken, probably, it is fair to add, because of his very imperfect knowledge of French. Outside the salons, however, he pleased the Parisians who admired the Spanish *grand seigneur*'s luxurious equipage.

Aranda's post as President of the Council of Castile was filled by Manuel Ventura Figueroa, a cunning courtier, an egoist and a miser, who died years later as Patriarch of the Indies and Commissary-General of the Crusade, and holding other high-sounding and remunerative offices.

Since the beginning of Carlos III's reign there had been a Moroccan question, and in 1765 negotiations began to bring about a treaty between the Sultan Sida Mohamed ben Abdala and the King of Spain. The first negotiator was Samuel Surnbel, a Jew from Marseilles, and after him the talks were continued by the Apostolic Prefect of Missions, Fray Bartolomé Girón de la Concepción, who obtained an audience with the Sultan on 2 February 1766, and who returned to Spain with the Moroccan ambassador Sidi Ahmed el Gazel.[67] The latter disembarked in Algeciras, visited Sevilla and arrived at Madrid, where he stayed first in the palace of Buen Retiro, and then in La Granja, having conversations with King Carlos until his departure on 4 October. As a compliment to the Sultan the naval authority Jorge Juan sailed, as ambassador-extraordinary, to Morocco five weeks later on 10 November. Jorge Juan landed at Tetuan and visited several cities including Rabat and on 28 May 1767 signed a treaty of friendship.[68]

In spite of the treaty, seven years later the Sultan wanted to expel the Spanish from the territory they occupied in Morocco and on 9 December 1774 besieged Melilla with 13,000 men. Mariscal del campo Juan Sherlock, supported by the fleet under Francisco Hidalgo de Cisneros, resisted the attacks of the Sultan's army. Losing heart, the Sultan asked for talks, and after some difficulties Grimaldi accepted his empty excuses.[69]

The Dey of Algiers had been the influence behind the Sultan's action, and Carlos III decided to attack the city of Algiers, a veritable nest of pirates, to avenge grievances and to make Mediterranean commerce secure. The King was told that the enterprise was very likely to succeed, and his confessor Fray Joaquín Eleta presented it to him as a holy one. After considering others, Carlos chose as the leader of the expedition Alejandro O'Reilly,[70] who was put in command of 20,000 men. O'Reilly, of Irish origin, served first in Spain and afterwards in France until 1760, when he returned to Spain, recommended by maréchal de Broglie, and protected by Ossun he gained the favour of Wall, a fellow Irishman. O'Reilly came to be the reformer of the Spanish army. Honours were now heaped on him: the King nominated him Inspector-General of Infantry, in 1771 ennobled him as conde, and in 1773 appointed him Military Governor of Madrid. Flexible, well-mannered and insinuating, by 1774 his influence in the Departments of War and of the Navy and the Indies was incontestable. Nonetheless, O'Reilly with all his excellent qualities lacked foresight. Moreover, the indiscretions of the Spanish cabinet militated against him, so that, time being allowed to lag, the Dey of Algiers was prepared when he appeared.

O'Reilly, having embarked at Cádiz, arrived before Algiers in the flagship *El Velasco* full of confidence—too much so.[71] On 7 July 1775 preparations were made to disembark, and the ships' guns destroyed the cannon of the fort of Algiers. On the following day Spanish landing-craft in seven columns, each one preceded by a gunboat, made for the shore between Algiers and El Harrach. With great difficulty the troops disembarked, but the cannon sank in the sand, and from the little hills which dominated the strand the Algerians attacked and fell on the Spanish. O'Reilly's troops advanced as far as some aloes which surmounted the hillocks, and the Algerians tried to encircle them. The Spanish fleet trained its guns on the enemy, but their shots fell on their own men. O'Reilly's troops now fell back to some entrenchments; but this was of no avail, and the order was given for retreat. This disaster cost Spain twenty-seven officers and 500 men dead, and 191 officers and 2,088 men wounded. The expedition returned to Spain and disembarked at Alicante.[72]

Public opinion thundered against those held responsible for the disaster, and Grimaldi and O'Reilly were the targets for popular indignation, which vented itself in prose and verse and rose to a still greater height when minister and commander were officially defended in the *Gaceta*.[73] The príncipe and princesa de las Asturias encouraged the opposition against the minister, but the true leader of the plot was Canónigo Ramón Pignatelli, brother of the conde de Fuentes,[74] who wanted to take Grimaldi's place. One of the friends of Asturias, the duque de Villahermosa openly censured the ministry's conduct.

Grimaldi during all his time as minister had fought against the Aragonese party[75] led by Aranda. Although Grimaldi was of the party of the *golillas*,[76] at the time of the attack on Algiers he could not count on much support from his fellow ministers, a typical example being Manuel de Roda who, although a *golilla* by profession, belonged to the Aragonese party. Miguel Muzquiz, Minister of Finance, did not sympathise with him, while the conde de Ricola, Minister of War, owed his position to his relative Aranda. As for Julián de Arriaga, Minister of Marine and of the Indies, he was an octogenarian and died six months after the Algerian disaster on 5 February 1776, when the two posts he had held were divided. That of Marine went to the marqués Pedro González de Castejón, enemy of O'Reilly and above all of Grimaldi, and that of the Indies to José de Gálvez, so active in South American affairs. Abandoned by all, Grimaldi was saved by the King who reprimanded the Aragonese faction and wrote a severe letter to his son the príncipe de las Asturias. The fall of Grimaldi was postponed.

Relations between Spain and Portugal at this period were not very cordial.

The roots of the trouble lay in the terms of the treaty of 1750 concerning Spanish-Portuguese American boundaries, which had always been ill-interpreted by Portugal, and this attitude had been increased by the Portuguese minister Pombal's bad faith. Trusting in the support of Great Britain Pombal manifested apparently peaceful intentions to the Spanish ambassador, the marqués of Almodóvar, while secretly encouraging the abuses which the Portuguese were causing in the area of Río de la Plata. In 1766 a Spanish officer, José Molina, came upon a Portuguese detachment in the Sierra de los Tapes, north of the Río Pardo. Molina protested about this and at their headquarters he and the Portuguese commanding officer came to an understanding which was drawn up in writing on 24 May 1767. In spite of this, five days later the Portuguese seized the area of the Río Grande de San Pedro where it enters the Laguna de los Patos and turned it into a centre for their further infiltration into Spanish territory.

Carlos III, with other matters on his mind, did nothing about this, and so an abnormal situation continued until 1773, when Juan José Vertiz, Governor of Buenos Aires, went to Montevideo and from there set out on a reconnaissance of the area. He then discovered that on the outskirts of Monte Grande a Spanish detachment composed of Indians and of the militia of the town of Corrientes had been partly exterminated and the rest taken prisoner with all their goods. There was no doubt at all that this was the work of the Portuguese. Pombal made out that he was the victim of Spanish greed and managed to convince Britain. It was useless that Escarano, the Spanish ambassador in London, explained the situation to Lord Rochford in November 1774, and the only result was that it was believed that Spain wanted to conquer Brazil. All the same, Britain with the growing trouble in North America on her hands was not now ready to back up Pombal, and the cabinet declared that Britain was not going to become involved in the Spanish-Portuguese quarrel.

The French minister Vergennes encouraged King Carlos to counter the Portuguese outrage by sending a fleet to Buenos Aires; but now Pombal pretended nothing but pacific motives and friendship towards Spain, and that and the faint-heartedness of Grimaldi delayed any action being taken. An energetic letter from Aranda to the King's confessor Eleta, dated 11 October 1776, drove the latter to present a memorandum to Carlos in which he accused Grimaldi of inexplicable timidity, bordering on incapacity. This produced immediate effects, and on 13 November 1776 a squadron under the marqués de Casa-Tilly set out from Cádiz. It was composed of seven ships-of-the-line, eight frigates and four packet boats escorting the transport, and with them went fourteen infantry battalions and four squadrons of cavalry under Pedro Ceballos. At the same time another fleet, under Miguel Gastón, entered the Tajo and stood off Lisbon. Pombal, dissimulating his anxiety, received the officers splendidly.

The first fleet set out for Buenos Aires but, having captured some

Portuguese ships on the way, it changed direction and proceeded towards the island of Santa Catalina, which was captured without resistance, the Portuguese governor being allowed to leave for the Brazilian mainland. Having lost one ship, the *San Agustín*, taken by the Portuguese, the fleet arrived at the Río de la Plata, and for the second time Ceballos conquered the Colonia del Sacramento.[77]

King José I of Portugal died on 22 February 1777, and Pombal fell from power. María Francisca, the daughter of King José and Queen María Victoria, Carlos III's much-loved sister, succeeded and was married to her uncle the Infante Dom Pedro, who shared the throne with his consort on an equal basis as Pedro III. On 1 October 1777, Floridablanca for Spain and Francisco de Souza Countinho for Portugal signed a preliminary treaty at San Ildefonso, and this was ratified in the Escorial by Carlos III ten days later.[78] By means of this treaty adjustments to the unsatisfactory treaty of 1750 were made, and the whole question of Spanish and Portuguese boundaries in the New World was clarified. On the successful termination of these negotiations, Carlos III invited his sister, the Queen-Mother of Portugal, to pay him a visit. She accepted and spent a year in Spain. This peace with Portugal was of great benefit to Spain on the eve of a war with Great Britain, now fighting the American Colonies.

A bad relationship between the colonists and the mother country had become overt in 1765 and increased in the following years. The situation was critical in 1774, and in that year at the Congress of Philadelphia the colonists published the Declaration of Colonial Rights. Negotiations between London and the Colonies began, but were broken off in 1775. Hostilities opened, Washington took command of the rebels, and the battle of Bunker Hill followed.

The struggle which broke out in North America was of the utmost interest to France and Spain, though for different reasons. As to France, Choiseul during his ministry had been preoccupied with the onset of the disaccord between Britain and her colonies, and sent a M. Kalb as special agent to North America to keep him informed of developments there. With the death of Louis XV in 1774 and the succession of his young grandson Louis XVI a new era began for France. In the place of a decadent court, new and vigorous ministers such as Turgot and Vergennes appeared, alive to the present and eager to make France once again a power in the world. Britain's formidable warlike preparations in 1775 alarmed France and Spain. Grimaldi decided that the Spanish ambassador in London, Masserano, should seek explanations of the situation from the British cabinet, since it was being whispered that the preparations were against the Family Compact which to British minds seemed to be an alliance which might well encourage the rebellion. If the Family Compact were detroyed, then this would help to break the revolt.

Lord Rochford, Secretary of State for the Southern Department, provided full explanations, signifying that the armaments were destined for America. The French minister Vergennes became warlike in his attitude, and Aranda, still Spanish ambassador to France, sent despatches home in which he pointed out that here was a good opportunity to attack Britain.

Spain, no less than France, wanted revenge for what was for them the shameful Treaty of Paris of 1763, and it appeared that both governments were, in principle, of a like mind to aid the rebel colonists in some way, since it was in the interests of both to weaken British power. Nonetheless France did not behave with any clarity towards her ally, secretly, without the knowledge of Spain, sending two secret agents, one Beaumarchais, the well-known dramatist, to London, and the other de Bonvouloir to North America. Spain[79] copied France, and the Minister of the Navy, José de Gálvez, ordered the Governor of La Habana to send agents to Pensacola, Florida and Jamaica. Vergennes and Grimaldi, judging by their despatches between October 1775 and February 1776 seemed about to declare war on Britain, and on 27 June Grimaldi wrote a half-hearted letter to Aranda in Paris saying that Spain as much as France wanted to 'Keep the rebellion alive' and sending a bill of credit for one million '*livres tournois*',[80] but they did nothing more and by October 1776 their ardour had cooled. It was, however, a pointer to the future, and it is interesting to notice that in these despatches the conquest of Portugal, Menorca and Gibraltar was discussed. Aranda considered at attack on Ireland. Vergennes acceded to the conquest of Portugal as provisional, keeping this exploit in reserve as a guarantee of further agreements between France and Spain; but he did not like the idea of its annexation by Spain. Grimaldi proposed the sending of a force of between ten and twelve thousand men to defend Santo Domingo. The projects for a direct attack on Great Britain, considered in the first flush of receiving the news of the colonists' victory in Long Island, was abandoned in favour of sending detachments to strengthen the rebel armies rather than despatching a separate Spanish force.

Meanwhile a ministerial upheaval was taking place in Spain. At first Carlos III was able to support Grimaldi, as has been mentioned above, but the public clamour against him, seconded by the Aragonese faction, forced him to retire. The Aragonese party now felt sure that one of their number would succeed as Minister, but the King still resented Aranda and his followers and, remaining faithful to the *golillas*, chose one of them, Floridablanca, and recalled him from his embassy in Rome to take office. Grimaldi resigned on 7 November 1776, and changed places with Floridablanca, becoming ambassador at Rome. Floridablanca assumed his post as Minister.

On 4 July 1776 the North American colonists proclaimed their independence at the Congress of Philadelphia. Already the month before

France and Spain had set about giving pecuniary assistance to the rebels,[81] whose spokesman Silas Deane had come to Paris to see the minister Vergennes. He was soon in communication with Aranda as Spanish ambassador.[82]

At the head of an organisation called Rodérique Hortalès et Cie. was the famous Beaumarchais who had founded it to send aid to the rebels. Meanwhile, the American George Gibson had visited the Governor of Louisiana, Luis de Unzaga y Amézaga, asking for a commercial treaty between the revolting states and his territory. By December 1776 Unzaga had received arms, munitions, clothing and quinine with orders to send them to the rebels. Powder and guns were also sent to them from La Habana and Mexico. Early in 1777 a packet-boat set out from La Coruña bringing other goods for the Americans, but it was very late, months late, in arriving.

The British ambassador in Madrid, Lord Grantham, had already complained to the Spanish government for giving refuge to rebel shipping in Spanish harbours; but, when Grimaldi made excuses, he did not insist. Carlos III did not want war since he was fully occupied with the problems which Portugal was giving Spain in the New World. He had certainly aided the Americans in secret, but now they wanted more.

On 26 October 1776 Benjamin Franklin arrived in France as a commissioner of the American rebels. Lee who was in London, moved to Paris, and now Deane, Franklin and Lee formed a triumvirate of American commissioners in Paris. The three of them had two talks, one on 29 December 1776 and the other on 4 January 1777, with the Spanish ambassador Aranda. They proposed to Vergennes and Aranda nothing less than an alliance between the rebels and France and Spain. Vergennes was very cautious, and said that though the day might well come for this, the moment had not yet arrived. Instead he proposed a policy of preparation and menace against Britain, and the Spanish government seemed to agree. Not so Aranda, who in his despatches to Madrid showed himself decidedly in favour of an out-and-out alliance with the insurgent Americans.

Aranda's words struck home to a wavering Spanish government, the headship of which Floridablanca had just taken over from Grimaldi; and at the end of January 1777 the proposition for such an alliance was discussed by a council of the secretaries of the various governmental departments. The Spanish ministers refused an immediate treaty with the Americans; but they proposed to aid them secretly and meanwhile to keep themselves in readiness against the eventuality.[83] Carlos III wanted to weaken British power, but his position was not so clear and free as that of France, since the latter did not now have much territory in America; but, in the case of Spain, openly to help the colonists could be a disastrous example to Spanish America to try to throw off the Spanish yoke in the same way as the North Americans were attempting to throw off that of

their mother country. This was how it appeared to the Spanish government, and this is why its policy seemed to be equivocal and vacillating.
France took this attitude in bad part and resented the fact that Spain did
not frankly second her views, which, however, were not clear either.

Arthur Lee left Paris on 7 February 1777, and the news of his coming to
Spain caused great annoyance. Already Aranda had warned Lee to appear
incognito. He journeyed from Bilbao to Burgos, where on his arrival on 28
February a letter from the banker Diego Gardoqui awaited him. On 2
March Gardoqui himself arrived. Two days afterwards the lately retired
Minister, Grimaldi, arrived in Burgos and saw Lee. In his conversations
with the American, Grimaldi tried to dissuade him from going to Madrid
since King Carlos had no intention of breaking with Great Britain. The
pushing Lee, with that rough self-assertiveness so much in evidence among
the American colonists, insisted that he would not leave Spain without a
satisfactory reply, at least as regards the pecuniary help for which the
American Congress asked. Grimaldi allowed himself to be browbeaten
into letting Lee go to Vitoria to await the King's reply. The very day that
he had seen Grimaldi, Lee wrote to the Spanish court setting out the
reasons for the American Revolution.[84]

Grimaldi wrote to his successor, Floridablanca, about the result of his
conversations with Lee, and this led to Floridablanca's policy. It was
twofold: to content Lee and to get him out of Spain! Lee while in Vitoria
had another meeting with Grimaldi, when the latter assured him that the
colonists would be helped directly from Spain or from New Orleans,
principally by Gardoqui's banking-house. Moreover, said Grimaldi,
Aranda could help them by raising some credit on Holland or on a French
port, but the Americans must keep absolutely quiet about these proceedings. Lee went back to Paris satisfied; but Aranda had to counter a new
difficulty, since Franklin had meanwhile received full powers from the
American Congress to make a treaty of alliance with Spain[85] and was
ready to go to Madrid; but Aranda managed to dissuade him from it.

What had happened to Lee in Spain produced a certain uneasiness in
the minds of the French ministers Vergennes and Maurepas. They blamed
Spain for underhand conduct, for France's attitude to the American
deputies had become truly enthusiastic. Floridablanca, like his predecessor
Grimaldi, called for an expedition to Santo Domingo and for putting the
Windward Islands and Spanish America in general in a state of defence.
The French cabinet ignored these actions and did not build up its
armaments in support of Spain with much activity. Meanwhile Great
Britain, with greatly increased reinforcements, prepared for a second
campaign against the rebels. In the summer of 1777, however, the French
cabinet, owing to the information of Noailles, ambassador in London,
became bellicose and agreed to send troops to Saint Domingue (Haiti) and
Martinique. What is particularly notable is the effect that this had on
Floridablanca who, in face of the sudden change of attitude of France,

became more circumspect. He said that it was necessary to wait for the return of the fishing-fleet from Newfoundland, that of the fleet from Mexico, which would not arrive until the spring of 1778, and that of the Spanish troops sent to South America. By September 1777, as the document drawn up by the American deputies for France and Spain as their allies, or hoped-for allies, shows, Spain was continuing her policy of pecuniary help to the rebels. We see from it that Diego de Gardoqui received from the Spanish Treasury 70,000 *pesos* first and then another 50,000 *pesos* to be sent to the Americans. Drafts to the value of 50,000 *pesos* were also sent to Lee, and Gardoqui himself sent merchandise worth 946,906 *reales*. In December 1777 news was received of General Burgoyne's capitulation at Saratoga, and France thought that the time had come to join forces with the Americans before a Chatham administration tried to bring about a reconciliation with the colonists. Aranda thought that France was right. Vergennes brought pressure to bear on Spain to ally herself with the Americans, but Floridablanca said that the time was inopportune since the fleet sent to South America had not yet returned. The French answer was that, whatever Spain might or might not do, she would bring about the alliance, which she did on 6 February 1778, announcing the fact to the British cabinet. France would not accept Floridablanca's good reasons for refusing to follow; but the Spanish Minister knew what he was doing; for one thing, Spain was not on a sufficiently strong war-footing; secondly, for the present, Spanish popular feeling was against war with Britain, as was not the case in France.

George III took a personal and impassioned interest in the war against the rebels, and used all his power to drive the nation along a road opposed to the insurgents. Masserano resigned as Spanish ambassador in London, his place being taken by Pedro de Góngora y Luján, marqués de Almodóvar, assisted as First Secretary by Escarano, whose knowledge of Britain, gained through his long stay there, was valuable. Spain now offered to intervene with Carlos III as mediator between the mother country and the colonists, and France agreed, but when the Spanish embassy bargained for Gibraltar as the price for Spain's mediation, Britain beat off friendly Spanish overtures, for the giving up of the fortress was something that was in no way to be considered. Lord Weymouth, Secretary of State for the Southern Department, kept up the same ambiguous diplomacy, of which Floridablanca complained to the British ambassador, Grantham, on 1 June 1778. The Spanish cabinet reprimanded Escarano for having gone beyond his orders.

The cannonade between the French *Belle-Poule* and the British *Arethusa* posed the question of a *casus belli*. Lord North had decided on war to the death with the Americans, and the *Belle-Poule* episode served Vergennes as an occasion to advise Floridablanca that here was a good opportunity for the Family Compact to come into action; but the Spanish ambassador in London, marqués de Almodóvar, encouraged by Floridablanca, continued to believe that the war could be stopped by Spanish mediation. Yet it was difficult for Spain, since British privateers were now insulting the Spanish flag, and Lord Weymouth behaved as arrogantly as ever. Britain sought to exploit Spain's neutrality and yet repelled Spanish mediation, since, he said, that would have been at the probable price of recognising the independence of the North Americans. The result was that at last Spain grew tired of the delay and declared war on Britain on 3 April 1779, at the same time recognising the independence of the thirteen States. On 12 April Floridablanca signed a treaty with France to make common cause in the war.[86]

France and Spain now planned an attack on the Isle of Wight. The combined fleet consisted of sixty-six ships-of-the-line, without counting frigates and light craft, and was commanded by comte d'Orvilliers, hero of the battle of Ushant. Spain's position in 1779 was more favourable than in 1761, for she was at peace with Portugal, there was no danger now from Moroccan pirates, the moral prestige of Carlos III was felt by all social classes, and so popular now was the war against the British that even beggars made gifts of their very alms to the government. Spain addressed to the new enemy a list of grievances, which was answered, it is averred, by no less a person than the historian, Edward Gibbon.

The French and Spanish fleets, now united, did not, however, attack a Plymouth ungarrisoned and gunless, owing to d'Orvilliers' timidity and the audacity of Admiral Hardy, who in August 1779 appeared with a fleet near the Scilly Isles, saving Britain from an attack that would have proved serious.[87] Meanwhile Aranda, as warlike as ever, worried and furiously anti-British, drew up war-plans and censured the conduct of Floridablanca, until the latter in measured but firm language called him to order. The inaction of the fleet in Brest, caused by an epidemic among the crews, obliged the admirals, on the French side du Chaffault, de Vaux and Guichen and on the Spanish side Arce, Gastón, and Córdoba, to hold a council of war on 4 October 1779, at which it was decided that Luis de Córdoba should sail with part of the Spanish fleet to Cádiz, while Miguel Gastón, with the other part, should stay in Brest, because the direction of the wind and the state of the sea made it impossible to decide on a date for the combined navies to put to sea. Guichen was to sail to the West Indies.

Spain had now decided on one thing, and this was to blockade Gibraltar.[88] Martín Álvarez de Sotomayor was placed in command with 8,000 men and he was supported by the ships of Admiral Antonio Barceló, a man of outstanding value and well known for his heroic daring. Sir George Elliot, Governor of Gibraltar, had a garrison of 3,800 men and with them made frequent sorties. On 10 June 1779 the Spanish government announced officially to the diplomatic corps that all shipping was prohibited from sailing in the vicinity of Gibraltar.

Britain fitted out a fleet of twenty-four ships-of-the-line under the command of Admiral Rodney who, thanks to the continued inaction of the French at Brest and to the bad weather, set sail to the aid of Gibraltar. Córdoba sought to join forces with a fleet under Juan de Lángara, but a storm obliged him to take refuge in Cádiz, and it was Lángara alone who clashed with Rodney between Capes Espartel and Trafalgar on 16 January 1780[89] Lángara, who had only nine ships-of-the-line and two frigates, gave orders to make for the nearest port. With three times the number of ships the British attacked the *Santo Domingo*, whose captain, Ignazio Mendizábal, sank the ship rather than let it fall into enemy hands. The frigates *Santa Cecilia* and *Santa Rosalia* and the ships *San Lorenzo* and *San Agustín* were able to save themselves thanks to their speed. The *San Julián* and the *San Eugenio* owed their escape to the skilfulness of their captains. The marqués de Medina, in command of the *San Julián*, afterwards caught in a sudden storm and obliged to surrender to the British, was in the strange position of being able to tell his victors that they had the choice of perishing in that very storm, or being taken to port by the Spanish themselves, who alone know those waters, where the British would be made prisoner on arrival. Rodney, however, sailed gloriously into Gibraltar, leading in his prizes, the *Princesa*, the *Diligente*, the *Monarca* and the *Fénix*, in which last the brave Lángara had been wounded. Carlos III compensated all the survivors of the disaster. In February 1780 Gastón arrived at Cádiz; and the worst of it was that not only had Rodney arrived at Gibraltar, but that Córdoba did not prevent his leaving it again while fifty Spanish ships remained impotent in Cádiz.

José Gálvez, Minister of the Indies, wanted to find an opportunity which would allow his nephew, Bernardo, Governor of Louisiana,[90] to distinguish himself, and proposed that he should lead the fight against the British in America. The result was that a fleet, commanded by José Solano, sailed to the West Indies to join forces with the French squadron under Guichen. The objective of the expedition was to recover Florida from the British. Solano's fleet was composed of twelve ships-of-the-line, three frigates, a packet-boat and 114 transport craft with 10,000 men on board. The Spanish and French fleets, now united, formed a force vastly superior to the British, an advantage that the allies did not profit by owing to the opposing views of the two commanders, Solano and Guichen; for the former insisted on making La Habana the base for the operations, while the latter was equally insistent on making Martinique his headquarters, and each sailed his own way. Meanwhile one blow had been struck against Britain when on 9 August 1780 Luis de Córdoba captured sixty British merchant ships in the Azores.

On the American continent hostilities between Spain and Britain had begun in 1779, when Roberto de Rivas Betancourt, Governor of Campeche, sent two detachments against the British forces in the area. One of these detachments under José Rosado took Cayo Cocina, the most important British settlement in the area; while the other under Colonel

Francisco Piñeiro destroyed the factories of Río Hondo, and drove the British out of the Campeche region. As for Bernardo Gálvez, Governor of Louisiana, he did not waste the opportunity given him by his uncle and in August 1779 captured from the British the cities of Manchak, Bâton-Rouge and Natchez. The Chacta Indians with their seventeen chiefs and 480 leading warriors now made a pact with Bernardo Gálvez, promising him a contingent of 4,000 men. At the beginning of 1780 Gálvez with 1,200 men marched on Mobile and besieged it, and in March Colonel Dunford surrendered with his garrison.

Gálvez's next objective was Pensacola, but to take it he would need more men, which would mean going to La Habana. He did so, and on 16 October 1780 returned from La Habana to the scene of action with a fleet of seven warships and five frigates commanded by José Solano. A storm scattered the fleet, but the tenacious Gálvez gathered another together and, on 28 February 1781, put to sea again with five warships, the crews numbering 1,300 men. On 9 March he reached Pensacola and, after unending difficulties, took the fortress on 10 May, making General Campbell and Admiral Chester prisoner, together with 1,400 soldiers of the garrison, a great number of negroes and 153 pieces of artillery.[91]

Meanwhile in Central America another campaign was taking place. The hero there was also a member of the Gálvez family, Matías Gálvez, President of the Audiencia of Guatemala, brother José Gálvez, Minister of the Indies, and father of Bernardo, the organiser of the Pensacola expedition. His first exploit was to capture the fortress of San Fernando de Ornoa, held by the British, on 28 November 1779, which success led to a general attack on the British settlements on the Gulf of Honduras and the Mosquito Coast. The British had a temporary success when they took San Juan de Nicaragua; but Matías Gálvez organised an expedition to recover it, making Masaya his headquarters and ordering Tomás López de Corral to keep a watch on enemy movements in Costa Rica. López not only kept watch, but also captured the British settlements of Tortuguero and Boca de Toro, while early in 1781 Matías Gálvez clinched the campaign with the capture of San Juan de Nicaragua.

In Madrid, Floridablanca was passing through a difficult time, surrounded by hostile politicians, even his own ministers, who accused him of being the cause of the naval disasters in the Channel and in the Straits of Gibraltar. The leader of the intrigues against him was Castejón, Minister of Marine, who owed his position entirely to Floridablanca, but who ungratefully turned against his old patron. Another of Floridablanca's enemies was José Gálvez, but his most serious enemy was the King's confessor, Padre Joaquín Eleta, who called Floridablanca 'the Criminal of the State'. Carlos III, however, was not to be shaken and stood by his Minister.

A further word should now be said of Floridablanca, who stands before us

tall and dignified in Goya's portrait. José Moñino, conde de Floridablanca,[92] was by temperament cold and reserved, although at times he
could become animated in conversation. He was clear-minded and
methodical, of balanced judgement and prudent, in manner ceremonious
and solemn, basically authoritarian, even despotic. He had the supreme
ability to hold the king's confidence, to the point, it was said, of Carlos III's
considering his word 'as Gospel truth'. He was known as 'the Old Fox' for
his subtlety. In politics his particular standpoint was to make Spain
completely independent, above all of France, for he regarded the Family
Compact as fatal for Spain—an attitude which history has fully
vindicated.[93]

Britain sought at all costs to part the two allies Spain and France, for
what with these and the American rebels her position in the world was
being ruined. Commodore Johnstone, by an intermediary, a certain
Cantoffer, initiated negotiations for peace with Spain, which, according to
Floridablanca, were spoilt by the French ambassador in Madrid,
Montmorin. Another figure in such a move for peace was the Irish priest
Hussey, the marqués de Almodóvar's chaplain. Hussey, representing Lord
George Germaine, came to Madrid and saw Floridablanca, soon learning
from him that Spain was not so bound to France that she could not
conclude a separate peace with Great Britain. The stumbling-block,
however, was the question of Gibraltar, which Carlos III on entering the
war had vowed to win back; and no peace with Britain was likely to be
possible without a clause by which the Rock would be returned to Spain.
Early in 1780 Lord Germaine sent his secretary Richard Cumberland, the
well-known dramatist already known for his lachrymose tragedy *The West
Indian* in which the slave-question was the leading theme, to Spain where
he settled down in Aranjuez to await his opportunity. Unfortunately his
character was in no way satisfactory for a diplomat, for he was so well
known for his particularly jealous and irritable nature that he was the
prototype of Sheridan's 'Sir Fitful Plagiary'! What was more, just at this
movement a rival appeared, none other than the American deputy, John
Jay.

Spanish relations with the American rebels were now much more
intense, and Spanish financial and armed aid sent to the colonists by
Bernardo Gálvez was more openly given than formerly; but Madrid still
had its scruples. This approach showed clearly in the behaviour of Juan
Miralles, the agent now sent by Spain to the North American Congress.
John Jay and his secretary, Carmichael, as soon as they reached Madrid
began to make a series of petitions for continuing pecuniary help, which up
to then had been maintained by Spain in spite of the difficulties caused by
the lack of the resources of the Spanish American Empire which could not
reach Spain because of the war. Even so, on one—perhaps unguarded—
occasion in conversation with Jay, Floridablanca promised him a sum of
the equivalent of £40,000 (sterling still being used by the colonists) by the

end of 1780. At this point Miralles died and Diego Gardoqui was nominated to take his place. He accepted unwillingly and put difficulties in the way, since he did not wish to leave the Compañía de Comercio of which he was director.

Gardoqui adopted a different attitude from Miralles in his dealings with Jay. He was straightforward and businesslike in his diplomacy, and the American soon learnt that his emerging country would have to pay a price for Spanish aid. Since Spain now recognised the independence of the North American colonies, then the Americans must make sure that Spanish territory contiguous to the thirteen whilom British colonies should be run in an orderly manner and that there should be no attempt to infiltrate into Spanish Florida and Louisiana. It was a very reasonable requirement, but one which France, now with no territory to speak of in North America, unthinkingly condemned. Spain had good reason to doubt the colonists' intentions, as before the war the North Americans had already made claims to control the navigation of the Mississippi; and now here was Spain helping the rebels and aiding in the destruction of a European empire in the New World like her own. Hence the bargaining with Jay, an attempt, while helping to destroy Britain's American power, to preserve hers. Whatever might be said of it in a European context (and when anyway had there been a true idea of European unity since the Middle Ages?), in a nationalistic one it was legitimate enough, for it was merely the extension of the rivalry of two European powers into the New World.

Richard Cumberland in the meantime had become the nightmare of the French ambassador Montmorin's life; and yet the latter had no reason to be suspicious of the Spanish Minister or the Spanish court, for Florida-blanca had come to no agreement with the British agent and he countered Montmorin's complaints with characteristic impassivity. For the French, the comte d'Estaing, victorious admiral at the battle off the Island of Grenada, now in residence in Madrid, did his utmost to rouse the war-spirit among the Spanish war-party. The abrupt attitude of Necker, the French Minister of Finance, when negotiating a Spanish loan soured relations between the two countries during the autumn of 1780; but it was finally resolved thanks to the intervention of the bankers Cabarrus and Drouillet. The danger of Russian participation passed, Cumberland left Madrid in March 1781, and shortly afterwards the peace negotiations of Kaunitz, the Austrian Chancellor, failed.

At the beginning of 1781 the war began to languish. Admiral Darby had managed to break the blockade and siege of Gibraltar; but if the Spanish had failed there perhaps they could take Menorca. Preparations were made in Cádiz, and on 23 July 1781 a fleet consisting of two ships-of-the-line, two frigates, two gunboats, two fireships and two sloops, which convoyed sixty-three transport ships, embarked. The commander of the expeditionary force was the duc de Crillon, now in Spanish service. Navigation was difficult, but in spite of that the British were taken unawares. Crillon disembarked and, well supported by the marqués de Casa-Cagigal and the marqués de Avites, laid siege to the castle of San Felipe.

Crillon soon realised that he needed more men than he had brought and begged France for aid. France responded in October 1781 with 4,000 men under the command of comte de Falkenhayn and the marquis de Bouzols. On 5 February 1782 General Murray surrended San Felipe, and Crillon was loaded with honours as Captain-General, grandee of Spain and duque de Mahón. Menorca was Spanish again.[94]

Gibraltar still remained to be taken, and King Carlos had set his heart on winning it; but up to 1782 the blockade had been unsuccessful in spite of Barceló's zeal, since Portugal as Britain's ally kept the Rock supplied with provisions, outwitting all Spanish vigilance. It was now decided to turn the blockade into a siege. There was no lack of plans for attacking the place: Aranda proposed artificial reefs just below the water-level, d'Estaing suggested a system of bombardment, while Barceló was in favour of fast craft armed with cannon. Late in 1781, a French engineer named Michaud d'Arçon,[95] recommended by Aranda, came to Madrid suggesting floating batteries. Floridablanca now summoned Crillon to court, where Carlos III nominated him commander of the besieging forces at Gibraltar, on the condition that he carried out the plans of siege drawn up by Michaud d'Arçon; but Crillon was annoyed at the idea of being forced to carry out someone else's plans and declined his appointment.

France now became more active than ever in joining in the siege, and outstanding personages, such as Louis XVI's brother, the comte d'Artois, the duc de Bourbon, and other nobles, were eager to throw in their lot. As Crillon had foreseen, however, the floating batteries were as disaster, for the red-hot cannon balls set on fire the very batteries that launched them. Nor were the allies much more successful at sea, since Admiral Luis de Córdoba with the Spanish fleet was unable to prevent the British fleet under Admiral Howe from bringing supplies to Gibraltar. Although he chased after him, he was unable to bring him to battle. At most Córdoba could be said to have gained a moral victory by forcing Howe to return to England. British losses were insignificant.[96] The siege nonetheless continued.

Peace negotiations were now in sight, for all the belligerents except Spain wanted it by 1782. On 20 March Lord North's administration fell, and the Whigs, so hated by George III, succeeded it. The leaders of the new government were the Marquess of Rockingham and Franklin's friend, Lord Shelburne. The latter sent a Scottish agent called Oswald to Paris to begin negotiations with Vergennes on 12 April 1782. Thomas Grenville replaced Oswald and, thanks to the recent victory of Lord Rodney at the Battle of the Saints, was a much more aggressive and intractable negotiator. On 16 July Fitz-Herbert succeeded Grenville and the comte de Grasse went to London. Britain and France, now that the American colonists had to all intents and purposes won their freedom, were at last on good terms; it was the warlike attitude of Spain which was the obstacle. Carlos III was as adamant as ever about the possession of Gibraltar, and his offer of Oran and Mazalquivir in exchange held no inducements for Britain. When during the summer the French envoy Rayneval went to London to try to come to some agreement he found Shelburne little disposed even to consider the question of giving up Gibraltar. He maintained that Spain had no right to it, since she had not captured it, and after stating that he found Spanish claims excessive he refused to talk of the subject any more.[97]

Aranda, with the permission of Floridablanca, next sent one of his secretaries, Ignacio de Heredia, to London, and bargaining began. The matter of Gibraltar, in spite of all, came up again, but the price that Britain expected Spain to pay for it makes one feel that her intention was to keep it anyway; for how could Spain be expected to make over to her enemy in exchange for the Rock, however much it was desired by Carlos III, all the territory such as Florida which she had won in the war, with the addition of Puerto Rico? At this point Louis XVI made a generous gesture by offering Britain French colonies in exchange for Gibraltar, hoping thereby to placate Spain and entice Britain; but Britain did not accept. Finally Vergennes offered to agree to Gibraltar remaining in British hands if Spain kept Menorca and Florida, and with this Britain, troubled by political changes and problems, concurred.

Aranda claimed that he was responsible for this agreement, and it is true that in his own way he had wanted to save Carlos III's face and for the moment Floridablanca's government, which in fact was not grateful to him and lamented his actions. Surely, however, the Treaty of Versailles, which was signed by Spain and Great Britain on 3 September 1783,[98] was a success for Spain, which had won back Menorca and had strengthened her hold on Florida, although the Bahamas and Providence Island, conquered by Casa-Cagigal during the war, were returned to Great Britain. The area in which campeachy wood could be cut was defined and limited and the British were confined to a corner of Honduras, Belize. A doubtful clause, which seemed to allow the British to keep their factories on Cayo Cocina and in various other stations along the coast, was not ironed out until 1786 when a special commission under Bernardo Gálvez met in London. Long before this, on 30 November 1782, a private treaty between Britain and the United States recognised the latter's independence.

As to the North Americans, their plenipotentiary Jay[99] in conversation with Aranda showed himself to be intransigent over the question of the navigation of the Mississippi, and an agreement with Spain could not be reached. The American attitude was the more wounding to Spain because Spain had been outstandingly generous to the colonists, having given them nearly eight million *reales* and 30,000 articles of clothing, besides the generous personal gift of Carlos III amounting to one and a half million *reales*, an advance of 284,480 *reales* to the commander of the South Carolina squadron, the 9,612 *pesos* furnished on another occasion, and the quantity of cash payments made to Jay. Spain had been too good to a spoilt, selfish and spiteful child.

During the last years of his reign Carlos III turned to home affairs, to those reforms which he had very much at heart.[100] The other concern of these later years was the Moroccan question.

On 30 May 1780 the Moroccan ambassador Sidi Mohammed ben Othman signed a treaty with Spain, which was ratified by the Sultan on the following Christmas Day. By it Morocco obliged the British to keep their shipping away from the coast of Tetuan and Tangier. Nonetheless the contraband with Gibraltar continued. Now that the war between Morocco and Spain was over, Francisco Salinas went as ambassador to Morocco on 27 April 1785, drew up a map of the coast from Tetuan to Cape Espartel, and returned to Spain with presents for Carlos III.

The Dey of Algiers, however, showed himself to be intractable and did not wish to conclude anything with Spain, excusing himself by saying that he could not do so without the agreement of the Porte. This being the case Floridablanca decided to reach an understanding with the Sultan of Turkey and sent to Constantinople Juan de Bouligny, who was so successful that a treaty between Spain and Turkey was signed on 14 September 1782.[101] By it Spain was allowed to establish consulates in Turkish ports and Spanish subjects were allowed to visit the holy places. The Sultan gave notice of the treaty to his North African regents, the result of this being that a treaty was immediately made with the Regency of Tripoli on 19 September, thanks to the efforts of the conde de Cifuentes, Captain-General of the Balearic Islands, aided by Pedro, Juan and Jaime Soler, the sons of the well-known merchant José Soler, their part being most important for that section of the agreement which dealt with trade.

Algiers, however, was another matter. There were still difficulties there, since the treaty was not recognised by the Dey. Spain's response was therefore to send a heavily armed squadron against Algiers in July 1783 under Antonio Barceló. On 1 August a bombardment of the city began, but with meagre results, and the Spanish fleet retired.

The following year another attack on the city was made with a Spanish fleet of about the same strength as before, but this time Spain was supported by a Portuguese squadron and some Neapolitan and Maltese ships,[102] for after all it was in their interest too that piracy should be destroyed and trade should flourish in the south-western Mediterranean without interference. This operation, however, was more risky than that of 1783 because the Algerians had prepared an important line of armed craft, and the allied fleet was badly mauled and had to withdraw.[103]

In 1785, Spain decided to make a third attack on Algiers, but at the moment of departure the conde de Cifuentes sent Floridablanca a letter from a certain Bartolomé Escudero, in which he wrote that the Dey wanted peace. Carlos III therefore ordered Mazarredo, commanding a small squadron, to sail to Algiers showing the white flag.[104] Setting sail from Cartagena, Mazarredo arrived before Algiers on 14 June 1785, and on 16 July peace negotiations began. The final obstacles to an agreed treaty were overcome by Brother Álvaro López, Administrator of the Spanish Hospital at Algiers, and a mercenary soldier calling himself conde de Expili. A merchant captain, Alejandro Baselini concluded a truce with the Dey of Tunis, which Jaime Soler converted into a definitive treaty of peace in June 1786; but the commericial demands of the Dey made Soler's efforts vain, and trade and shipping problems continued to trouble Spain in the south-western Mediterranean.

Dynastic questions occupied Carlos III in 1783, since the male line through his second son[105] the príncipe de las Asturias (afterwards Carlos IV) was not secure, and even for Asturias there was the complication of his having been born in Naples and not on Spanish soil; but King Carlos successfully contested the vexed clause in the law of 1713.[106] The Infante Carlos Eusebio died on 11 June of this year, and although María Luisa de las Asturias gave birth to twins on 5 September, these also died two months later; but the birth on 14 October, 1784 of Fernando, afterwards King Fernando VII, at last made the succession sure. Floridablance had convinced the King that it was desirable to have a close link between the two Iberian royal families. He had already arranged the marriage of King Carlos's fourth son, the Infante Gabriel to María Ana Victoria of Portugal, and he now pushed on with a plan for the marriage of Carlota, elder daughter of Carlos of Asturias (afterwards Carlos IV), to príncipe João of Portugal. His plan was to strengthen Iberian unity and to destroy France's tutelage of Spain.

The European powers were worried about this close alliance between Spain and Portugal, particularly when they saw that it was leading to Spain's interference in external politics on the side of Portugal, as, for example, when Spain acted as mediator between France and Portugal over North African affairs. On the other hand, the alliance with Portugal brought worries to Spain. The health of Pedro III of Portugal, who had suffered a stroke, gave cause for alarm, and since the males of his family, who might have been likely to succeed him, all died prematurely, King Pedro began to set his hopes on his daughter María Ana Victoria. Moves to bring her to Madrid were scotched by Carlos III, who saw the danger of a possible union of the crowns in favour of Portugal, and also the probable hostility of the European states.

Meanwhile Charles III's relationship with his third son Fernando I, King of Naples and Sicily, had become more and more bitter. Fernando was dominated by his wife, Maria Carolina, who helped to draw father and son apart. The cause of the antagonism was Maria Carolina's ambition to be the future Queen of Spain, and she saw her illusions frustrated by the marriage of príncipe João of Portugal and Carlota de las Asturias. Spaniards living in Naples had come to be the least-favoured foreigners, and it was an Englishman, Acton, who filled the post of Minister of the Kingdom of the Two Sicilies when Spain went to war with Great Britain. The death of Frederick the Great of Prussia in August 1786 led to the danger of renewed war between Britain and Spain, since, unlike his old uncle who of recent years had taken no part in any matter in which Spain and Britain were involved, Frederick William II was very pro-British, and in the Austrian Netherlands political parties were divided in their adherence, some to France and some to Britain. France prepared for war, and Carlos III made it known that he would support her. This energetic and decided attitude resulted in a treaty between Britain and France, signed on 17 October 1787.

On 8 July 1787 Floridablanca had created the *Junta Suprema del Estado*, which reform brought about a union of his enemies, bent on his political destruction. Aranda was foremost among these opponents, attacking him with his customary violence. Domestic events had brought Aranda back to Spain at last, for his first wife had died, and he had married his niece María del Pilar Silva y Palafox, whose illness obliged him to leave Paris for Spain to be at her side. Moreover, Aranda was tired of his French ambassador-ship, which he regarded as an honourable exile. Floridablanca acceded to his request to be relieved of his post and on 29 January 1788 appointed as his successor the duque de Fernán-Núñez. Hardly had he arrived in Madrid than Aranda's restless character appeared. Indignant that the *golilla* Floridablanca should still be at the head of affairs, Aranda, heading the Aragonese cabal, began to intrigue against him.

Aranda had not long to wait to a find a motive for attacking Florida-blanca. Exasperated by a decree which extended the style of Excellency to those who wore the Grand Cross of Carlos III, such as Floridablanca, he wrote to the King and then to Jerónimo Caballero, Minister of War. Shortly afterwards an anonymous and libellous pamphlet appeared, entitled *Conversación que tuvieron los condes Floridablanca y Campomanes el 20 de junio de 1788*. The pamphlet gained great popularity, equal to that of the story called *El Raposo (The Fox)*, which appeared in the *Diario de Madrid* and which alluded to Floridablanca.[107] María Luisa de las Asturias, future Queen of Spain, detested Floridablanca and carried her weak husband, the future Carlos IV, along with her. As a result Floridablanca took action against his Aragonese enemies. The marqués de Rubí was sent to Prussia as ambassador, while O'Reilly, involved in circulating the satire, was sent on a mission to Galicia, and his brother-in-law Luis de las Casas, Governor of Oran, who was on leave in Madrid, returned hastily to his post. Finally, Aranda himself, in whose house gatherings of Floridablanca's enemies were held, was severely reprimanded by Campomanes, President of the Council of Castile.

Other pamphleteering attacks followed, and Floridablanca, weary of the thrusts against him, drew up a memorial justifying his political conduct since 1777, when he first became Minister, and asked the King to allow him to resign; but Carlos III would not hear of it.[108]

Family misfortunes embittered Carlos's last days with the death of the Infanta María Ana Victoria, her husband Gabriel and their son Carlos José. The King who according to his invariable timetable was due to go to spend some time in the Escorial, stayed on in the palace of San Lorenzo, having a presentiment of his approaching end. On 12 December 1788 he took to his bed with a strong cold, which quickly developed into a high fever, and he died on the fourteenth, having made his will and sealed it. Two days before his death he had recommended the loyal Floridablanca to his son, who now became Carlos IV.

Carlos III was a monarch who truly governed. Already in Naples (until 1759) he had shown himself to be one of the keenest enlightened despots. When he became King of Spain he was a man of mature judgement, influenced in great measure by the intelligent Tanucci, his chief minister in Naples and a vigorous exponent of enlightened ideas. Upright, inflexible and reasonable, he always fulfilled his kingly duties with mechanical exactitude. He united a sincere religious faith with a surprising freedom of mind. Without outstanding talents, he had a correct judgement, a real feeling for the nation at large and the perception to choose men of merit, and he was very loyal to his ministers. Strongly bent on reforms, he was wont to say of his Spanish subjects: *Mis vasallos son como los niños, lloran cuando los lavan* (my subjects are like children, who cry when they are washed).[109] Apart from these qualities, his measures have been much discussed. There has been an abundance of panegyrists and some detractors of Carlos III. His external policy was often dictated by prejudice, such as his hatred of Great Britain; and this hate led him unwisely to participate in the American War of Independence, whose successful outcome did much to bring about the loss of the Spanish Empire on the continent of America one generation later. He was much more successful in his home policy, and many of his reforms were of outstanding value. In his expulsion of the Jesuits, which deserves much criticism, he simply followed the policy of enlightened despots everywhere, who saw in the Society a spiritual and political rivalry to threaten their own. It was also a blow against the Papacy, for the Society was always known as the strong arm and support of the Vatican, and this at a time when nationalistic tendencies were nurtured by the enlightened despots who wished to keep the Pope's influence as something distant and vague, while they were left free to wield their autocracy. Furthermore, it was an action which members of all the other religious orders approved of as removing from the scene a hated and powerful rival, having the ear of Rome and controlling education. In the long run, however, it was an unwise deed which caused untold harm to Spain in the New World.

Granted some imperfections, it is safe to state that Carlos was a good king, the best that Spain had had since the sixteenth century (although Ferdinand VI in his earlier years was responsible for a rule as attractive as it is underestimated), and such a one as the country was not to enjoy again until the third quarter of the nineteenth century with Alfonso XII. Carlos III was devoted to an enlightened policy of material and cultural progress but, like Joseph II of Austria, another in many ways attractive enlightened despot, he sowed his seed in soil that was not ready for it, as can, sadly enough, be so clearly seen in the dismal reign of his incompetent son and in the reigns that followed.

Notes

INTRODUCTION

1. The two great classical works on the *Consejo de Castilla* are: A. Martínez Salazar, *Colección de memorias y noticias del gobierno y político del Consejo* (Madrid, 1764); and P. Escolano de Arrieta, *Práctica del Consejo Real en el despacho de los negocios consultativos, instructivos y contenciosos* . . . (Madrid, 1796). They contain a wealth of information and are essential for the subject of statecraft.

2. G. N. Desdevises du Dézert, 'Les Institutions de l'Espagne au XVIIIe Siècle', *Revue Hispanique*, June and August, 1927.

3. The *comuneros* troubles.

4. Carlos III very soon after his Spanish succession became a widower.

5. For a survey of Spanish institutions in the eighteenth century see G. N. Desdevises du Dézert, *op. cit.*

6. P. R. Campomanes, *Cartas politico-económicas*, ed. A. Rodríguez Villa (Madrid, 1878).

7. For an account of its history, its complicated constitution and a plan of reform addressed to Carlos IV see G. M. de Jovellanos, 'Consulta del real y supremo Consejo de las Órdenes', *Bibl. Aut. Esp.*, vol. XLVI, 1858 (rep. 1963), pp. 457–76.

8. Decree of 8 July.

9. A. Baudrillart, *Philippe V et la cour de France*, 5 vols. (Paris, 1890) vol. I, pp. 575–7.

10. Such dress is to be seen in portraits of, for example, Francisco de Urquijo (Museo de Vitoria, Álava) and Ramón de Pignatelli (Col. Pano, Zaragoza).

11. Many examples and facts mentioned here are to be found in that mine of information, J. Santos Sánchez, *Extracto puntual de todas las pragmáticas, cédulas, provisiones, circulares, publicadas en el reinado del señor Don Carlos III* (Madrid, 1792–93).

12. J. Mercader Riba, 'La ordenación de Cataluña por Felipe V: la Nueva Planta', *Hispania*, XLIII, pp. 257–366.

13. G. N. Desdevises du Dézert, *L'Espagne de l'ancien régime*, 3 vols. (Paris, 1897–1904) vol. I, pp. 122ff.

14. J. Santos Sánchez, *op. cit.*, real cédula, 12 enero de 1740.

15. J. Santos Sánchez, *op. cit.*, 28 noviembre.

16. *Novísima recopilación de las leyes de España*, Bk. V, tit. X, (Madrid, 1805).

17. G. N. Desdevises du Dézert, *Rev. Hisp.*, June 1927, p. 149.

18. Ibid., p. 150.

19. J. Yanguas y Miranda, *Diccionario de Antigüedades del reino de Navarra* (3 vols.), (Madrid, 1840), vol. III, p. 527.

20. J. Santos Sánchez, *op. cit.*, ordenanza, 13 octubre de 1749.

21. Until 30 November 1800 when they were placed under military authority.

22. G. N. Desdevises du Dézert, *L'Espagne de l'ancien régime*, vol. I, pp. 121–40, for the different officers and institutions.

23. *Ibid.*, pp. 52–3 and 61.
24. But in fairness to him it must be taken into account that the Archduke Charles had presided over the Catalan *cortes* in 1705.
25. The future Luis I.
26. W. Coxe, *Historical Memoirs of the Kings of Spain of the House of Bourbon*, vol. II, pp. 137–40 (London, 1815).
27. *Ibid.*, p. 142.
28. M. Dánvila y Collado, *Historia del Reinado de Carlos III*, vol. II, pp. 92–3 (Madrid, 1893–95).

PART ONE   THE REIGN OF FELIPE V (1700–46)

1. For this will see: F. Nicolini, *L'Europa durante la guerra*, pp. 167–8, trans. in W. N. Hargreaves-Mawdsley, *Spain under the Bourbons, 1700–1833*, pp. 1ff. Louis was most surprised at the will of Carlos, never expecting he would favour France, see duque de Maura, *Vida y reinado de Carlos II*, vol. III, p. 417.
2. For a personal account of the question of the Spanish succession see L. de Saint-Simon, *Historical Memoirs* (ed. and trans. Lucy Norton, 3 vols., London, 1967–72), vol. I, pp. 136ff.
3. A constant source of reference on French influence on Spain in the eighteenth century is F. Mérimée, *L'influence français en Espagne au XVIIIe siècle* (Paris, 1936).
4. For a contemporary account of the very beginning of Felipe V's reign (1700–01) see B. M., MS Sloane 3958, especially fos. 31 and 33. Much valuable contemporary evidence, used in the following pages, is to be found in B. M. MS Add. 34,142 (fos. 1–254 *in toto*), 'Historia Politica y secreta del Rey Philipe [*sic*] V desde su ingreso a la Corona de España en 1701 hasta la Paz general, celebrada en 1719'.
5. A. Baudrillart, *Philippe V et la cour de France*, 5 vols. (Paris, 1890) vol. I, p. 566.
6. F. Rousseau, *Un réformateur français en Espagne au XVIIIe siècle: Orry, 1701–1714*, (Paris, 1912), p. 16.
7. A quaint amateur study, most laudatory to the subject, is: Constance Hill, *Story of the Princess des Ursins* (New York, 1899).
8. F. Combes, *La Princesse des Ursins: essai sur sa vie et son caractère politique* (Paris, 1858), p. 17.
9. For an account of the War's origins see M. A. Thompson, 'Louis XIV and the Origin of the War of the Spanish Succession', *Transactions of the Royal Historical Society*, 5th Ser., iv (1954), pp. 111–34. For a detailed account of the conduct of the war behind the scenes see H. A. F. Kamen, *The War of Succession in Spain, 1700–15*, (London, 1969) pp. 60–80. See also: A. Parnell, *The War of Succession in Spain during the Reign of Queen Anne, 1702–1711* (London, 1905), a work interpreting the English standpoint, to be set against which is V. Bacallar y Sanna, *Comentarios de la guerra de España e historia de su rey Felipe V, el Animoso* (Madrid, 1957).
10. A vivid account of the War by a French courtier, and so seen from a distance, is to be found in L. de Saint-Simon, *op. cit.*, vol. I. pp. 173ff. For Felipe V's part in it, see *Ibid.* pp. 267ff. and 461ff. See also Rousset de Courcy (marquis M. R.), *La Coalition de 1701 contre la France (1700–1715)*, 2 vols. (Paris, 1886).

11. [F. Wrangham], *The British Plutarch*, 8 vols. (Perth, 1795), V, pp. 58ff.
12. From 1703 to 1706 one is aided by an interesting and informative, if somewhat rambling, account of the War to be found in 'Noticias individuales de los sucesos más particulares tanto de Estado como de Guerra, acontecidos en el Reynado de Felipe V . . .'. They are in the form of four letters purporting to be written by a monk to a gentleman, but are by Melchor de Macanaz (B. M. MS Egerton 390, fos. 19–112).
13. For an account of the conquest of Gibraltar from the Allies' point of view, see W. N. Hargreaves-Mawdsley, *op. cit.*, pp. 21–5; [F. Wrangham,] *op. cit.*, V, pp. 65–7.
14. [F. Wrangham,] *op. cit.*, V, p. 50.
15. A. Baudrillart, *Philippe V et la cour de France*, vol. I, p. 80.
16. A. Baudrillart, *op. cit.*, vol. I, pp. 216ff.
17. P. Voltes Bou, *El archiduque Carlos de Austria, rey de los catalanes*, (Barcelona, 1953) pp. 86–101.
18. For the campaign in Barcelona, Valencia and adjacent theatres of war from 1705 to 1708 from the Allies' point of view, see B. M. MS Add. 28,058, 'Official Papers relating to military operations in Spain sent to Sidney Godolphin, 1st Earl Godolphin, Lord High Treasurer of Great Britain', § 1, fos. 1–29.
19. For an account of this siege see: W. N. Hargreaves-Mawdsley, *op. cit.*, pp. 26–34. See also A. Baudrillart, *op. cit.*, vol. I, pp. 251–5; A. Vovard, 'Le siège de Barcelone en 1706', *Communications et Mémoires de l'Académie de Marine*, XIV (1935), pp. 139–161.
20. A. Baudrillart, *op. cit.*, vol. I pp. 267–71.
21. Felipe's delight is shown in his address to the University of Salamanca (W. N. Hargreaves-Mawdsley, *op. cit.*, pp. 34–5).
22. For Berwick in Spain, see L. de Saint-Simon, *op. cit.*, vol. II, pp. 86–7.
23. For the siege and capture of Lérida, see A. L. Javierre, 'Las cartas del duque de Orleans a Felipe V sobre el sitio de Lérida en 1707', *Ilerda*, IV (1946), pp. 93–119.
24. The treatment meted out to Aragón and Valencia appears in N. de J. Belando, *Historia civil de España*, pt. 1, pp. 316ff., trans. W. N. Hargreaves-Mawdsley, *op. cit.*, pp. 35–6.
25. A. Baudrillart, *op. cit.*, vol. II, pp. 17ff.
26. He was to become Regent of France on the death of Louis XIV in 1715.
27. The Archduke Charles had been in correspondence with Queen Anne, certainly since 1704; see B. M. Add. MS 29,548, fol. 43, Charles III, titular King of Spain to Q. Anne, 9 Feb. 1704.
28. M. Menéndez y Pelayo, *Historia de los Heterodoxos españoles*, (Madrid, 1880–82), vol. III, cap. i, § ii–v.
29. For the relationship between Felipe V and the Vatican, see B. M., MS Add. 21, 535, 'Papeles especiales sobre puntos ecclesiásticos y controversias con la corte Romana, 1508–1736', the second part of which contains letters addressed to Antonio Ibanes de' la Riva Herrera, Archbishop of Zaragoza, Inquisitor General. See especially § 2, fos. 222–24 and 242–50, being letters written by Felipe V from Madrid on 19 June and 10 July 1709.
30. For Villars, see C. C. Sturgill, *Marshal Villars and the War of the Spanish Succession* (London, 1966).

31. Province of Cáceres. This fine old bridge was built in 1552 to open a communication with La Mancha.

32. For Felipe V at these battles, see L. de Saint-Simon, *op. cit.*, vol. II, pp. 99–101.

33. For Vendôme in Spain, a highly unflattering portrait by one who hated him, see L. de Saint-Simon, *op. cit.*, vol. II, pp. 96ff.

34. See A. Baudrillart, *op. cit.*, vol. I, pp. 409ff. for a general account of this campaign.

35. For the Peace Treaties see: A. Robledo, *Tratados de Utrecht. Reseña histórica de la paz general de 1713* (Madrid, 1846); O. Weber, *Der Friede von Utrecht. Verhandlungen zwischen England, Frankreich, der Kaiser und die General Staaten, 1710–1713* (Gotha, 1892); *Tratados de España. Colección desde Felipe V hasta el presente*, 3 vols. (Madrid, 1796–1801); and M. R. Rousset de Courcy, *Renonciation des Bourbons au trône de France* (Paris, 1889).

36. A Baudrillart, *op. cit.*, vol. I, pp. 409ff.

37. A. Baudrillart, *op. cit.*, vol. I, pp. 475–7.

38. A. Baudrillart, *ibid.*, pp. 488–501. There is little doubt, however, that Felipe regretted this decision in later years. His later mental illness was increased by a longing for France, from which he was now for ever exiled.

39. A. Baudrillart, *ibid.*, pp. 502–14; N. de J. Belando, *Historia civil de España*, pt. 1, pp. 542ff.

40. A. Baudrillart, *op. cit.*, p. 516.

41. The main articles of the Treaty of Utrecht are given in N. de J. Belando, *Historia civil de España*, pt. 1, pp. 650ff, trans. W. N. Hargreaves-Mawdsley, *op. cit.*, pp. 48–52. The clauses concerning the Netherlands, particularly the trade agreements, are given in N. de J. Belando, *op. cit.*, pt. 4, pp. 48ff, trans. W. N. Hargreaves-Mawdsley, *op. cit.*, pp. 53–7. For political reasons Belando's generally very impartial review of Spanish affairs between 1713 and 1733 was unfairly attacked after its publication in 1740. Melchor de Macanaz flew to its defence and exposed the criticisms for what they were. See B. M., MS 28,479, 'Defensa de la Historia civil de España de el Reynado del Señor Don Felipe V escrita por Fray Nicolás de Jesús Belando de la Descalzé de S. Francisco' by Melchor Rafael de Macanaz, preceded by a complaint of Belando to Felipe V, with notes by Macanaz (?1744).

42. The consequences of the War for Spain are well summed up in H. A. F. Kamen, *The War of Succession in Spain, 1700–15* (London, 1969), pp. 361ff.

43. Although he half-heartedly pledged himself to do so in an article of the Quadruple Alliance (1718).

44. For a particularly vivid account of affairs in Barcelona, 1711–14 see B. M. MS Egerton 363 (suppl.) *in toto*.

45. He wrote in praise of the Catalans, calling them a 'valiant people', to Queen Anne declaring that they must not be abandoned 'to the yoke of the Bourbon House' (S. Sanpere y Miquel, *El fin de la nación catalana*, p. 6).

46. T. A. T. de Belmont, *Histoire de la dernière revolte des catalans et du siège de Barcelone* (Lyon, 1714).

47. S. Sanpere y Miquel, *op. cit.*, p. 66. She had held court in Barcelona for several years.

48. F. Soldevila, *Historia de Catalunya* (3 vols. Barcelona, 1934–35), vol. II, p. 391.

49. N. de J. Belando, *Historia civil de España*, pt. 1, pp. 650ff, trans. W. N. Hargreaves-Mawdsley, *op. cit.*, p. 50.

50. S. Sanpere y Miquel, *op. cit.*, pp. 564–5; F. Soldevila, *op. cit.*, vol. II, pp. 422–9.

51. A. Baudrillart, *op. cit.*, vol. I, p. 561.

52. For the popular hatred of him, see Bibliothèque nationale, Paris, Archives Espagnoles, Correspondence politique (Espagne) MS 237, fo. 99.

53. A. Baudrillart, *op. cit.*, vol. I, pp. 571–3.

54. A. Baudrillart, *op. cit.*, vol. I, pp. 579–90.

55. N. de J. Belando, *op. cit.*, pt. IV, pp. 48ff, trans. W. N. Hargreaves-Mawdsley, *op. cit.*, pp. 53–7. For a very detailed account of the effect of the whole war on Spain see H. A. F. Kamen, *op. cit.*, pp. 361ff.

56. For his career see S. Harcourt-Smith, *Alberoni, or The Spanish Conspiracy* (London, 1943), an attractively written book and easily available. The standard work is P. Castagnoli, *Il Cardinale Giulio Alberoni*, (3 vols., Piacenza/Rome, 1929–32).

57. A. Baudrillart, *op. cit.*, pp. 595–614.

58. E. Rosseew-Saint-Hilaire, *La princesse des Ursins* (Paris, 1875).

59. E. Armstrong, *Elisabeth Farnese 'The termagant of Spain'* (London, 1892).

60. A. Baudrillart, *op. cit.*, vol. I, p. 603.

61. S. Sanpere y Miquel, *op. cit.*, pp. 595–618.

62. Article V of the Treaty of Utrecht, W. N. Hargreaves-Mawdsley, *op. cit.*, p. 49.

63. A. Baudrillart; *op. cit.*, vol. II, pp. 236–48. For the period 1717–22 I have made use of B. M., MS Add. 10,240, Anon. 'Historia de España, 1712–25', fos. 68–144. The earlier and later part of this MS is rather perfunctory, while the middle section is detailed.

64. A. Baudrillart, *op. cit.*, vol. II, pp. 265–76.

65. A. Baudrillart, *op. cit.*, vol. II, pp. 276–313.

66. W. N. Hargreaves-Mawdsley, *op. cit.*, pp. 61–2. This, of course, was the father of the unfortunate Admiral George Byng of the ill-starred Menorca expedition (1756).

67. N. de J. Belando, *op. cit.*, pt. 4, pp. 191–3, trans. W. N. Hargreaves-Mawdsley, *op. cit.*, pp. 65–8.

68. A. Baudrillart, *op. cit.*, vol. II, pp. 326ff.

69. Who was that very year killed at the siege of Fredrikshald (Halden), Norway.

70. F. Soldevila, *op. cit.*, vol. III, pp. 23–4; J. Mercader Riba, 'El valle de Arán, la Nueva Planta y la invasión anglofrancesa de 1719', *Primer congreso Internacional del Pirineo* (Zaragoza, 1952).

71. A. Baudrillart, *op. cit.*, vol. II, p. 400.

72. A striking face to face portrait of Felipe V and an account of his private life and character at this time are to be found in L. de Saint-Simon, *op. cit.*, vol. III, pp. 326ff and 352–7.

73. N. de J. Belando, *op. cit.*, pt. 4, pp. 253–5, trans. W. N. Hargreaves-Mawdsley, *op. cit.*, pp. 69–70.

74. The terms of this treaty are set out in A. Baudrillart, *op. cit.*, vol. II, pp. 403–57.

75. A. Baudrillart, *op. cit.*, vol. II, p. 467; P. Bliard, 'La question de Gibraltar au

temps du Régent, d'après les correspondances officielles, 1720–1721', *Revue des Questions historiques*, LVII (1895), pp. 192–209.

76. A. Baudrillart, *op. cit.*, vol. II, pp. 469–502.

77. A. Baudrillart, *op. cit.*, vol. II, p. 539.

78. B. M., MS Add. 10,252, 'Papeles varios', fos. 21–23, 'Renuncia de Felipe V, 1724'.

79. N. de J. Belando, *op. cit.*, pt. 4, pp. 320–1, trans. W. N. Hargreaves-Mawdsley, *op. cit.*, pp. 83–4; J. Maldonado Macanaz, Voto y renuncia del Rey don Felipe V', *Discursos leidos ante la Real Academia de la Historia* (Madrid, 1894), pp. 41–6.

80. M. Dánvila y Collado, *El reinado relámpago: Luis I y Luisa Isabel de Orléans, 1707–42* (Madrid, 1952).

81. Cartas de don Juan Bautista Orendayn, 1724–33 (B. M. Egerton MSS 365–6). The following are especially important: Egerton 365 (vol. i), §§ 6, 8, 19, 28, 35, 39 and Egerton 366 (vol. ii), §§ 49, 55, 61, 72, 78, 85, 96.

82. A. Baudrillart, 'L'influence française en Espagne au temps de Louis I; mission du maréchal de Tessé' in *Revue des Questions historiques*, LVIII (1896), p. 485.

83. A. Pimodan, *Louise-Elisabeth d'Orléans, reine d'Espagne (1709–1742)*, 2nd edn (Paris, 1923).

84. A. Baudrillart, *op. cit.*, vol. III, p. 19.

85. J. Olmedilla y Puig, *Noticias históricas acerca de la última enfermedad del Rey de España Luis I* (Madrid, 1909).

86. J. Maldonado Macanaz, 'Voto y renuncia del Rey don Felipe V', *Discursor leidos ante la Real Academia de la Historia* (Madrid, 1894), p. 46.

87. W. N. Hargreaves-Mawdsley, *op. cit.*, pp. 85–6; J. Maldonado Macanaz, *op. cit.*, pp. 47–55.

88. On Ripperdá, see: G. Syveton, *Une cour et un aventurier au XVIIIe siècle. Le Baron de Ripperdá d'après des documents inédits des archives impériales de Vienne et des archives du Ministère des Affaires étrangères de Paris.* (Paris, 1896). S. A. Mañer, *Historia del Duque de Ripperdá* (Madrid, 1796).

89. For these early years see A. Rodríguez Villa, 'Informaciones del Marqués de Berreti-Landy [sic] sobre antecedentes del barón de Ripperdá antes de su embajada en Viena', *Boletín de la Real Academia de la Historia*, XXXI (1897), pp. 221–5.

90. A. Rodríguez Villa, *ibid*.

91. A. Rodríguez Villa, 'La embajada del barón de Ripperdá en Viena (1725); *Revue Historique*, XXX, 1897.

92. N. de J. Belando, *op. cit.*, pt. 4, pp. 382–9, trans. W. N. Hargreaves-Mawdsley, *op. cit.*, pp. 86–90. They are discussed in A. del Cantillo, *Tratados* (Madrid, 1843), pp. 202ff.

93. N. de J. Belando, *op. cit.*, pt. 4, pp. 383–9; W. N. Hargreaves-Mawdsley, *op. cit.*, pp. 88–90. Here and elsewhere below use has been made of additions to Belando's published work, often of value, to be found in B. M., MS Add. 28,480, 'Breve Compendio con Adiciones al Tomo 3º de la Historia Civil de España desde el año de 1713 al de 1733, escrita por el P. F. Nicolás de Jesús Belando, Francisco Descalzo', written by Melchor de Macanaz between 1740 and 1744.

94. A. del Cantillo, *Tratados, convenios y declaraciones de paz y de comercio que han hecho con las potencias extranjeras los Monarchas españoles de la Casa de Borbón desde el oño*

de 1700 hasta el dia, 4 parts (Madrid, 1843), pp. 231–6.

95. R. Beltrán y Rózpide, 'Ripperdá en Africa', *Ilustración Española y Americana*, 1894.

96. 1670 is also given.

97. A. Rodríguez Villa, *Patiño y Campillo. Reseña histórico-biográfica de estos dos ministros de Felipe V* (Madrid, 1882). 'Fragmentos históricos para la vida del señor D. José Patiño', *Seminario Erúdito*, XXVIII, p. 72.

98. A. Baudrillart, *op. cit.*, vol. III, p. 251.

99. C. A. Montgon, *Mémoires* (9 vols., The Hague, 1745–53). It contains much that is interesting, but should be used with some caution.

100. T. A. Girard, 'La folie de Philippe V', *Feuilles d'histoire du XVIIIe au XIXe siècle*, vol. III (*Revue Historique*, Paris, 1910).

101. M. Fernández. *Diario de lo ocurrido en el sitio de Gibraltar, que se principió en Febrero de 1727* (Madrid, 1781).

102. A. del Cantillo, *op. cit.*, pp. 243–4.

103. T. A. Girard, *op. cit.*

104. Felipe V was always homesick for France, and this was one of the contributory factors of his illness. For the illness at this stage, see J. -L. Jacquet, *Les Bourbons d'Espagne* (Lausanne, 1968), pp. 104–8. 'He would have preferred to rule and live in France', states Saint-Simon, *op. cit.*, vol. III, p. 358.

105. A del Cantillo, *op. cit.*, pp. 247–60.

106. T. A. Girard, *op. cit.*,

107. He had died on 20 January 1731.

108. On 6 June at Sevilla, Great Britain promised to support Spain's claims in Italy.

109. A. del Cantillo, *op. cit.*, pp. 263ff. This is known as the Second Treaty of Vienna.

110. For the wretched plight of Gian Gastone as the diplomatic pawn of the rivals of Austria and Spain, see G. F. Young, *The Medici* (N.Y. Modern Library, 1930), pp. 731–5.

111. A. Baudrillart, *op. cit.*, vol. IV, p. 117, where he mistakenly refers to *Miguel Reggio* as *Andrés*.

112. P. de la Cueva, *Iconismos o verdadera descripción de la expedición de Africa, en que las Reales Armas de S. M. recobraron a Mazalquivir, Oran y sus castillos* (Granada, n. d.); N. de J. Belando, *op. cit.*, pt. 4, p. 540; W. N. Hargreaves-Mawdsley, *op. cit.*, pp. 91–7.

113. P. Cardona, *La guerra tra Spagna ed Austria in Italia durante la lotta per la successione al trono di Polonia* (Catania, 1913).

114. P. Boyé, *Stanislas Leszczinski et le troisième traité de Vienne* (Paris, 1898).

115. E. de Ferrater, *Código de derecho internacional*, vol. I, pp. 154ff; the most important articles are translated in W. N. Hargreaves-Mawdsley, *op. cit.*, pp. 97–8.

116. For this part of the campaign, see A. Baudrillart, *op. cit.*, vol. IV, pp. 202–14.

117. A. Baudrillart, *op. cit.*, vol. IV, pp. 226–39.

118. A. Baudrillart, *op. cit.*, vol. IV, pp. 239–40ff.

119. A. Gadaleta, *Relazione de Spagna del cav. A. Cappello, ambasciatore a Filippo V dall'anno 1735 al 1738* (Florence, 1896). Baudrillart, *op. cit.*, vol. IV, p. 456.

120. For diplomatic relations between Great Britain and Spain, see J. Rousset de

Missy, *Le procès entre la Grande-Bretagne et l'Espagne, ou Recueil des Traitez, Conventions, Mémoires et autres Pièces touchant les Démélez entre ces deux couronnes* (The Hague, 1740).

121. For Britain's naval history at this time, see H. W. Richmond, 'The Navy in the War of 1739–1748' in *History*, Oct., 1924.
122. A. Baudrillart, *op. cit.*, vol. V, pp. 48–57; W. Coxe, *Historical Memoirs of the Kings of Spain of the House of Bourbon,* (London, 1815), vol. III, pp. 428–38.
123. A. Rodríguez Villa, *Patiño y Campillo* (Madrid, 1882).
124. A. del Cantillo, *op. cit.*, pp. 346–9.
125. A. Baudrillart, *op. cit.*, vol. V, p. 106.
126. That he had in mind a comprehensive programme for Spain and saw its affairs in the round can be seen in the two masterly treatises which he wrote between August 1741 and February 1742, 'Lo que hay de mas y de menos en España paraque sea lo que debir ser y no lo es' and 'España despierta. Criticas e instructivas reflexiones Correspondientes a varios e importantísimos asumptos para la mejor organización y regimen de la Monarchía Española'. (B. M. MS Add 25,684, §§ 1 and 2, 'Obras inéditas del Ministro Campillo, transcr. por Francisco Maldonado, enero de 1804).
127. A. Rodríguez Villa, *Don Cenón de Somodevilla, marqués de la Ensenada* (Madrid, 1878).
128. W. N. Hargreaves-Mawdsley, *op. cit.*, p. 107.
129. R. Auñón y Villalón, *Episodios maritimos* (Cartagena, 1913), § 'El combate de Cabo Sicié (1744)'.
130. E. Zévort, *Le marquis d'Argenson* (Paris, 1880).
131. A. Baudrillart, *op. cit.*, vol. V, pp. 364ff.
132. A. Baudrillart, *op. cit.*, vol. V, p. 392.
133. A. Baudrillart, *op. cit.*, vol. V, pp. 436–8.
134. A. Baudrillart, *op. cit.*, vol. V, p. 437.
135. V. Vignau y Ballester, 'Papeles referentes a la muerte de Felipe V y coronación de Fernando VI', in *Revista de Archivos, Bibliotecas y Museos,* III (1899).

PART TWO   THE REIGN OF FERNANDO VI (1746–59)

1. For the personality and reign of Fernando VI, see M. Dánvila y Collado, *Estudios españoles del siglo XVIII. Fernando VI y Doña Bárbara de Braganza* (Madrid, 1905); A. García Rives, *Fernando VI y Doña Bárbara de Braganza. Apuntes sobre su reinado* (Madrid, 1917). Some of the following information is to be found in the latter part of the important document (B. M. Add MS 15,576) 'Historia del Reynado de Felipe 5' (which actually goes to 1762), fos. 58–212. For a summary of court affairs during this reign see P. Zabala y Lera, *España bajo los Borbones*, 5th edn (Barcelona, 1955), pp. 45–9.
2. Her complicated will, 'Testamento de la Reyna Bárbara' is to be found in B. M. Add. MS 10,252, 'Papeles varios', fos. 24–49.
3. Like Felipe V he suffered from priapism.
4. For this aspect of Fernando, see the first-hand account of his physician Piquer 'Discurso sobre la enfermedad del Rey Fernando VI', *Colección de documentos*

inéditos, XVIII, pp. 156–7; & that of his confessor in C. Pérez Bustamente, *Correspondencia privada e inédita del P. Rávago confesor de Fernando VI* (Madrid, 1936). See also C. Stryienski, 'Fernand VI, roi d'Espagne' in *Chronique Médicale*, 15 Nov. 1902.

5. A. Baudrillart, *Philippe V et la cour de France* (Paris, 1890), vol. V, pp. 485–9.

6. W. N. Hargreaves-Mawdsley, *Spain under the Bourbons, 1700–1833. A Collection of Documents* (London, 1973), pp. 109–13. It is noticeable (p. 113) that Sotomayor's name is not among the signatories. Thus Spain did not sign.

7. Much that is interesting about him, especially the influence of Spanish popular music on his own, is to be found in G. Chase, *The Music of Spain*, 2nd edn rev., (New York 1972), pp. 108–14. See also R. Kirkpatrick, *Domenico Scarlatti* (Princeton, 1952), pp. 81–133.

8. M. Mozas Mesa, *Don José de Carvajal y Láncaster, Ministro de Fernando VI* (Jaén, 1924). Mª. D. Gómez Molleda, 'El pensamiento de Carvajal y la política internacional española del siglo XVIII in *Hispania*, XV (1955), pp. 117–37.

9. In thus setting down his 'political testament' he displays the influence of his mentor Campillo, who had drawn up his in 1742 (B. M. MS Add. 25,684), see above n. 126.

10. A. Rodríguez Villa, *Don Cenón de Somodevilla, marqués de la Ensenada* (Madrid, 1878). J. M. de Aranda, *El marqués de la Ensenada. Estudios sobre su administración* (Madrid, 1898). R. Bouvier and C. Soldevila, *Ensenada et son temps* (Paris, 1941).

11. A. del Cantillo, *Tratados convenios y declaraciones de paz y de comercio que han hecho con las potencias extranjeras los Monarchas españoles de la Casa de Borbón desde el año de 1700 hasta el dia*, 4 pts., (Madrid, 1843), pp. 400–8.

12. C. Calvo, *Colección completa de los tratados de la América Latina* (Paris, 1862), vol. II, pp. 241–60.

13. A. Bermejo de la Rica, *La colonia del Sacramento* (Toledo, 1920), pp. 55–6.

14. W. Coxe, *Historical Memoirs of the Kings of Spain of the House of Bourbon* (London, 1815), vol. IV, p. 180.

15. A. Rodríguez Villa, *op. cit.*, p. 281.

16. M. Menéndez y Pelayo, *Historia de los Heterodoxos españoles* (3 vols.), (Madrid, 1880–82), vol. III, pp. 45–67; R. S. de Lamadrid, *El concordato español de 1753, según los documentos originales de su negociación* (Jérez, 1937). A short appraisal of it is to be found in R. Herr, *The Eighteenth-Century Revolution in Spain* (Princeton, 1958), p. 13.

17. The text of the concordat is given in *Mercurio Histórico y Político*, Madrid, marzo, 1753, pp. 63–8 and 70–9; it is translated in W. N. Hargreaves-Mawdsley, *op. cit.*, pp. 113–21.

18. M. Fraile Miguélez, *Jansenismo y Regalismo en España (datos para la historia). Cartas al señor Menéndez Pelayo* (Valladolid, 1895).

19. C. Pérez Bustamente, *op. cit.*

20. H. W. Richmond, *Papers relating to the Loss of Minorca in 1756* (London, 1913).

21. For this and similar negotiations between Pitt's government and Spain see V. Palacio Atard, 'Las embajadas de Abreu y Fuentes en Londres, 1754–1761', *Simancas*, I (1950), pp. 55–122.

22. See B. M. Add. 10,252, 'Papeles varios', fos. 24–49, 'Testamento de la Reyna Bárbara'.

23. A. Piquer, *op. cit.*, p. 156; C. Pérez Bustamente, *op. cit.*; C. Stryienski, *op. cit.*

24. The cold relationship between Carlos and Fernando VI is noted in C. Petrie, *King Charles III of Spain: an Enlightened Despot* (London, 1971), pp. 61–62.

25. M. Menéndez y Pelayo, *op. cit.*, vol. III, p. 60.

26. L. de Saint-Simon, *Historical Memoirs of the Duke de Saint-Simon* (ed. and trans. Lucy Norton), (3 vols.), (London, 1967–72), p. 109, n. 1.

PART THREE   THE REIGN OF CARLOS III (1759–88)

1. For Carlos III see, M. Dánvila y Collado, *Historia del Reinado de Carlos III* (6 vols.), (Madrid, 1891–96); F. Rousseau, *Règne de Charles III d'Espagne (1759–1788)* (2 vols.), (Paris, 1907); A. Baudrillart, 'Le roi d'Espagne Charles III' (review of Rousseau's work), *La Correspondant*, 25 avril 1907; J. Addison, *Charles III of Spain* (Oxford, 1900).

2. *Real cédula* 23 de junio de 1768.

3. The review of Spain's naval power which he ordered to be drawn up appears in B. M. MS Add. 20,926, § 3. (fos. 19–21), 'Estado actual de las fuerzas navales de S. M. Católico en primero de agosto de 1760'.

4. V. Palacio Atard, 'Las embajadas de Abreu y Fuentes en Londres, 1754–1761, *Simancas*, I (1950), pp. 55–122.

5. F. Rousseau, *Règne de Charles III d'Espagne, 1759–88* (2 vols.), (Paris, 1907), vol. I, p. 52.

6. *Ibid.*, p. 69.

7. F. Rousseau, *op. cit.*, vol. I, pp. 54ff.

8. F. Rousseau, *op. cit.*, vol. I, pp. 61–4.

9. V. Palacio Atard, *El tercer Pacto de Familia*, pp. 121ff and 348ff; the Third Family Compact (4 Feb. 1762) is translated in W. N. Hargreaves-Mawdsley, *op. cit.*, pp. 126–31.

10. M. Dánvila y Collado, *op. cit.*, vol. II, pp. 148ff.

11. W. N. Hargreaves-Mawdsley, *op. cit.*, p. 122.

12. M. Dánvila y Collado, *op. cit.*, vol. II, pp. 148–58; F. Rousseau, *op. cit.*, vol. I, pp. 69–72. L. Cahen, 'Le Pacte de famille', *Revue Historique* (1925).

13. For the diplomatic treatment of Portugal by the French and Spanish, see A. Bourget, 'Le duc de Choiseul et l'alliance espagnole: un ultimation franco-espagnol au Portugal (1761–1762)', *Revue d'histoire diplomatique*, XXIV (1910), pp. 25–38.

14. For a full account of the campaign in Portugal see conde de Fernán Nuñez, *Vida de Carlos III* (Madrid, 1898), vol. I, pp. 164ff.

15. V. Palacio Atard, *Simancas*, I (1950), pp. 55–122.

16. M. Dánvila y Collado, *op. cit.*, vol. II, p. 186.

17. For a contemporary account of the siege and capture of Manila see N. P. Cushner (ed.) *Documents illustrating the British Conquest of Manila 1762–1763*, *Transactions of the Royal Historical Society, Camden Fourth Series*, vol. 8 (London, 1971).

18. F. Rousseau, *op. cit.*, vol. I, pp. 89–90.

19. Sometimes called Jacob.

20. F. Rousseau, *op. cit.*, vol. I, pp. 106–7.

21. About that time beginning to be thus spelt, a corruption of Peñiscola.

22. But of course, they still had Belize.

23. For the terms of the Treaty of Paris, see *Tratados de España*, vol. III, pp. 235ff. Translations of the most important articles are given in W. N. Hargreaves-Mawdsley, *op. cit.*, pp. 132–4.

24. Bibliotèque nationale (Paris), MS Espagne 424, fo. 284.

25. W. marqués del Villa-Urrutia, *Mujeres de antaño: la reina María Luisa, esposa de Carlos IV* (Madrid, 1927).

26. J. Pérez de Guzmán y Gallo, *La Historia Inédita: estudios de la vida, reinado, proscripción y muerte de Carlos IV y María Luisa* (Madrid, 1908); J. Pérez de Guzmán y Gallo, 'Reparaciones a la vida de Carlos IV y María Luisa', *Rev. de Arch. Bibl. Mus.*, X (1904).

27. The Order is given in *Novísima recopilación de las leyes de España*, Bk. III, § XIX, Law XIII; W. N. Hargreaves-Mawdsley, *op. cit.* pp. 134–5. The two different dresses are illustrated in J. Cayetano Rosell, 'Motín contra Esquilache', *Seminario Pintoresco Español*, 1 (Madrid, 1836), p. 201.

28. Blue bands were often at this time worn with full dress by high officers of state. It was a French fashion in the first place, so must have spread to Spain.

29. 'The marqués de Esquilache hasn't prohibited this!'

30. For the initial riots on 15 and 16 March see the letter written from Madrid (B. M., MS Add. 10,252, fos. 289–297).

31. 'Why don't you observe the order and not wear your hat?'

32. For a general account of the *motín* see M. Dánvila y Collado, *op. cit.*, vol. II, cap. vi; F. Rousseau, *op. cit.*, vol. I, pp. 176ff.

33. *Relación verdadera y circumstanciada de todo lo acaecido en la ciudad de Zaragoza*; W. N. Hargreaves-Mawdsley, *op. cit.*, pp. 136–8.

34. For a short summary of the *motín*, see P. Zabala y Lera, *España bajo los Borbones*, 5th edn. (Barcelona, 1955), pp. 61–63.

35. For Carlos III's appointment of Aranda to be President of the Council of Castile, see M. Dánvila y Collado, *op. cit.*, vol. II, p. 358; W. N. Hargreaves-Mawdsley, *op. cit.*, p. 138.

36. A. Rodriguez Villa, *Don Cenón de Somodevilla, marqués de la Ensenada* (Madrid, 1878), pp. 286–7.

37. C. Eguía Ruiz, *Los jesuítas y el motín de Esquilache* (Madrid, 1947); R. Herr, *The Eighteenth-Century Revolution in Spain* (Princeton, 1958), p. 14, where he points out that the Society of Jesus and the Inquisition were the chief opponents of royal authority.

38. V. Rodríguez Casado, 'La "revolución burguesa" del siglo XVIII español', *Historia de España* (ed. Arbor), pp. 379–81.

39. C. Eguia Ruiz, *El Padre Isidro López y el motín de Esquilache* (Madrid, 1935).

40. F. Espinosa, 'El conde de Aranda', *España Moderna*, CXLIX (1909), p. 5.

41. F. Rousseau, *Expulsion des Jesuites en Espagne. Démarches de Charles III pour leur sécularisation* (Paris, 1904).

42. For the Papacy during the whole of this period, see L. von Pastor, *History of the Popes from the Close of the Middle Ages* (London, 1950).

43. For the Royal Decree of Carlos III regarding Papal authority (1761) see B. M., MS Add. 10,252, fos. 195–201.

44. J. F. de Isla, *Obras Escogidas*, vol. I (Biblioteca de Autores Españoles, XV, Madrid, 1945).

45. P. Fraile Miguélez, *El Jansenismo y Regalismo en España* (Valladolid, 1895), pp. 330ff.

46. M. Menéndez y Pelayo, *Historia de los Heterodoxos españoles* (Madrid, 1880–82), vol. III, pp. 84ff.

47. J. Sarrailh, *L'Espagne éclairée de la seconde moitié du siècle XVIII* (Paris, 1964).

48. L. von Pastor, *op. cit.*, vol. 37, p. 311.

49. *Pragmática sanción de su Majestad en fuerza de ley*; W. N. Hargreaves-Mawdsley, *op. cit.*, pp. 138–44.

50. For the relationship between Carlos III and Aranda, see C. Petrie, *King Charles III of Spain: an Enlightened Despot* (London, 1971), pp. 151–5.

51. For an account of the expulsion in Spanish America, when it was sometimes ruthlessly and cruelly carried out and greatly upset the Indians, see B. Moses, *Spain's Declining Power in South America, 1730–1806* (London, 1965), pp. 97–152.

52. J. de Manterola, *La disolución en España de la Compañía de Jesús* (Barcelona, 1934).

53. A vivid account of the sufferings endured by the Jesuits driven from Spain is to be found in the 'Life of Padre José de Isla', a fine example of a member of the Society (*Obras escogidas del P. José Francisco de Isla*, vol. I, pp. vii–xiv (*Bibl. Aut. Esp.* XV)).

54. See A. Rodríguez Villa, *Introducción a las 'Cartas político-económicas' de Campomanes* (Madrid, 1878), for his general attitude.

55. He had had a change of heart.

56. L. von Pastor, *op. cit.*, vol. 38, p. 73.

57. Such as Theiner.

58. F. Rousseau, *Règne de Charles III*, vol. I, caps. ix–xv.

59. For him and his work as ambassador to the Holy See see M. Cayetano Alcázar, *El conde de Floridablanca* (Madrid, 1929) and J. Sarrailh, *op. cit.*, pp. 588ff.

60. L. von Pastor, *op. cit.*, vol. 38, p. 533.

61. L. von Pastor, *op. cit.*, vol. 39, p. 21.

62. Although Britain had ceded it to Spain at the Treaty of Paris (1763).

63. Of 1762, surrendering Manila, saying that those documents had been superseded by the Treaty of Paris. These documents are given in N. P. Cushner, *op. cit.*, pp. 122–5 and 140–2.

64. J. Goebel, *The Struggle for the Falkland Islands* (New Haven, 1927).

65. L. Blart, *Les rapports de la France et de l'Espagne après le pacte de famille jusqu'à la fin du ministère du duc de Choiseul*, (Paris, 1915).

66. O. Gil Munilla, *El conflicto anglo-español en 1770* (Sevilla, 1948).

67. V. Rodríguez Casado, 'Política marroquí de Carlos III: las misiones diplomaticas de Boltas y Girón . . .', *Hispania*, II (1942), pp. 101–22 and 236–78.

68. A. Rodriguez Villa, 'Una embajada española en Marruecos y estado de este imperio en tiempo de Carlos III (1767)', *Revista Contemporánea*, XXVII (1880), pp. 257–308.

69. F. S. Miranda, *El sitio de Melilla de 1774 a 1775* (ed. R. Fernández de Castro) (Tangier, 1939).

70. For O'Reilly and the expedition see C. Petrie, *op. cit.*, pp. 158–60.

71. See B. M., MS Add. 21,445, 'Papeles históricos', fos. 96–99, 'Noticias de Cádiz: Expedición a Argel'.

72. M. Dánvila y Collado, *Historia del reinado de Carlos III* (Madrid, 1891–96), vol. IV, pp. 206–59.

73. *Gaceta de Madrid,* 18 de julio de 1775; W. N. Hargreaves-Mawdsley, *op. cit.* pp. 149–50.
74. The former ambassador in London.
75. Narrowly patriotic nobles.
76. The lawyers, the new professional men of the Enlightenment.
77. M. Dánvila y Collado, *op. cit.*, vol IV, pp. 317ff; A. Bermejo de la Rica, *La colonia del Sacramento* (Toledo, 1920), pp. 67–73. It was now that the Viceroyalty of La Plata was created.
78. W. N. Hargreaves-Mawdsley, *op. cit.*, pp. 157–8.
79. For a general survey of Spain's part, see F. Morales Padrón, *La Participación de España en la independencia de los Estados Unidos* (Madrid, 1952).
80. J. F. Yela Utrilla, *España ante la independencia de los Estados Unidos* (Lérida, 1925), vol. II, pp. 9–10.
81. *Ibid.*
82. *Ibid.*, pp. 26ff; W. N. Hargreaves-Mawdsley, *op. cit.*, p. 152.
83. J. F. Yela Utrilla, *op. cit.*, vol. II, p. 144.
84. *Ibid.*, pp. 72ff; W. N. Hargreaves-Mawdsley *op. cit.*, pp. 152–5.
85. *Ibid.*, II, p. 94; W. N. Hargreaves-Mawdsley, *op. cit.* pp. 155–6.
86. M. Dánvila y Collado, *op. cit.*, vol. IV, pp. 448ff and vol. V, pp. 1ff.
87. A. Temple Patterson, *The Other Armada. The Franco-Spanish Attempt to invade Britain in 1779* (Manchester, 1960).
88. B. M., MS 10,252, 'Papeles varios', fos. 70–73, 'Letter from Algeciras on News of the Siege of Gibraltar (1779)'; C. Petrie, *op. cit.*, pp. 170ff and 191–5.
89. F. Rousseau, *Règne de Charles III*, vol. II, cap. v, § 2.
90. For Gálvez's exploits, see J. Caughey, *Bernardo de Gálvez in Louisiana, 1776–1783* (Berkeley, 1934).
91. *Diario de la expedición contra la plaza de Panzacola*; W. N. Hargreaves-Mawdsley, *op. cit.*, pp. 159–60.
92. For an earlier and fine account of him see A. Farrer del Río, 'Estudio sobre el conde de Floridablanca', introduction to Floridablanca. *Obras originales* vol. LIX, pp. v–xlv (*Obras originales de Floridablanca, Biblioteca de Autores Españoles*, Madrid, 1867).
93. For his interesting 'political testament' written in 1788 see 'Representación hecha al Sr. Rey Don Carlos 3°' (B. M. MS Add. 29, 299). It is a review of his administration in self-justification against the attacks of his opponents. Following it is an appendix in the form of a letter to Carlos IV recommending it to his judgement, 1789.
94. M. Dánvila y Collado, *op. cit.*, vol. V, pp. 164ff; F. Rousseau, *Règne de Charles III*, vol. II, pp. 189–95; eyewitness account in Bibl. Nat., Paris, Espagne, MS No. 423.
95. F. Rousseau, *Règne de Charles III*, vol. II, pp. 198–202; C. Petrie, *op. cit.*, pp. 201–2.
96. S. Ancell, *A Circumstantial Journal of the Siege of Gibraltar* (London, 1784), for a general account.
97. M. Dánvila y Collado, *op. cit.*, vol. V, pp. 370–1, F. Rousseau, *Règne de Charles III*, II, pp. 216–7.
98. Main clauses given in W. N. Hargreaves-Mawdsley, *op. cit.*, p. 167.
99. See the excerpts from Aranda's diary given in J. F. Yela Utrilla, *op. cit.*, vol. II, pp. 355ff; W. N. Hargreaves-Mawdsley, *op. cit.*, pp. 163–5.

100. For these see the Introduction to this work.
101. W. N. Hargreaves-Mawdsley, *op. cit.*, pp. 165–6 (selected articles only).
102. *Gaceta de Madrid* 20 de julio de 1784; W. N. Hargreaves-Mawdsley, *op. cit.*, p. 168.
103. G. Guastavino Gallent, *Los bombardeos de Argel en 1783–1784 y su repercusión literaria* (Madrid, 1950), pp. 12–17.
104. *Ibid.* p. 19.
105. Carlos III's eldest son Felipe was insane.
106. See the Introduction to this work (p. 2), Asturias had been born in Italy, and according to the law of 1713 those born outside Spain might not be able to succeed to the throne.
107. Whose nickname was '*el viejo zorro*'—'the Old Fox'.
108. The 'political testament' referred to above (n. 93) (B. M. MS Add. 29,299).
109. For his popular character see R. Herr, *The Eighteenth-Century Revolution in Spain* (Princeton, 1958), p. 233; for a contemporary account see J. Townshend, *A Journey through Spain in 1786 and 1787* (London, 1791), vol. II, pp. 123–6.

Bibliography

(a) Manuscripts as detailed in the notes; (b) printed books.

Addison, J., *Charles III of Spain* (Oxford, 1900).

Ancell, S., *A Circumstantial Journal of the Siege of Gibraltar* (London, 1784).

Armstrong, E., *Elisabeth Farnese 'The termagant of Spain'* (London, 1892).

Auñón y Villalón, R., *Episodios maritimos* (Cartagena, 1913).

Bacallar y Sanna, V., *Comentarios de la guerra de España e historia de su rey Felipe V, el Animoso* (Madrid, 1957).

Baudrillart, A., *Philippe V et la cour de France*, 5 vols. (Paris, 1890).

Baudrillart, A., 'L'influence française en Espagne au temps de Louis I; mission du maréchal de Tessé', *Revue des Questions historiques*, LVIII (1896).

Baudrillart, A., 'Le roi d'Espagne Charles III', *Le Correspondant* (25 avril 1907).

Belando, Padre N. de J., *Historia civil de España y sucesos de la guerra y tratados de la paz*, 3 vols. (Madrid, 1740).

Beltrán y Rózpide, R., 'Ripperdá en Africa', *Ilustracion Española y Americana* (1894).

Bermejo de la Rica, A., *La colonia del Sacramento* (Toledo, 1920).

Blart, L., *Les rapports de la France at de l'Espagne après le pacte de famille jusqu' à la fin du ministère du duc de Choiseul* (Paris, 1915).

Bliart, P., 'La question de Gibraltar, au temps du Régent, d'après les correspondances officielles, 1720–1721', *Revue des Questions historiques*, LVII (1895).

Bourget, A., 'Le duc de Choiseul et l'alliance espagnole: un ultimation franco-espagnol au Portugal (1761–1762)', *Revue de l'histoire diplomatique*, XXIV (1910).

Bouvier, R. and Soldevila, C., *Ensenada et son temps* (Paris, 1941).

Boye, P., *Stanislas Leszczinski et le troisième traité de Vienne* (Paris, 1898).

Cahen, L., 'Le Pacte de famille', *Revue Historique*, (1925).

Calvo, C., *Collección completa de los tractados de la América Latina* (Paris, 1862).

Campomanes, P. Rodríguez, *Cartas politico-económicas*, ed. A. Rodríguez Villa (Madrid, 1878).

Cantillo, A del, *Tratados, convenios y declaraciones de paz y de comercio que han hecho con las potencias extranjeras los Monarchas españoles de la Casa de Borbón desde el año de 1700 hasta el dia*, 4 pts (Madrid, 1843).

Cardona, P., *La guerra tra Spagna ed Austria in Italia durante la lotta per la successione al trono di Polonia* (Catania, 1913).

Castagnoli, P., *Il Cardinale Giulio Alberoni*, 3 vols (Piacenza/Rome, 1929–32).

Caughey, J., *Bernardo de Gálvez in Louisiana, 1776–1783* (Berkeley, 1934).

Cayetano, Alcázar, M., *El conde de Floridablanca*, (Madrid, 1929).

Cayetano Rosell, J., 'El Motín contra Esquilache', *Seminario Pintoresco Español*, 1 (Madrid, 1836).

Chase, G., *The Music of Spain* (2nd edn rev.) (New York, 1972).

Combes, F., *La Princesse des Ursins: essai sur la vie et son caractère politique* (Paris, 1858).

Coxe, W., *Historical Memoirs of the Kings of Spain of the House of Bourbon* (2nd. edn), 5 vols (London, 1815).

Cushner, N. P. (ed.), *Documents illustrating the British Conquest of Manila 1762–1763, Transactions of the Royal Historical Society, Camden Fourth Series*, vol. 8 (1971).

Dánvila y Collado, M., *Estudios españoles del siglo XVIII. Fernando VI y Doña Bárbara de Braganza* (Madrid, 1905).

Dánvila y Collado, M., *El reinado relámpago: Luis I y Luisa Isabel de Orleans, 1707–42* (Madrid, 1952).

Dánvila y Collado, M., *Historia del reinado de Carlos III*, 6 vols (Madrid, 1891–96).

de Aranda, J. M., *El marqués de la Ensenada. Estudios sobre su administración* (Madrid, 1898).

de Belmont, T. A. T., *Histoire de la dernière revolte des catalans et du siège de Barcelone* (Lyon, 1714).

de Courcy, marquis M. R. Rousset, *Renonciation des Bourbons au trône de France* (Paris, 1889).

de Courcy, marquis M. R. Rousset, *La Coalition de 1701 contre la France (1700–1715)*, 2 vols (Paris, 1886).

de Ferrater, E., *Código de derecho internacional, o sea colección metódica de los Tratados de paz, amistad y comercio entre España y las demas naciones* (Barcelona, 1846).

de la Cueva, P., *Iconismos o verdadera descripción de la expedición de Africa, en que las Reales Armas de S.M. recobaron a Mazalquivir, Orán y sus castillos* (Granada, n.d.).

de Lamadrid, R. S., *El concordato español de 1753, según los documentos originales de su negociación* (Jérez, 1937).

Desdevises du Dézert, G. N., *L'Espagne de l'ancien régime*, 3 vols (i, La société; ii, Les institutions; iii, La richesse et la civilisation), (Paris, 1897–1904).

Desdevises du Dézert, G. N., a revision of the above as articles in *Revue hispanique*, lxiv (1925), pp. 225–656; lxx (1927), pp. 1–556; lxxiii (1928), pp. 1–488.

Diario de la expedición contra la plaza de Panzacola concluida por las armas de S. M. Católica bajo las órdenes del Mariscal del Campo D. Bernardo de Gálvez (no place of publication and no date [1781]).

Eguía Ruiz, C., *Los jesuitas y el motín de Esquilache* (Madrid, 1947).

Eguía Ruiz, C., *El Padre Isidro López y el motín de Esquilache* (Madrid, 1935).

Escolano de Arrieta, P., *Práctica del Consejo Real en el despacho de los negocios consultativos, instructivos y contenciosos* (Madrid, 1796).

Espinosa, F., 'El conde de Aranda', *España Moderna*, CXLIX (1909).

Farrer de Rio, A., 'Estudio sobre el conde de Floridablanca', introduction to Floridablanca, *Obras originales*, vol. LIX *Biblioteca de Autores Españoles* (Madrid, 1867).

Fernán Nuñez, conde de, *Vida de Carlos III* (ed. A. Morel-Fatio and A. Paz y Mélia) 2 vols (Madrid, 1898).

Fernández, M., *Diario de lo ocurrido en el sitio de Gibraltar, que se principió en Febrero de 1727* (Madrid, 1781).

Gaceta de Madrid, 18 de julio de 1775.

Gadaleta, A., *Relazione de Spagna del cav. A. Cappello, ambasciatore a Filippo V dall'anno 1735 al 1738* (Florence, 1896).

García Rives, A., *Fernando VI y Doña Bárbara de Braganza. Apuntes sobre su reinado* (Madrid, 1917).

Gil Munilla, O., *El conflicto anglo-español en 1770* (Sevilla, 1948).

Girard, T. A., 'La folie de Philippe V' (Feuilles d'histoire du XVIIIe au XIXe siécle), *Revue historique*, III (Paris, 1910).

Goebel, J., *The Struggle for the Falkland Islands* (New Haven, 1927).

Gómez Molleda, Mª. D., 'El pensamiento de Carvajal y la política internacional española del siglo XVIII', *Hispania*, XV (1955).

Guastavino Gallent, G., *Los bombardeos de Argel en 1783–1784 y su repercusión literaria* (Madrid, 1950).

Harcourt-Smith, S., *Alberoni, or The Spanish Conspiracy* (London, 1943).

Hargreaves-Mawdsley, W. N., *Spain under the Bourbons, 1700–1833. A Collection of Documents* (London, 1973).

Herr, R., *The Eighteenth-Century Revolution in Spain* (Princeton, 1958).

Hill, C., *The Story of the Princess des Ursins* (New York, 1899).

Isla, Padre J. F. de, *Obras escogidas*, I, *Biblioteca de Autores Españoles*, XV (Madrid, 1945).

Jacquet, J.-L., *Les Bourbons d'Espagne* (Lausanne, 1968).

Javierre, A. L., 'Las cartas del duque de Orleans a Felipe V sobre el sitio de Lérida en 1707', *Ilerda*, IV (1946).

Kamen, H. A. F., *The War of Succession in Spain, 1700–15* (London, 1969).

Kirkpatrick, R., *Domenico Scarlatti* (Princeton, 1952).

Maldonado Macanaz, J., 'Voto y renuncia del Rey don Felipe V', *Discursos leidos ante la Real Academia de la Historia* (Madrid, 1894).

Manterola, J. de, *La disolución en España de la Compañía de Jesús* (Barcelona, 1934).

Mañer, S. A., *Historia del Duque de Ripperdá* (Madrid, 1796).

Martínez Salazar, A., *Colección de memorias y noticias del gobierno y politico del Consejo* (Madrid, 1764).

Maura, duque de, *Vida y reinado de Carlos II*, 3 vols. (Madrid, 1942).

Menéndez y Pelayo, M., *Historia de los Heterodoxos españoles*, 3 vols (Madrid, 1880–82).

Mercader Riba, J., 'La ordenación de Cataluña por Felipe V: la Nueva Planta', *Hispania XLIII* (1950).

Mercader Riba, J., 'El Valle de Arán, la Nueva Planta y la invasión anglofrancesa de 1719', *Primer congreso internacional del Pirineo* (Zaragoza, 1952).

Mercurio Historico y Politico, marzo 1753, Madrid.

Mérimée, F., *L'influence française en Espagne au XVIIIe siecle* (Paris, 1936).

Miguélez, M. Fraile, *El Jansensismo y Regalismo en España (datos para la historia). Cartas al señor Menéndez Pelayo* (Valladolid, 1895).

Miranda, F. S., *El sitio de Melilla de 1774 a 1775* (ed. R. Fernández de Castro) (Tangier, 1939).

Montgon, C. A., *Memoires*, 9 vols (The Hague, 1745–53).

Morales Padrón, F., *La Participación de España en la independencia de los Estados Unidos*, Madrid, 1952.

Moses, B., *Spain's Declining Power in South America, 1730–1806*, London, 1965.

Mozas Mesa, M., *Don José de Carvajal y Láncaster, Ministro de Fernando VI*, Jaén, 1924.

Nicolini, F., *L' Europa durante la guerra di successione di Spagna*, 3 vols., Naples, 1937–39.

Novísima recopilación de las leyes de España (Madrid, 1805).

Olmedilla y Puig, J., *Noticias históricas acerca de la última enfermedad del Rey de Espana Luis I* (Madrid, 1909).

Palacio Atard, V., *El tercer Pacto de Familia* (Madrid, 1945).

Palacio Atard, V., 'Las embajadas de Abreu y Fuentes en Londres, 1754–1761', *Simancas*, I (1950).

Parnell, A., *The War of Succession in Spain during the Reign of Queen Anne, 1702–11*, 2 vols (London, 1905).

Pastor, L. Freiherr von, *The History of the Popes from the close of The Middle Ages*, 40 vols (London, 1950).

Pérez Bustamente, C., *Correspondencia privada e inéditá del P. Rávago confesor de Fernando VI* (Madrid, 1936).

Pérez de Gúzman y Gallo, J., *La Historia Inédita: estudios de la vida, reinado, proscripción y muerte de Carlos IV y María Luisa* (Madrid, 1908).

Pérez de Gúzman y Gallo, J., 'Reparaciones a la vida de Carlos IV y María Luisa', *Revista de Archivos, Bibliotecas y Museos*, X (1904).

Petrie, Sir C., *King Charles III of Spain: an Enlightened Despot* (London, 1971).

Pimodan, A., *Louise-Élizabeth d'Orléans, reine d'Espagne (1709–1742)*, 2nd edn (Paris, 1923).

Piquer, A., 'Discurso sobre la enfermedad del Rey Fernando VI', *Colección de documentos inéditos*, XVIII (1928).

Prágmatica sanción de su Majestad en fuerza de ley (Madrid, 1767).

Relación verdadera y circumstanciada de todo lo acaecido en la ciudad de Zaragoza (Zaragoza, 1766).

Richmond, H. W., *Papers relating to the Loss of Minorca* (London, 1913).

Richmond, H. W., 'The Navy in the War of 1739–1748', *History*, Oct, 1924.

Robledo, A., *Tratados de Utrecht. Reseña histórica de la paz general de 1713* (Madrid, 1846).

Rodríguez Casado, V., 'Política marroquí de Carlos III: las misiones diplomaticas de Boltas y Girón', *Hispania*, II (1942).

Rodríguez Casado, V., 'La "revolución burguesa" del siglo XVIII español', in *Historia de España* (Ann Arbor, 1944).

Rodríguez Villa, A., *Introducción a las "Cartas político-económicas" de Campomanes* (Madrid, 1878).

Rodríguez Villa, A., *Don Cenón de Somodevilla, marqués de la Ensenada* (Madrid, 1878).

Rodríguez Villa, A., *Patiño y Campillo. Reseña histórico-biográfica de estos dos ministros de Felipe V* (Madrid, 1882).

Rodríguez Villa, A., 'Una embajada española en Marruecos y estado de este imperio en tiempo de Carlos III (1767)', *Revista Contemporánea*, XXVII (1880).

Rodríguez Villa, A., 'Informaciones del marqués de Berreti-Landy [sic] sobre antecedentes del barón de Ripperdá antes de su embajada en Viena', *Boletín de la Real Academia de la Historia*, XXXI (1897).

Rosseew-Saint-Hilaire, E., *La princesse des Ursins* (Paris, 1875).

Rousseau, F., *L'Expulsion des Jesuites en Espagne. Démarches de Charles III pour leur sécularisation* (Paris, 1904)

Rousseau, F., *Le Règne de Charles III d'Espagne (1759–1788)*, 2 vols (Paris, 1907).

Rousseau, F., *Un reformateur français en Espagne au XVIIIe siècle: Orry, 1701–1714* (Paris, 1912).

Rousset de Missy, J., *Le procès entre la Grande-Bretagne et l'Espagne, ou Recueil des Traitez, Conventions, Mémoires et autres Pièces touchant les Demelez entre ces deux couronnes* (The Hague, 1740).

Saint-Simon, L. duc de, *Historical Memoirs of the Duke de Saint-Simon* (ed. and trans. by Lucy Norton), 3 vols (London, 1967–72).

Sanpere y Miquel, S., *El fin de la nación catalana* (Barcelona, 1905).

Santos Sánchez, J., *Extracto puntual de todas les pragmáticas, cédulas, provisiones, circulares, publicadas en el reinado del señor Don Carlos III*, 2 vols (Madrid, 1792–93).

Sarrailh, J., *L'Espagne éclairée de la seconde moitié du siècle XVIII* (Paris, 1964).

Seminario Erúdito, vol. XXVIII, 'Fragmentos históricos para la vida del señor D. José Patiño'.

Soldevila, F., *Historia de Catalunya*, 3 vols (Barcelona, 1934–35).

Stryienski, C., 'Fernand VI roi d'Espagne', *Chronique Médicale*, xi, 15 Nov. 1902.

Sturgill, C. C., *Marshal Villars and the War of the Spanish Succession* (London, 1966).

Syveton, G., *Une cour et un aventurier au XVIIIe siècle. Le Baron de Ripperdá d'après des documents inédits des archives impériales de Vienne et des archives du Ministère des Affaires étrangères de Paris* (Paris, 1896).

Temple Patterson, A., *The Other Armada. The Franco-Spanish attempt to invade Britain in 1779* (Manchester, 1960).

Thompson, M. A., 'Louis XIV and the Origin of the War of the Spanish Succession', *Transactions of the Royal Historical Society*, 5th ser., IV (1954).

Townshend, J., *A Journey through Spain in 1786 and 1787*, 2 vols (London, 1791).

Tratados de España. Colección desde Felipe V hasta el presente, 3 vols (Madrid, 1796–1801).

Vignau y Ballester, V., 'Papeles referentes a la muerte de Felipe V y coronación de Fernando VI', *Revista de Archivos, Bibliotecas y Museos*, III (1899).

Villa-Urrutia, W. marqués de, *Mujeres de antaño: la reina María Luisa, esposa de Carlos IV* (Madrid, 1927).

Voltes Bou, P., *El archiduque Carlos de Austria, rey de los catalanes* (Barcelona, 1953).

Vovard, A., 'Le siège de Barcelone en 1706', *Communications et Mémoires de l'Académie de Marine*, XIV (1935).

Weber, O., *Der Friede von Utrecht. Verhandlungen zwischen England, Frankreich, der Kaiser und die General Staaten, 1710–1713* (Gotha, 1892).

[Wrangham, F.], *The British Plutarch*, 8 vols (Perth, 1795).

Yanguas y Miranda, J., *Diccionario de Antigüedades del reino de Navarra*, 3 vols. (Madrid, 1840).

Yela Utrilla, J. F., *España ante la independencia de los Estados Unidos* (Lérida, 1925).

Young, G. F., *The Medici* (New York, 1930).

Zabala y Lera, P., *España bajo los Borbones* 5th edn (Barcelona, 1955).

Zévort, E., *Le marquis d'Argenson* (Paris, 1880).

Index